STAGE
and the
SCHOOL

Teacher's Manual

GLENCOE
McGraw-Hill

New York, New York   Columbus, Ohio   Woodland Hills, California   Peoria, Illinois

Glencoe/McGraw-Hill

A Division of The McGraw·Hill Companies

Printed in the United States of America.

Send all inquiries to:
Glencoe/McGraw-Hill
8787 Orion Place
Columbus, OH 43240

ISBN 0-02-817235-3
Teacher's Manual

3 4 5 6 7 8 047 02 01

Table of Contents

PART ONE
Interpreting the Drama   3

    CHAPTER 1   Improvisation   4
    CHAPTER 2   Pantomime and Mime   12
    CHAPTER 3   Voice and Diction   22
    CHAPTER 4   Acting   32
    Theater Etiquette   46

PART TWO
A Treasury of Scenes and Monologues   47

    Readers Theater   50

PART THREE
Appreciating the Drama   51

    CHAPTER 5   The Structure of Drama   52
    CHAPTER 6   Varieties of Drama   60
    CHAPTER 7   History of Drama   70
    Puppet Theater   80

Table of Contents

PART FOUR
Producing the Drama   **81**

CHAPTER 8   **Producing the Play**   82

CHAPTER 9   **Producing the Musical Play**   90

CHAPTER 10   **Stage Settings**   100

CHAPTER 11   **Lighting and Sound**   108

CHAPTER 12   **Costuming**   116

CHAPTER 13   **Makeup**   124

How to Judge a Play   131

PART FIVE
Adapting and Interpreting Drama   **132**

CHAPTER 14   **Theater and Other Media**   133

CHAPTER 15   **Theater and Other Art Forms**   143

Media and Culture   153

Part One

Interpreting the Drama

CHAPTER 1
Improvisation   4

CHAPTER 2
Pantomime and Mime   12

CHAPTER 3
Voice and Diction   22

CHAPTER 4
Acting   32

Theater Etiquette   46

1 Improvisation

Framework

The word improvise comes from the Latin improvisus, meaning "unforeseen." We may improvise dinner when unforeseen guests drop in or use a newspaper to improvise an umbrella in an unforeseen rainstorm. In drama, however, improvisation refers to the portrayal of a character or scene without a script or rehearsal.

This book begins with improvisation because improvisation demands the coordinated use of voice and movement, which is an important first step in mastering acting skills and building confidence. Improvisation helps students develop an ability to interpret a situation and to create a character that is both recognizable and unique.

For many of your students this will probably be their first experience with acting, therefore, they may need a little time to overcome their inhibitions and self-consciousness. Patience and ample opportunities to observe and enjoy the improvisations of classmates are often all that are required. Once they are comfortable, most students readily take to improvising. You will probably find improvisation to be one of the most enjoyable and productive areas of study, one that you may wish to return to periodically to refocus attention on interpretation.

Teaching Note

- Not to be confused with the ad-libbing that occurs when an actor forgets a line or misses a cue, improvisation lies at the very foundation of the actor's craft.

- Activities found in the **Review Workshop** at the end of the chapter often require some planning or preliminary work by students. Be sure to check these activities, and make sure students have adequate time in which to complete them.

Instructional Objectives

- To develop the basic acting skills of interpretation, voice, movement, and timing through improvisation
- To create freshness and the "illusion of the first time" in acting situations through practice with the unpredictability inherent in improvisation
- To function successfully as part of an acting team
- To develop a number of successful improvisational techniques for establishing character, such as visualizing, working out stage settings in advance, and using actions to suggest entrances and props

Vocabulary

improvisation the impromptu portrayal of a character or scene without any rehearsal or preparation

spontaneity naturalness

"illusion of the first time" a situation in which the audience is led to believe that each performance is the first

scene-stealing calling attention to one's presence onstage and diverting attention away from the main actors

character-centered approach an approach to telling a story that focuses on a character or a group of characters who experience different situations

situation-centered approach an approach to telling a story that takes a single situation or series of situations and places characters into them

motivated sequence the natural way in which a person responds to an external stimulus—the brain registers, the body responds and then reacts—as mirrored by an actor in an improvisation

Ancillaries

Forms, Models, and Activities Blackline Masters, pages 1–3

Chapter Test, page 1

Transparency 1

Motivating Activity

This activity will provide an opportunity for students to observe the difference between actual behavior and improvisation.

Ask three students to leave the room. Explain to the rest of the class that you are going to conduct an experiment. They are to observe the results and to be prepared to discuss what they have seen. Emphasize that it is extremely important that they remain completely quiet and serious during the entire experiment. Then place a box with a lid, such as a shoe box, on the desk in front of the room. Inside the box, place an egg. Then have the three students return to the room one at a time. Tell each student the following:

> I have placed in this box something that can be extremely fragile if not handled with the utmost care. I want you to pick up the box and very carefully carry it out of the room.

Without smiling or otherwise hinting at the contents, the class is to observe the actions of each student as he or she approaches the box, picks it up, and carries it out of the room.

After the experiment has been completed, discuss with the class the behavior of the students. Have one student or groups of students improvise similar situations, incorporating and modifying the behaviors they observed. Then discuss how the "real" behavior compares with the improvised behavior.

EXERCISES: *Improvisation, page 10*

The Mirror Emphasize that this is a cooperative effort, not a contest to see who can trick her or his partner. It may be helpful to demonstrate the exercise with a student partner. Call attention to the fact that they should begin slowly, moving the hands in predictable patterns before involving other parts of their bodies.

The Machine You may wish to divide the class into groups of four or five students and have each group work independently on an improvisation. Isolating each group will ensure that the group prepares an original improvisation.

EXERCISES: *Improvising, page 13*

Some students may respond more readily if the action and the reason for urgency are provided. You might therefore prefer to write each action and the circumstance on a 3" × 5" card. Have students choose cards. As each performs, the rest of the class can attempt to guess the action.

Extension Some additional actions and circumstances:

- packing a suitcase when you are late for an important trip
- washing dishes when you are anxious to get out of the house before you are given another job to do
- eating a pizza before your brother gets home and sees it
- looking for a phone number in the telephone book so that you can call a radio station within thirty seconds and win a prize
- cleaning up a mess you made on the kitchen floor before a parent arrives home

▶ Additional Improvising Exercise

Pitch and Catch Have students work in pairs to improvise a game of catch. One student takes the part of the pitcher; the other takes the part of the catcher. The pitcher decides on the size, weight, velocity, and direction of the ball and improvises the throw accordingly. The catcher must interpret the action of the pitcher and improvise catching such a ball. Then the roles are reversed and the catcher becomes the pitcher. The new pitcher can change the size, weight, velocity, and direction of the ball when returning the throw.

EXERCISES: *Motivated Sequence, page 14*

You might want to have students work in small groups for this assignment. One student can improvise the action described in each exercise, and the remaining group members can act as friends or family members reacting to the situation.

Extension Additional situations might include the following:

- You are slowly driving home one night after an exhausting rehearsal when you look in the rearview mirror and see the flashing lights of a police car.
- You have just completed your homework and settled into a comfortable chair with a bowl of popcorn, ready to watch your favorite television program. Suddenly the television screen flashes the message: "Sorry! Technical Difficulties. We will resume the broadcast as soon as possible."
- You are baby-sitting in your home for a neighbor's two-year-old child. While you are answering the telephone, you notice the child has wandered off. Suddenly you hear a crashing sound coming from the kitchen.

EXERCISES: *Characterizations, page 15*

Have students establish their characters prior to engaging in this exercise. Use the questions on page 14. After each reenactment has been completed, have the class discuss their perceptions of the character and compare their perceptions to the one the actor envisioned.

Extension Additional events for reenactment might include the following:

- You are waiting for an important call. When the telephone finally rings, you find it is only someone trying to sell you a magazine subscription that you have no interest in buying. You want to conclude the conversation as quickly as possible so your phone will be free for the call you are expecting.

- After finishing your meal in a restaurant, your server presents you with your bill. You reach for your wallet, which contains your cash and credit cards, but find that it is missing. The server returns for your payment.

- You have taken refuge in a basement during a tornado. The storm rages above you, shaking the room and occasionally causing tremendous bursts of noise as trees fall, windows break, and flying debris hits the building.

▶ Additional Characterization Exercise

Show a video of the movie *Twelve Angry Men.* Then have students profile one of the characters by answering the questions on page 14 as the character might answer them.

EXERCISES: Group Improvisations, page 17

In exercises 1 and 3, allow each pair ample time to prepare the assigned improvisation. Be prepared to spend a little time with each, helping them decide on the situation or characters.

You may wish to assign several groups to perform exercise 2. If so, do not allow the groups to observe the improvisations of another group prior to their own performance. This will allow each group to arrive at its own interpretation instead of attempting to imitate the work of another group.

EXERCISES: Individual Improvisations, page 19

▶ Additional Variations

Exercises 1 and 2 Divide the class into groups of three to five members. Give each member a prop or costume. Participants should develop a character around the item given them; then the group should improvise a scene depicting the character in a situation you describe.

Application Activities, pages 19–21

Emotional Responses

Activity 1 You might have students work in pairs, one delivering the line and the other responding. Then have students switch roles. Afterward, have the class discuss the elements that make an improvisation convincing.

Activity 2 Facial and verbal expressions should reinforce each other in this activity and be specific to the object. The best sentences will be expressive of a particular reaction, rather than a generalized "Yuk!" or "Ummmm."

Activity 3 Look for facial expressions and actions that differentiate the specified feeling from all the others. One strategy might be to write the feelings on 3" x 5" cards, mix them, place them facedown on your desk, and have students select a card with an emotion they are to improvise. If the improvisation is successful, students should be able to identify the emotion being portrayed.

Vocal Responses

Activity 1 A good response will include an appropriate statement with proper emphasis and body language. You may wish to review the Motivated Sequence on page 13 prior to this activity.

Activity 2 With practice students should learn to move immediately into the prescribed emotion without hesitation or reflection. Facial and verbal expressions should reinforce each other in this activity and should change when the director specifies a new emotion. Hand and arm movements will complement the emotion.

Activity 3 The emphasis in this activity is on creativity. Unusual and unexpected approaches should be encouraged and rewarded. Conflict can be heightened if students "misunderstand" the gestures of the partner.

Activity 4 The success of this activity depends on how smoothly and completely the student taking part B is able to move from one conversation to another. This might take some practice. Allow students to work on their improvisations until they are satisfied with them. Encourage the development of convincing dialogue and characterization in both conversations. After completing the activity, students might want to trade parts and do the activity again. Good responses by B will include appropriate statements with proper emphasis and body language.

Scripts

Activity 1 The dialogue in the student scripts should reveal a sense of character. A superior response will go beyond a general and stereo-typical idea of the character and will provide individual characteristics, using stage directions and similar notations. Facial expressions and gestures should amplify the characters' emotions.

Activity 2 Remind students that a situation-centered approach works best when the characters exhibit unique responses. The conclusion should represent logical outcomes considering the characters, the situations, and the dialogue.

Creating the Improvised Play

Observe the work of each group to note the contribution level of individual students. Try to configure and guide the groups so that all students make contributions. Occasionally a group may tend to be dominated by one or two students. If this occurs, you might have these students act as "evaluators" or "stage managers" for the improvisations. This will allow others to come forward with ideas.

▶ Additional Application Activity

Involve as many students as possible in a group improvisation about a day at school. It can include situations such as a session with a counselor, a job or college interview, a conversation with a teacher about an overdue assignment, or a meeting of the school newspaper staff.

<hr>

ASSESS

Chapter Review, page 22

Summary and Key Ideas Sample Responses

1. Improvisation is the portrayal of a character or a scene without rehearsal or preparation. Characterization, dialogue, and action are created without the benefit of a script.

2. Actors create the "illusion of the first time" when they convey the spontaneity, naturalness, and freshness that give the audience the feeling that each performance is the first. It is sometimes difficult to capture this illusion after weeks of rehearsal and many performances.

3. To "do nothing" effectively is a challenge because it demands that an actor be visible onstage without playing an active part in the scene. The actor must get the audience to accept his or her presence without distracting attention from the focus of the scene. An actor who seeks attention at the expense of the scene is guilty of scene-stealing.

4. One basic approach to telling a story is the character-centered approach, which focuses on a character or a group of characters who experience different situations one after another. This approach emphasizes each character's response to those situations as they occur. *Man of LaMancha* and *Big River* are examples of this approach. The other basic approach is the situation-centered approach, which takes a single situation or a series of situations and places a number of characters into the situation to demonstrate how different personalities will respond to the same event. *Arsenic and Old Lace* and *Little Shop of Horrors* are situation centered.

5. The motivated sequence progresses through the following steps:
   • You experience the stimulus.
   • You respond instinctively.
   • The idea "connects." Your brain registers the stimulus—this usually takes only a fraction of a second.

- If the stimulus is the kind that causes a reflex action, you might jerk back your head, or you might make a sound. Your eyes look in that direction. Then your body reacts; your chest moves in the direction of the stimulus.
- You react vocally and/or physically with your main response.

6. When establishing a character, ask the following questions:
- Who am I?
- What kind of person am I?
- How am I different from the other characters?
- What are the fewest things I can do to convey the most information about my character?
- What does my character want?

7. A list of essential things to keep in mind while improvising might include the following:
- Speak loudly enough to be heard throughout the theater or auditorium.
- Do not hide behind pieces of furniture or other people.
- Move about freely. Try not to stand beside other characters all the time.
- Take plenty of time to speak and to move so that you can create a definite impression.
- While onstage, stay in character at all times.

Discussing Ideas

1. A discussion of character should touch on the fact that characterization, whether conveyed through voice, body language, or movement, is often more precisely revealed through a subtle movement or vocal inflection than through sweeping actions and speeches. As stated on page 14, ". . . a raised eyebrow, a silent stare, a one-word response, or a groan might convey more information about your character than a dozen sentences."

2. A good discussion will bring out the fact that a performer must visualize character, situation, and setting. Once this is done, the actor's actions will allow the audience to see what the actor visualizes.

3. It is important that the students recognize the distinction between feeling an emotion and portraying an emotion. Be certain students recognize that acting is pretending, not being. An actor simply cannot be a character, but he or she can always portray the character by recalling similar emotions from personal experiences and by using imagination.

4. Through discussion, students should be able to infer that allowing an experienced actor to improvise a characterization may be advantageous in developing a role. However, such improvisations must be tempered and guided by the director's perception of the character.

Review Workshop, page 23

Independent Activities

Using a Prop   You might want to bring several items to class for students to use. This activity should be judged on the basis of originality and the students' abilities to convey emotional attachments to various objects.

Masking Physical Irritation   This activity should be quite entertaining for the class. The key to its success lies in the student's ability to portray the dramatic contrast between the poised outward appearance and the irritation that is being masked with only limited success. A convincing and entertaining portrayal will require exaggerated movements and gestures.

▶ **Additional Activity**   Select a student to be a salesperson. Then have that student improvise a series of sales calls on customers, which are played by other students. The salesperson should decide what product or service he or she will be selling. Each student playing the role of a customer should improvise an objection or obstacle to the sale. The salesperson will need to improvise a response to the objection and attempt to complete the sale.

For example, if the salesperson is selling a vacuum cleaner, the customer may assume the role of a wealthy woman who hires a cleaning service to clean her home. If the salesperson is selling magazines, the customer may assume the role of a recent immigrant who is unable to speak or read English. The customer should give the salesperson the greatest challenge possible. The salesperson's creativity and ability to improvise will then be put to the test.

Cooperative Learning Activity

Characterization This activity provides an opportunity for students to develop a character and analyze the results of their portrayal. Note the insights students demonstrate in the nature of the character and the elements that portray that character.

Extension Two archaeologists have discovered the tomb of an ancient pharaoh. An inscription above the tomb warns of danger to those who disturb it. One archaeologist wants to leave immediately. The other wants to open the tomb.

Across the Curriculum Activity

Art Students should demonstrate an insight into the emotional context of the painting by analyzing its expressive elements—the use of light and color to express emotion, or the expressiveness of people in the picture, for example. The "picture window" should be a logical context for the "snapshot" represented by the painting. If called upon, students should be able to defend their choices by sharing their analysis of the painting.

CLOSE

Final Activity

Have each student create a character, using the questions on page 14. Allow sufficient time for students to reflect on each question and to clarify the character by writing out answers to each question. Then, using the situation-centered model described on pages 9 and 10, have students take turns improvising their character in the following situation:

> The character is standing in a long check-out line at the grocery store. As the line slowly moves, the character notices another customer attempting to sneak into the front of the line.

Organize students into groups of four. Try to include contrasting characters in each group. Remind them to stay in character and then describe the following situation:

> Each group of characters is seated in the waiting room of a bus terminal. The bus will not arrive for hours due to mechanical problems. There are no books or magazines to read, but there is a television set. While remaining in character, improvise a discussion wherein the group decides which television program to watch.

After the improvisations have been completed, engage the class in a discussion of the characters. Focus on how the students think the questions on page 14 were answered.

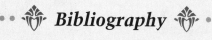 Bibliography

Books

Appel, Libby. *Mask Characterization: An Acting Process.* Carbondale, IL: Southern Illinois University Press, 1982. Appel shows how using masks can help students feel less vulnerable and freer to develop their creativity.

Caruso, Sandra, and Paul Clemens. *The Actor's Book of Improvisation.* New York, NY: Penguin Books, 1992. This comprehensive collection of material on which to base improvisations is organized around specific aspects of the acting job, such as being aware of subtext. Improvisation can be used to solve specific acting problems; however, some suggested scenes may not be appropriate for high school.

Dezseran, Louis John. *The Student Actors Handbook.* Palo Alto, CA: Mayfield Publishing Co., 1975. This book describes a series of exercises and games designed to help the student actor portray conflict, comedy, and period-style acting. Dezseran also includes relaxation exercises.

Goldberg, Andy. *Improv Comedy.* Hollywood, CA: Samuel French, 1992. Goldberg discusses the challenging task of being funny and provides the reader with advice on improvisation and stand-up comedy. The foreword is by actor John Ritter.

Halpern, Charna, et al. *Truth in Comedy: The Manual for Improvisation.* Colorado Springs, CO: Meriwether Publishing, 1994. Halpern focuses on honing the skills needed to produce spontaneous comedy. She covers both the art of improvisation and stand-up comedy.

Held, Jack Preston. *Improvisational Acting: A Handbook of Exercises for the Student Actor.* Belmont, CA: Wadsworth Publishing Company, 1971. This is a book of exercises leading students to the discovery of their own potential in creative acting. There are four major parts to the book: Daily Exercises, Ensemble Exercises, Characterization Exercises, and Rehearsal Techniques.

Hodgson, John Reed. *Improvisation,* 2d ed. New York, NY: Harper & Row, 1983. This book shows how improvisation enables actors to connect with their imaginations and become more aware of themselves and others. Hodgson also demonstrates how to use improvisation to better understand a script.

Johnstone, Keith. *Improv: Improvisation and the Theatre.* New York, NY: Theatre Arts Books, 1979. Johnstone's source book of ideas for discovering creativity offers techniques and exercises to foster students' spontaneity and narrative skills.

Polsky, Milton E. *Let's Improvise: Becoming Creative, Expressive & Spontaneous Through Drama.* Englewood Cliffs, NJ: Prentice Hall, 1980. Polsky guides the beginning actor through a step-by-step creative process. In addition to helpful exercises and illustrations, simple ways to guide, encourage, and evaluate performances are described. A Player's Diary is included for actors to record their reactions during the acting process.

Rudlin, John. *Commedia dell'Arte: An Actor's Handbook.* London; New York, NY: Routledge, 1994. Both history and criticism of this genre are provided. It is also a practical guide to how this type of comic theater was performed.

Spolin, Viola. *Improvisation for the Theater: A Handbook of Teaching and Directing Techniques.* Evanston, IL: Northwestern University Press, 1994. This handbook describes the nature of spontaneity and outlines workshop procedures that are conducive to the practice of improvisation. There are hundreds of catalogued acting exercises in progressive sequences. Spolin comments about understanding children in the theater and directing plays for the community. Many problem-solving insights are offered as well.

Wirth, Jeff. *Interactive Acting: Acting, Improvisation, and Interacting for Audience Participatory Theatre.* Fall Creek, OR: Fall Creek Press, 1994. This book includes descriptions of interactive performances, methods of encouraging audience participation, a concise review of improvisation skills, and other topics of information. There are also lists of questions that help establish characters and settings for improvisations.

Videotapes and Films

Monster in a Box. This is Spalding Gray's 1992 film version of his stage show. It is listed in Viewfinder's Catalog of Uncommon Video 1-800-342-3342. Video, color; 90 minutes.

Swimming to Cambodia. In this monologue Gray relates his experiences in Southeast Asia during the filming of *The Killing Fields.* It is listed in Viewfinder's Catalog of Uncommon Video 1-800-342-3342. Video, color; 85 minutes.

Internet

Improv Across America. If you are interested in improvisational comedy troupes, this site lists dates and locations of performances in cities throughout the United States. The Internet address is http://http.tamu.edu:8000/~fslip/ ImprovAmerica/

The Improv Page. This Internet site functions as a clearinghouse for information about improvisational theater. The Internet address is http://sunee.uwater loo.ca/~broehl/improv/index.html

CHAPTER

2 Pantomime and Mime

Framework

The art of acting without words began to develop centuries ago when hunters and warriors returned to their villages and used movements, gestures, and facial expressions to retell their adventures. Modern drama includes two forms of silent acting: pantomime and mime. Although many people use the terms interchangeably, they are not identical. Mime is far more stylized, focusing on conveying an abstract theme; pantomime focuses on conveying a particular action.

Nonverbal communication is the core of both pantomime and mime. We use nonverbal communication every day to convey thoughts, emotions, and ideas. For example, we smile when we are pleased, we blow a kiss when a loved one leaves, and we hold a finger to our lips when we want silence. When an actor incorporates gestures and facial expressions into a performance, the character is believable. This chapter will teach your students, through a study of pantomime and mime, how to use body language to produce a convincing characterization.

Many students enjoy performing pantomimes and mimes that involve strong emotions and dramatic movements and gestures. Students might need prompting, however, to notice and practice ordinary actions, such as walking, sitting, and standing. This chapter includes detailed descriptions of how to accomplish these things onstage, as well as activities and exercises that encourage creativity and imagination. You will probably find that pantomime and mime not only act as building blocks for acting techniques, but also act as vehicles that unleash your students' creativity.

Teaching Note

Activities found in the **Review Workshop** at the end of the chapter might require planning or preliminary work by students. Be sure to check these activities, and make sure students have adequate time in which to complete them.

Instructional Objectives

- To master the basic principles of pantomime and apply them to common stage actions
- To recognize and practice conventional mime actions and exercises
- To use facial expressions and gestures to enhance a characterization
- To differentiate between mime and pantomime

Vocabulary

pantomime the art of acting without words

nonverbal communication communicating without words, using facial expressions, gestures, and body language

cross to move from one position to another onstage

gesture a movement of any part of the body to help express an idea

kinesthesis sometimes called "muscle memory"; the neuromuscular sense the body has in a particular physical position

mime an offspring of pantomime that often conveys abstract ideas

inclination the bending of the body to the front, the side, or the rear

rotation turning or pivoting a body part in smooth circles

isolation the process of separating parts of the body for individual development and expression

Ancillaries

Forms, Models, and Activities Blackline Masters, pages 4–6

Chapter Test, page 2

Motivating Activity

This activity will encourage students who are new to pantomime and mime to work without inhibition by providing them with the security of a group. It will also demonstrate to students that they already have experiences they can draw on to perform successful pantomimes.

Ask students to sit quietly and visualize watching a live sporting event. Ask them to describe details of both the actual sport and the actions of the audience. Then select a small group of students to pantomime a particular sport. The remaining students should try to name the sport they are watching. They should then describe details from the pantomime that are indicative of that particular sport, such as head movements, hand gestures, and facial expressions. (As a variation, have the seated students act as an audience, doing improvisational pantomimes in response to the action of the sporting event.)

After this activity is completed, discuss with students the importance of nonverbal communication, not only in acting but in life as well. Have students list examples of nonverbal communication they use or observe daily.

EXERCISES: *Relaxation, page 28*

You might wish to point out that not only is relaxation useful in various aspects of acting, but it also improves both mental and physical well-being. Explain to students that relaxation is a foundation of acting; they will use relaxation techniques in voice and diction and throughout the course.

EXERCISE: *Posture, page 30*

Before students begin the exercise, have them identify a person or a group of people who typically have good posture, such as a dancer or people in the military services. Encourage students to visualize someone with excellent posture as they do their own posture exercises. Discuss the benefits of having good posture, onstage and offstage.

Demonstrate to students how they can check their posture by standing with their backs and shoulders touching a wall and their heels approximately three inches from the wall.

EXERCISES: *Walking, page 31*

You might want to organize students into small groups to perform this exercise. Have one group perform as the rest of the class observes. Have the audience guess which type of walk is being portrayed.

Extension Some additional situations students might enjoy portraying include the following:

- walking barefoot across a gravel road
- walking on the surface of the moon
- walking into the cafeteria on your first day at a new school
- walking down a sidewalk holding the leash of a large, rambunctious dog

EXERCISES: *Crossing, Turning, and Falling, page 34*

Some students might find these exercises easier if they first visualize a character who might be in a situation in which he or she would have to cross, turn, or fall. You might encourage students to look at the chart on page 27 of the text and study the actions that usually indicate a strong-willed and confident person or a shy and retiring person. Have students practice crossing and turning as both of these types of characters.

Extension For added variety, allow students to experiment with different types of falls: a comic fall, a melodramatic fall, a heroic or tragic fall, and so on.

▶ *Additional Falling Exercise*

To achieve controlled action in falling, have students control their falls to a count of five. The students should begin their falls on the one count and complete the action on the five count. Gradually increase the count to ten or fifteen for even more control.

EXERCISES: *Gestures, page 36*

You might want to divide the class into four groups, each group performing an exercise. After each group performs, discuss the many different ways individuals react to the same stimulus.

Extension Additional situations might include the following:

- You have picked up a bottle of ketchup and unscrewed the lid in order to pour some on a hamburger. At first no ketchup comes out, but then suddenly a large quantity floods your food.
- You are a police officer at a busy intersection that has lost its traffic light due to a power outage. Traffic is backed up in all directions, and drivers are impatient. You try to conceal your hostility for the honking drivers while calmly directing traffic.

- For this exercise have students work in pairs; one student will be the native, the other a foreigner. If time permits, have them switch roles.

> You are in a foreign country where you do not speak the language. You hesitate to approach a stranger, but finally you see a friendly looking person. Using hand and arm gestures as well as facial expressions, try to show that you are hungry and would like to know of any nearby restaurants.

EXERCISES: *Pantomime Expressions, page 40*

Students who are unsure of how to begin might find it easier to work in pairs. As one student follows the instructions in the text, have the other student pantomime reactions to that emotion. For example, if one student pantomimes rage in the first exercise, the other might react either with aggression, fear, or scorn. Have students take turns being the initiator and the reactor. Add interest to the exercises by inviting other students to identify the emotion being portrayed.

EXERCISES: *Characterization, page 41*

For exercise 2, have students enact these scenes in different ways—melodramatically or comically, for example. This will allow students to recognize the different ways any scene can be performed.

You might encourage students to take notes on the effectiveness of certain movements and to critique each performance. Commend originality.

▶ *Additional Characterization Exercise*

Have individual students pantomime the actions of a baseball player, a chef, a dentist, a carpenter, a salesclerk, or a mail carrier. Have the class discuss the significant means of non-verbal communication used to portray these characters.

EXERCISES: *Objects in Pantomime, page 43*

Before beginning the activity, discuss the physical properties of items: size, shape, weight, resistance, texture, placement, and condition (refer students to page 44 for an explanation of condition). Emphasize the importance of establishing these characteristics at the beginning of a skit and not altering them unless the object changes.

▶ *Additional Objects in Pantomime Exercises*

Write the words *size, shape, weight, resistance, texture, placement,* and *condition* on individual cards. Have students take turns naming an object and then choosing a card and describing that aspect of the item they have named.

List on the board a variety of different objects, such as a brick, an empty box, a soft pillow, a small stuffed animal, and a ball bearing. Discuss how an actor could pantomime the distinctive properties of each item.

Bring a variety of balls to class and pass them around for students to examine and feel. The balls might include any of those used in the following games: jacks, lacrosse, racquetball, tennis, golf, softball, baseball, basketball, football, or bowling. After they have examined and lifted the balls, divide the class into pairs. Have each pair choose one type of ball and pantomime rolling it, tossing it, serving it, and hitting it. Other students can then guess what type of ball the pair pantomimed using.

Have students pantomime handling or eating foods of different sizes, temperatures, and textures. These might include crisp crackers, sloppy sandwiches, sticky taffy, scalding soup, or mashed potatoes.

EXERCISES: *Pantomiming Imaginary People, pages 45–46*

Before students perform a pantomime of an individual character, encourage them to establish a character profile that includes physical and behavioral characteristics. For example, what is the character's height, weight, and age? How does he or she stand and walk? What gestures does the character typically make as he or she talks? Is the person quiet and shy or loud and aggressive? Answering questions such as these will help students visualize a character more realistically.

If you have a VCR available for use, you might have students watch scenes from several different movies with the sound turned off. For each character seen, have students discuss the attributes of the character and what clues suggest those attributes. Also, have students identify any emotions or ideas these characters exhibit through body language. Follow up with a discussion of the importance of nonverbal communication in acting.

EXERCISES: *Pantomiming a Real Activity, page 47*

Before students prepare their individual pantomimes, have them sit in groups and brainstorm some of their typical daily activities. Encourage students to name common activities that family members perform as well. Working from their brainstorming ideas, students should perform the exercises in the text. After the pantomimes are completed, have students identify details that struck them as particularly realistic.

EXERCISES: *Pantomiming a Real Person, page 48*

For this activity you might have students work in pairs, placing their individual characters in the same situation. This will emphasize the specific characteristics of each character pantomimed. Evaluate students' performances on the consistency of their characters' actions and reactions.

EXERCISES: *Group Pantomimes, page 49*

Have students who will be participating in each scene take turns describing how they imagine the situation. The group can then compare details and select the broad outlines of the scenes. They should take time to develop their individual characters before incorporating each character into the group performance.

▶ Additional Group Pantomime Exercises

- Have students work together to create a frozen picture depicting a particular scene. For example, they might show a moment in the life of a famous person, or they might show a scene from a novel, a poem, or a play. Students could work either in pairs or in groups.

- Have students pantomime four people sitting at a table building a house of cards. Emotions run high as the house gets taller. Give students only chairs for props. Their goal is to help others "see" the table, the cards, and the card house.

- Have students pantomime the following scene and situation: the guests at a fancy dinner party are seated around a lovely table while they are being served food and drink. One by one, each guest discovers that the food they were served tastes terrible. The hosts seem unaware of the problem, so the guests try to be gracious and polite. Each tries to avoid eating the food without calling attention to the action.

Application Activities, page 50

Activity 1 You might want to give students approximately five minutes to prepare the pantomime. Students should already be able to show moods and perform pantomime movements effectively.

Activity 2 Students will need more preparation time for activity 2. You might want to designate an entire class period to group pantomime preparation. You can present a list of group pantomimes from which students can choose, or have the class brainstorm ideas for the list.

A successful performance will exhibit the following elements:

- a definite beginning and end
- distinct characters whose expressions, gestures, and actions reveal character and mood
- clear, simple movements that are purposeful and motivated

Application Activities, page 59

You might have students choose and prepare only one of the first six activities. This will give them more time to focus, allowing them to concentrate on a particular situation.

Activity 1 Actions should be exaggerated, and each student should clearly shift weight from foot to foot as he or she pulls and is pulled. The length and diameter of the rope should appear to be constant.

Activity 2 Students should use a definite "click" to demonstrate the presence of the sides of the box. Their hands should snap into place as they contact the "hard surfaces."

Activity 3 Look for facial expressions and actions that express both the character's hopes and dashed expectations. The character's eyes should follow the kite as it flies away, and the character's posture should show a marked change from beginning to end.

Activity 4 Look for posture and gestures that show the strength of the wind not only outside but also against the closing door. Encourage humor and creativity.

Activity 5 Students should include actions that make the setting clear. Both facial expressions and posture should reflect the movement of the boat and the character's mounting malaise.

Activity 6 A good mime should have a clear central focus as well as a definite climax and conclusion. Major actions should be preceded by preparatory actions, and the entire performance should reflect a central theme.

Activity 7 For this activity, you might want to divide the class into small groups, having the students pantomime leaning on the same mantle. A student successfully performing this combination should appear almost like a jointed marionette. Make sure that each isolation and rotation is properly executed and the weight is properly shifted, leaving the audience with the desired effect of the actor leaning on a mantle. If students are working in groups, make sure that the height of the mantle is consistent.

▶ *Additional Application Activities*

Have students mime different kinds of changes:

- a flower breaking through the earth's surface, blooming, and then wilting in the hot sun
- a young child growing to adolescence, adulthood, and old age
- a person walking out of a dark room into bright sunlight
- a person changing from an exhausted worker into an energized marathon runner

FYI

Two important entertainers met by accident at a Paris airport in 1967. Silent film star Charlie Chaplin was 78, and mime Marcel Marceau was 43. Marceau told Chaplin that in one performance he had imitated the Tramp, a Chaplin character. Marceau then demonstrated his version of the Tramp's walk. Chaplin joined Marceau and did the walk himself. Out of consideration for Chaplin's privacy, Marceau told his photographer not to take a picture of the two artists waddling around the airport. Later, he regretted that decision. It was the only time the two men ever met, and unfortunately, no picture recorded the event.

Chapter Review, page 60

Summary and Key Ideas
Sample Responses

1. Pantomime helps students develop their nonverbal communication skills. An actor's nonverbal communication, which includes gestures, expressions, and actions, is the key to creating a character. Nonverbal communication is often more important than the words an actor speaks.

2. Facial expressions, gestures, and body language are the three types of nonverbal communication. For example, people commonly wink, point, or stomp out of a room angrily.

3. **Walking** Maintain good posture, keeping the chest high and the axis of the body over the feet. Walk in a straight line, keeping movements poised and rhythmical as the body swings easily from the hips. Let the arms swing in opposition to the legs, and place weight on the balls of the feet.

   Sitting Keep the spine at a ninety-degree angle to the seat; rest arms in the lap or on the chair arms; when rising, lead with the chest.

   Falling Fall in segments; be very close to the floor before actually collapsing; cushion the fall with the soft parts of the body.

4. An item's size, weight, shape, resistance, texture, condition, and placement should be clear.

5. Mime is more stylized than pantomime, and it attempts to express an idea or theme instead of reality.

6. The eyes and mouth are the most expressive facial features. Mimes emphasize these with makeup.

7. Mimes use gestures to convey themes and feelings rather than to express real actions.

8. Examples might include the mime walk, in which the body weight is shifted from one foot to the other and the arms swing rhythmically in opposition to the lifted foot, or the ladder climb, in which the actor alternates between arm or leg motion and looking up for the next rung.

Discussing Ideas

1. A discussion about an expressive body should emphasize the importance of the body as a means of communication. Actors use gestures, stances, and facial expressions to communicate thoughts, feelings, actions, and reactions.

2. Students should recognize that gestures should have a purpose, such as expressing a thought or feeling. No gesture at all is better than a gesture without a clear purpose. Not only is a gesture without a clear purpose confusing, it can also detract interest from another actor's purposeful gesture or from a sense of repose or watchfulness of a scene.

3. A good discussion will bring out the functions of both memory and imagination. Memory helps an actor recall and imitate reality. To be able to show the full range of emotions, an actor must observe people and store expressions, gestures, and body language in the memory. Imagination allows an actor to become a particular character, even though he or she might never have encountered such a character.

4. Through discussion, students should recognize that because mimes deal with universal themes and feelings, all audiences can understand and respond to the actions of mimes. Situations that imitate real and specific actions might have a more limited audience.

Review Workshop, page 61

Independent Activities

Emergence The key to the success of this activity lies in the student's ability to portray the posture and stillness of a typical mannequin, and then to make an engaging transformation. A convincing performance will heighten the contrast between the statue and the human.

Emotion   This activity provides an opportunity for students to focus on the postures and gestures that convey emotions. You might have the class try to guess which emotion is being portrayed and have students discuss the particular gestures that indicate the emotion. In a successful performance the emotion portrayed should be identified easily.

Extreme Temperatures   This activity could be presented for either serious evaluation of students' abilities or simply for fun. Pay attention to originality and each student's ability to communicate extreme heat or cold.

Other Possible Situations   building a fire outside on a cold day; walking to school during a fierce snowstorm; mowing a lawn on a hot summer day

▶ **Additional Activity**   Ask students to imagine that they are playing tug-of-war with a large dog that refuses to give up the sock in its mouth. A good performance will suggest the size of the dog, the frustration of the person, and the struggle between them.

Cooperative Learning Activities

Moving Day   Each character should exhibit a distinct personality by using expressions, gestures, and other movements. The activity should also demonstrate joint planning. For example, both characters should seem to be grasping the same box. Each should react to the other's movements.

The Sculptor and the Block of Wood   This is a challenging activity. The performance should be judged on the creativity of the solution to the problem of having a figure emerge from a block of wood.

▶ **Additional Activity**   Invite pairs of students to pantomime marionettes and puppeteers. This will require not only planning and rehearsal, but it also will require props, such as chairs or benches, to raise the students acting as puppeteers above the students acting as marionettes.

Across the Curriculum Activities

Physical Education   The activity provides an opportunity for students to plan and carry out actions and reactions. Note how well the performers demonstrate the size and feel of any sporting equipment. Evaluate the believability of their actions and reactions.

History   To be successful, students must first choose an event that other students will know. Look for a key action that establishes the characters and the setting. A successful routine will have a clear beginning and end, and each person's actions will be deliberate and will relate to the actions of the others.

CLOSE

Final Activity

The final activity is designed to incorporate many of the major themes of the chapter. Although it is not designed for evaluation, this activity will help you assess not only how successfully each student has mastered the material but also how successfully you have helped them meet the Instructional Objectives for the chapter.

Choose several students to perform a mime. Have the rest of the class imagine that they are walking through a park when they notice this mime performance. While the mimes are performing, the remaining students should act as an audience and pantomime their reactions to the mime. Aim for silence and expressive gestures, but encourage fun and creativity!

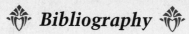

Books

Alberts, David. *Pantomime: Elements and Exercises.* Lawrence, KS: University of Kansas Press, 1971. Alberts gives both a philosophical discussion of the art of mime and a practical approach to performance. Pantomime techniques are described in detail and accompanied by ninety action photos. Four original pantomimes are included.

Bruford, Rose. *Teaching Mime.* New York, NY: Harper & Row, 1969. This book describes a sophisticated program in mime, including notes on how mime relates to other areas of a school curriculum. A number of mime for large groups are included.

Enters, Angna. *Angna Enters on Mime.* Middletown, CT: Wesleyan University Press, 1965. This book is a reflective log of the author's experiences teaching mime to young performers.

Fast, Julius. *Body Language.* New York, NY: Pocket Books, 1971. This is not a theater book per se, but it does inform the reader about body language and the science of kinetics. The author elaborates on body movements that amplify or contradict verbal expression.

Feder, Happy Jack. *Mime Time: 45 Complete Routines for Everyone.* Colorado Springs, CO: Meriwether Publishing, 1992. Written in a pleasant style, this book describes characters and situations in forty-five brief narratives, each suitable as an assignment.

Kipnis, Claude. *The Mime Book.* New York, NY: Harper & Row, 1976. This pictorial manual on the mechanics of mime contains isolation exercises, walks and runs, and an analysis of pantomime. It is divided into three parts: The Body, The Illusion, and Creating a World. The instructor who is interested in body work may find this manual useful.

Lessac, Arthur. *Body Wisdom: The Use and Training of the Human Body.* New York, NY: Drama Book Specialists, 1979. In this book the author sets forth a new way to use and train the human body and voice. Lessac describes an organic and sensory learning process. This work includes drawings on most pages.

Lustig, T.J. *Doubled Up: Or, My Life at the Back End of a Pantomime Horse.* London, England: Fourth Estate, 1990. This book concentrates on the British concept of pantomime.

Martin, Ben. *Marcel Marceau: Master of Mime.* New York, NY: Penguin, 1979. This book is an homage to Marceau and his character "Bip." There are 150 pages of photos with discussion of Marceau's life and ways in which he was influenced.

Martinez, J.D. *Combat Mime: A Non-violent Approach to Stage Violence.* Chicago, IL: Nelson-Hall, 1982. Martinez has compiled a detailed catalog of games, tricks, illusions, falls, punches, kicks, and special effects intended to promote safe fun and self-discipline.

Rolfe, Bari, ed. *Mimes on Miming: Writings on the Art of Mime.* Los Angeles, CA: Panjandrum Books, 1979. This anthology of statements about the art of mime includes illustrations as well as selections by Marceau, Chaplin, Keaton, Dick Van Dyke, Woody Allen, and many other artists.

Shepard, Richmond. *Mime: The Technique of Silence.* New York, NY: Drama Book Specialists, 1971. Designed as a classroom text, this book comprises a thirty-lesson course in mime, a brief history of mime, an explanation of mime makeup, and over one hundred drawings illustrating the text.

Stolzenberg, Mark. *Exploring Mime.* New York, NY: Sterling Publishing Co., 1979. Stolzenberg, a professional mime and clown, gives step-by-step directions for the development of mime skills, offers advice on creating an act and using makeup, and clarifies the ideas with many illustrations.

Videotapes and Films

The Art of Buster Keaton. This consists of two collections of silent features and short films starring Keaton. It is listed in The Video Catalog 1-800-733-2232. Collection I consists of 3 black-and-white videos; 348 minutes. Collection II contains 4 black-and-white videos; 414 minutes.

Cirque du Soleil: We Reinvent the Circus. This video won an Emmy and an Ace Award. It records Le Cirque's original world tour. It is listed in The Video Catalog 1-800-733-2232. Video, color; 55 minutes.

Isadora Duncan: Movement From the Soul. This portrait of the dancer, Isadora Duncan, presents her as a revolutionary choreographer, a scandalous performer, and an agent of social change. It is listed in The Video Catalog 1-800-733-2232. Video, color; 60 minutes.

Lady Windermere's Fan. This silent version of Oscar Wilde's play made in 1925 is directed by Ernst Lubitsch. Video, black and white; 80 minutes.

Martha Graham: The Dancer Revealed. This profile of the modern dancer covers her work as choreographer and teacher. Video, color; 60 minutes.

Pantomime: The Language of the Heart: An Introduction to Mime. Chicago, IL: Encyclopaedia Britannica Educational Corporation, 1973. This is the introductory film for a twelve-film series called *The Art of Silence.* It includes an explanation of mime by Marcel Marceau, as well as several performances. 16mm film, color; 10 minutes.

Slapstick. New York, NY: Sterling Educational Films, Inc., 1960. This film consists of clips from the performances of the top comics in the Slapstick era of the 1920s. It includes clips of Charie Chase, Monty Banks, Fatty Arbuckle, Larry Semon, and Andy Clyde. 16mm film, black and white; 27 minutes.

Journals

Ensemble. New York, NY: Corporeal Studio, Ltd. This journal contains reviews and critiques of mime, clown, and performance arts. Back issues are available.

Movement Theatre Quarterly. Portsmouth, National Movement Theatre Association. Formerly known as *Mime News,* this newsletter focuses exclusively on mime.

New Calliope. Lake Jackson: Olson Publishing. This magazine contains articles on clowning and includes photos, illustrations, and ideas for costuming and makeup.

Internet

Le Centre du Silence. This independent school offers theater and movement seminars and workshops. The school's mailing address is Le Centre du Silence, P.O. Box 1015, Boulder, CO 80306-1015. The Internet address is http://www.indranet.com/lcds.html

Drama*Share.* This Christian Drama Resource Center offers informative features on clowning, magic, mime, puppetry, and more. The Internet address is http://www3.sk.sympatico.ca/dramashr/index.htm

Pantomimes on the Web. This site offers information about the art form of pantomime and provides visitors with the opportunity to examine pantomimes written by Jon Keen for performance by a British theatrical group. The Internet address is http://www.ndirect.co.uk/~jgk/

The World of Mime Theatre. This site is devoted to promoting mime as a serious theatrical art by offering features such as mime resources and information, performance calendars, an index to search for mime-related topics, and links to other theatrical sites. The Internet address is http://www.geocities.com/Broadway/5222/

CHAPTER

3

Voice and Diction

Framework

An actor must use many tools to craft a compelling performance. Among these tools are voice and diction, which are essential when a characterization relies heavily on oral speech.

A strong, controlled voice and good diction can be wonderful attributes, helping people communicate thoughts, emotions, and instructions, onstage and in everyday life. With these an actor can assume a variety of characters and portray emotions that seem genuine to an audience. Voice quality, which is created by resonance and the formation of vowel sounds by the voice organs, is unique to an individual. Even though the voice is inherent, it can be developed with practice. Diction, the selection and pronunciation of words and their combination in speech, is completely a learned skill.

This chapter introduces students to methods for improving the effectiveness of their voices through the study and practice of pitch, inflection, volume, pause, and rate. In the section of the chapter dealing with diction, students will be instructed in correct pronunciation of vowel and consonant sounds. Finally, students will learn to use their improved voices and diction in clear, effective communication, both onstage and offstage.

Teaching Note

Activities found in the **Review Workshop** at the end of the chapter often require some planning or preliminary work by students. Be sure to check these activities, and make sure students have adequate time in which to complete them.

Instructional Objectives

- To develop a more effective speaking voice through relaxation, proper breathing, and good posture
- To learn habits of good diction in order to develop distinctive, effective voices
- To use voice quality, pitch, volume, pause, and rate effectively in interpreting character, mood, and meaning

Vocabulary

quality   the sound of a particular voice

resonance   the vibrant tone produced when sound waves strike the chambers of the throat, head, nose, and mouth

nasality   the sound produced through nasal passages, leaving the voice flat

pitch   the relative highness or lowness of the voice

inflection   modulation, variety in pitch

monotone   an unvaried speaking tone; lack of inflection throughout a speech

volume   the strength, force, or intensity with which sound is made

rate   the speed at which words are spoken

diction   the selection and pronunciation of words and their combinations in speech

schwa(ə)   a pronunciation symbol with the sound of "uh," as in *about*

voiceless   referring to consonants, such as *p*, *t*, and *f*, that do not cause vibration of the vocal folds when sounded

voiced   referring to consonants, such as *b*, *d*, and *v*, that cause vibration of the vocal folds when sounded

pronunciation   the manner of saying words using the correct sounds in words and placing the accent on the stressed syllables

Ancillaries

Forms, Models, and Activities Blackline Masters, pages 7–10

Chapter Test, page 3

Scenes and Monologues: From Euripides to August Wilson

Transparency 2

Motivating Activity

This activity is designed to show students that word choice, inflection, pause, and rate affect successful communication of ideas and emotions.

Show a videotape of a scene that features wordplay, such as Abbott and Costello's "Who's on First" or a scene from Groucho Marx's *Duck Soup.* After students watch the scene, generate a discussion that focuses on the reasons the dialogue is so confusing. Have them name specific words that cause confusion, and elicit from them suggestions of ways in which the dialogue might be spoken to avoid the confusion. Explain to students that the rate of delivery and the emphasis placed on words contribute to the comic success of the scene. Finally, inform students that in this chapter they will learn to improve their diction and use their voices more effectively. These skills will help students to communicate thoughts and ideas both on and off the stage.

EXERCISES: *Warm-up, page 66*

Before students begin these exercises, have them discuss the different techniques they use to relax. You might want to incorporate some of the students' ideas into the warm-up exercise. One simple technique that can be suggested is to lie flat on the back and beginning with the head, relax each part of the body in sequence, moving down to the shoulders, the torso, the arms, the hands, the legs, and the feet.

EXERCISES: *Relaxation, page 67*

Remind students of the importance of relaxing the entire body before focusing on a certain part of it. To begin this exercise, have students massage the points near their ears where their jaw is joined to the facial bones. Then massage around the mouth and chin. This helps relax facial muscles.

EXERCISES: *Breath Control, pages 68–69*

Students can work in pairs to serve as each other's coaches and monitors. This will prevent students from referring to the textbook in the middle of an exercise. For example, as one student does the exercises, the partner might name the different actions to be performed, remind the student of the proper placement of the hands, and emphasize the importance of avoiding muscular tension or strain.

EXERCISES: *Voice Quality, page 71*

Exercise 1 Before assigning this exercise, have students run their fingertips up and down the front of their necks. They should feel alternating bands. Explain that these bands are cartilage and smooth muscle that form the protective wall of the trachea, or windpipe. You might also explain that at the top of the trachea is the larynx, or voice box, and that inside the larynx are the vocal folds.

Exercises 3, 4, and 5 For these exercises, you might have students work in small groups, taking turns reciting the various words and lines. After each recitation, the other members of the group should discuss the person's delivery, noting the speech characteristics that were used to produce different emotions.

Application Activities, page 72

Students should read each selection silently before reading it aloud. They might also copy the passage and mark the accented syllables and the vowels within those syllables. Remind students that accented syllables are not necessarily spoken in a louder voice. Often a subtle emphasis on the vowel sounds can give them the desired stress. When discussing criteria for evaluation, emphasize that the best readings will preserve the selection's meaning while making each vowel sound in an accented syllable as full and rich as possible.

EXERCISES: *Pitch, page 74*

Before students begin these exercises, explain to them that the range of their pitch will most likely increase with practice. Emphasize the importance of relaxing the throat before beginning; tight muscles can cause strain, hoarseness, and a cracking voice.

Exercise 5 Extension The following sentences can be added:

- It was the most wonderful day of my life!
- You make me so angry!
- What did you say you saw in the window?
- I could not believe my eyes.

Exercise 6 Extension Use the following sentences to extend the exercise:

- It was the best of times; it was the worst of times.
- All's well that ends well.
- It is better to have loved and lost than never to have loved at all.

Application Activities, page 75

Before students begin, have them form small groups to discuss the mood and meaning of each passage. Then have members of each group take turns reading the selections aloud. Evaluate the readings on the basis of how well they reflect the appropriate meaning and mood by using inflections. If you use a tape recorder, demonstrate the adjustments one or more readers have made by playing the original and the revised readings. Also, compare the readings of several groups and discuss any differences in inflection and how the differences affect the mood or meaning.

EXERCISES: *Volume, page 77*

Exercise 5 Before students begin, remind them to use intensity, not merely loudness, to convey meaning; to use volume in combination with other voice qualities to suggest various feelings; and to emphasize key ideas through selected emphasis on words or phrases. Be sure to have students explain every interpretation they come up with for each sentence. For example, the first sentence can be read to mean "Someone else said it to her," "I said something else to her," and finally "I said that to someone else."

Application Activities, page 78

Suggest that students copy the passages and underline the words they want to emphasize. As the passages are being read, the other students might then write the words they hear being emphasized. Have them compare their lists with the reader's own underlined words. Readings should be evaluated on how well the meaning and mood are conveyed through the students' selections of words to be emphasized.

Application Activities, page 80

Assessment of each reading should center on the placement and length of the pauses as well as on the effectiveness of the different rates each student chooses. Ask students to give reasons for the pauses and the rate they selected. This activity offers an opportunity to demonstrate how dramatically the meaning of a sentence or passage can be altered by simply varying the pauses and rate. Remind students that a pause should never interrupt a thought group.

▶ **Additional Exercise**

For additional practice with rate and pauses, write this excerpt from *Hamlet* on the board, omitting all punctuation: "To be, or not to be: That is the question: . . ." As they read this excerpt aloud, encourage them to imply as many meanings as possible by changing the length and position of pauses and the rate at which various words are spoken. Remember that important words should be held longer than less important ones.

EXERCISES: *Voice Interpretation, page 82*

Exercise 1 Have students discuss the different voice techniques used to convey the emotions listed in the exercise.

Extension Have students use these additional words and exclamations to express a wide range of feelings and responses: *aaah, wow, but, hey, gee,* and *what.*

Exercise 2 Make sure students are relying on volume, not merely loudness, to project their voices. Remind students to keep the throat relaxed and open.

Extension Additional sentences might include the following:

- Call the doctor!
- Get over here!
- Can you breathe?
- What are you doing?

Application Activities, pages 82–83

Have each student describe the mood and meaning that he or she thinks each passage is trying to convey. Evaluate students on their ability to convey their interpretations of each passage. Remember that students are to be evaluated on their ability to convey the mood and meaning of a passage, not on their ability to interpret the mood and meaning of a passage.

Activity 1 Before attempting the first activity, encourage students to analyze the type of person speaking the passage and to write out their conclusions in order to clarify their thoughts. You might have students form small groups in which to brainstorm ideas and formulate their conclusions.

Activity 2 For the second activity, you might have students choose one of the three passages to study carefully. Encourage students to first read the passage silently in order to then make decisions about quality, volume, pitch, and rate. Next have students read the passage aloud based on their decisions, and finally, encourage students to revise their decisions and read the passage again.

Application Activities, page 84

These listening and analysis activities can be carried out on an ongoing basis throughout the school year. You might wish to have students write a detailed, formal analysis of one or more of these listening activities as a semester project. Be sure that any observations they report are supported by concrete evidence.

EXERCISES: Vowel Sounds, page 86

As students read the words, emphasize the importance of proper pronunciation, especially when using words such as *feel* and *fill* and *ten* and *tin*.

Extension Additional lists of words that focus attention on vowel sounds include: *bee, been, bin, ban, barn, born, burn, bow, bone, boon,* and *boil; dill, dell, dale, deal, dial, doubt,* and *down;* and *me, men, man, mince, mile, muck, mark, mount,* and *moon.*

For a challenge, have a student read several words at random. The rest of the class should listen carefully and record the pronunciation using the phonetic respellings on page 85.

Application Activities, page 87

Before beginning this activity, caution students about allowing the rhythm and rhyme of a poem to dominate the reading. There is always a danger of falling into a sing-song pattern at the expense of the meaning. Also, some students tend to pause at the end of a line, not realizing that the following line completes the thought.

Sometimes it is helpful to write a poem as prose in order to focus on meaning instead of on line breaks and rhyme. Assessment of each reading should be based on the student's ability to emphasize vowel sounds while conveying the meaning and mood of each passage.

For a careful assessment, tape-record a few students' readings, and play them back for the class. Have the other students identify which vowel sounds were pronounced most carefully and the reasons for focusing on these sounds.

EXERCISES: *Consonant Sounds,* page 89

You might want to have students work in pairs, with one student reading the lists of words and the other identifying the type of consonant spoken. Have students take turns reading and identifying.

Extension Additional words that focus attention on consonant sounds include: *coal* and *goal; toll* and *troll; drain* and *rain; sane* and *same;* and *stain* and *strain.* Have students use several similar words in a sentence and read it aloud: *Ben has ten pens,* for example. This will force students to differentiate between similar consonant sounds.

Application Activities, page 90

You might tape-record student readings and invite students to participate in self-assessment or a guided self-assessment (in which you participate). Evaluate students' ability to correctly pronounce similar words in the text, such as *whorls* and *world.*

EXERCISES: *Pronunciation,* page 91

These exercises might best be managed by having students select only a few sentences to concentrate on at one time. Suggest that students select one or two sentences in each exercise and practice them until they have eliminated any hint of mumbling, muttering, or dropping sounds or words.

EXERCISE: *Warm-up,* page 92

Students might be more successful if they concentrate on one or two tongue twisters, practicing until both rate and accuracy are substantially increased.

Application Activities, page 93

This activity might best be managed in pairs, with one student reading the poem and the other listening for clear pronunciation of vowel sounds and consonant sounds. To have students assess the reading, urge them to close their eyes as they listen and see whether—or to what degree—the sounds evoke images of water.

FYI

The designers of the ancient Greek amphitheaters used many devices to improve the audience's ability to hear the actors onstage. For example, to eliminate echoes, to create unobstructed sight lines, and to ensure clear sound projection from the stage to every audience member, theaters were positioned on hillsides with seating built on an incline. Behind the stage was a thick stone wall that prevented the sound of the actors' voices from drifting away from the audience. In addition to that wall, in front and slightly below the stage was a hard, flat floor that reflected sound up toward the audience. Modern designers have incorporated many of these devices into the construction of modern stages.

Chapter Review, page 94

Summary and Key Ideas Sample Responses

1. The keys to a good speaking voice are bodily relaxation, proper breathing, and good posture.

2. Resonance is the vibrant tone produced when sound waves strike the chambers of the throat, head, nose, and mouth. Resonance can be practiced by humming with an open and relaxed throat. It can also be practiced by repeating the same sentence from varying emotional points of view. A third way to practice resonance is by using personal experiences to "color" the meaning of a single word and listening for the special tone qualities that result.

3. Nasality occurs when vowel sounds are diverted from the nasal cavities, cutting down resonance and leaving the voice flat.

4. There are four characteristics of the voice that an effective speaker must use correctly: quality, or the individual sound of the particular voice; pitch, or the relative highness or lowness of the voice at any given time; volume, or the relative strength, force, or intensity with which sound is made; and rate, or the speed at which words are spoken.

5. The most valuable asset an actor or speaker can have is good diction. Good diction not only helps an actor to portray a convincing character onstage but also allows people to communicate their thoughts and ideas more effectively offstage.

6. Diction refers to the selection and pronunciation of words and their combination in speech. To have good diction, a person must avoid these common habits of sloppy speech: mumbling, muttering, or dropping words at the ends of sentences and letters at the ends of words; using the vocal apparatus, especially the tongue, in a lazy manner, resulting in indistinctness; being too meticulous, artificial, or theatrical.

7. Vowels are especially important because they aid an actor in interpretation. Vowels can be lengthened, shortened, and inflected to help change or emphasize meaning.

Discussing Ideas

1. Striving for good diction is important both on and off the stage. Good diction allows for clarity and effectiveness of speech, which improves communication of thoughts and emotions off the stage and also allows a greater emotional range on the stage. A successful discussion should include the benefits of being able to hold the attention and interest of an audience, small or large, and feeling self-confident during any speaking situation.

2. The discussion should touch on some or all of these points:
   - Onstage, actors must breathe for speech, taking quick breaths in through the mouth and controlling the release of breath over a period of time. During ordinary conversation, the same amount of time is typically given to inhalation and exhalation.
   - Ordinary conversation is likely to have a range of only four or five notes, but an actor needs to use two octaves or more.
   - Greater force, intensity, and strength should be employed onstage than in conversation; similarly, both pause and rate might vary more frequently and dramatically onstage.
   - An actor is likely to pronounce the vowel and consonant sounds more clearly and sharply onstage than someone in everyday conversation.

3. Students might mention breathing exercises, exercises to improve voice quality, exercises that build awareness of variation in pitch, exercises that help them widen their customary range, exercises that heighten awareness of volume, and exercises focusing on voice interpretation. Students might also mention pronunciation exercises, especially those that focus specifically on either vowel or consonant sounds.

Review Workshop, page 95

Independent Activities

Projecting Your Voice Evaluate the activity based on these criteria: clear pronunciation that could be heard from midway up a rock wall; a rate of delivery that conveys urgency but does not create hysteria or fear; pauses that effectively give the listener time to follow the instructions but not to become anxious; and volume that conveys energy, self-confidence, and optimism.

Communicating Assess this activity based on how well students are able to adjust their rate and diction to the requirements of people who need to be addressed at a slower rate of speed or with nearly perfect pronunciation.

Cooperative Learning Activity

Choral Reading In this activity, students select a poem, make decisions about reading it dramatically and chorally, and perform the poem. Note decisions students make about pitch, volume, emphasis, and rate, as well as about which lines should be read individually and which should be read chorally. Evaluate how well their reading dramatizes the poem, expresses its meaning, or brings its characters and actions to life.

Other Possible Choices of Texts Students might also select non-narrative poems, such as A. E. Housman's "When I was one-and-twenty" or W. H. Auden's "The Unknown Citizen." In these cases, students should concentrate more on the meaning, mood, and rhythm of the poems than on speakers or characterization.

Across the Curriculum Activity

History A well-executed revised speech will maintain the integrity of the historical figure so that the person's thoughts and feelings are recognizable and credible. The new version of the speech must also be expressed at a pitch, volume, and rate that reflect the seriousness or humor of the original speech as well as its purpose. Remind students that they should be prepared to defend choices they make about the delivery of their chosen speech.

CLOSE

Final Activity

This activity will give students a chance to demonstrate the skills they have acquired, especially those in projecting, pronouncing, inflecting, and timing.

Invite each student to select and memorize a short monologue, a short poem, or a part of a poem. Students may choose a selection from this book or from an outside source.

When students have memorized their selections, go to the school auditorium. Seat each student in a different place in the auditorium, being sure that some students occupy the seats farthest from the stage, while others sit in the center or in the front of the auditorium.

Have students take turns going onstage and reciting their memorized speeches. You might want to provide each student with a copy of the Voice and Diction Evaluation Form found on page 7 of the **Forms, Models and Activities Blackline Masters.** After each recitation, invite members of the audience to comment on how well they could hear the speech and on the strongest aspects of the speaker's voice and diction. Students might also reflect on the differences between practicing a poem or speech in a classroom and delivering the same piece to an audience in an auditorium.

As an extension of this activity, students might want to have their recitations tape-recorded. They can then listen and evaluate their own voices.

Books

Berry, Cicely. *Voice and the Actor.* New York, NY: Macmillan, 1973. Berry tells the reader how to set the voice free using a methodology that does not separate sounds and words from their meanings. Texts are an integral feature of the exercises.

Bowling, Evelyn Burge. *Voice Power.* Mechanicsburg, PA: Stackpole Books, 1980. Bowling shows the reader how to analyze hidden faults in the voice and also how to find a natural voice range. The book includes a test for monotony, as well as exercises to sharpen natural potential.

Fairbanks, Grant. *Voice and Articulation Drillbook.* New York, NY: Harper & Row, 1960. Fairbanks stresses auditory discrimination in which the phonetic and acoustic aspects of speech are the focal points. He includes numerous exercises that enhance voice quality and articulation.

Guralnick, Elissa S., ed. *Sight Unseen: Beckett, Pinter, Stoppard, and Other Contemporary Dramatists on Radio.* Athens, OH: Ohio University Press, 1996. Guralnick has compiled a collection of radio plays accompanied with background, history, and criticism.

King, Robert G., and Eleanor M. DiMichael. *Articulation and Voice: Improving Oral Communication.* New York, NY: Macmillan, 1978. This book addresses every student, not only drama students. The first part covers sounds of the American English language, and the second part is organized around four aspects of voice: quality, loudness, pitch, and rate. Exercises designed to overcome common voice problems are included.

Kuiper, Koenraad. *Smooth Talkers: The Linguistic Performance of Auctioneers and Sportscasters.* Mahwah, NJ: L. Erlbaum Associates, 1996. This book focuses on the particular verbal skills needed in these two professions and generates a new and deeper respect for people in these fields.

Robinson, Karl F. and Charlotte Lee. *Speech in Action.* Glenview, IL: Scott, Foresman, 1965. This text on speech for high school students covers the essentials in six sections and includes many exercises and activities.

Schindler, George. *Ventriloquism: Magic with Your Voice.* David McKay, 1979. Schindler presents a step-by-step guide to becoming a ventriloquist and reveals many tricks of the trade. The author also demonstrates his methods of writing an act and getting bookings. Many photos and line drawings are included.

Skinner, Edith. *Speak with Distinction.* New York, NY: Applause Theatre Book Publishers, 1990. This technical book documents many speech exercises for the actor aiming to improve voice production, vowels, consonants, diphthongs, syllabication, pronunciation, and phrasing.

Turner, Clifford J. *Voice & Speech in the Theatre.* New York, NY: Drama Book Specialists, 1977. This is considered one of the standard textbooks in Great Britain. The author suggests that voice training be based on correct physiological usage. Detailed training is provided, complete with a list of speeches for practice.

Withers-Wilson, Nan. *Vocal Direction for the Theatre: From Script Analysis to Opening Night.* New York, NY: Drama Book Publishers, 1993. This book documents how the theater voice specialist functions as a collaborative artist within the production process. The author stresses the importance of vocal excellence and shows how vocal directors analyze scenes.

Videotapes and Films

Acting: A Study of Life—Outer Techniques of Communication. 1971. Vermillion: University of South Dakota Educational Media Center. Alvina Kraus works with acting students to develop diction, proper use of lips, tongue, and teeth, as well as the body in communication. 16mm film, black and white; 25 minutes.

Cassettes and Recordings

Cassettes and LP recordings of drama are available from Caedmon/Harper & Row. The offerings include works by Beckett, Chekhov, Hansberry, Ibsen, Miller, Molière, O'Casey, O'Neill, Rostand, Shakespeare, Shaw, Sophocles, Wilde, and Williams, as well as many other notable playwrights. Catalog listings and information on the library subscription plan are available from Caedmon/Harper & Row, Keystone Industrial Park, Scranton, PA 18512.

Rosencrantz and Guildenstern Are Dead. The two hapless courtiers from *Hamlet* become central figures in this comic play. Listed in The AudioForum 1-800-243-1234. 2 audiocassettes.

She Stoops to Conquer. This classic comedy by Oliver Goldsmith stars Michael Williams and Judi Dench. Listed in The Audio Forum 1-800-243-1234. 2 audiocassettes.

Internet

Voice and Speech Page. Geared specifically for actors, teachers, trainers, and students, this site shares information on voice and speech research through features like anatomy, physiology, and care of the voice; speech and phonetics; and dialect sampling. The Internet address is http://www.uwindsor.ca/faculty/arts/dramatic/voice/v+s.html

CD-ROM

Theatre of the Imagination: Radio Stories by Orson Welles & the Mercury Theatre. Mac/Win (Hybrid). Recorded in the late 1930s and early 1940s, these fifteen programs reveal how Orson Welles transformed radio. There are a documentary component, program notes, and transcripts of the radio broadcasts. This CD-ROM is available from EDUCORP Multimedia 1-800-843-9497.

World's Greatest Speeches. Win. Published by SoftBit, this multimedia reference library contains over four-hundred speeches on CD-ROM. Key moments of history from ancient Greece to contemporary times are recreated. Audio, video, and text formats are supplemented by pictures and biographies of the speakers. Available from EDUCORP Multimedia 1-800-843-9497.

Multimedia

Skinner, Edith, and Timothy Monich. *Good Speech for the American Actor.* Drama Book Specialists, 1980. Skinner, who was a speech and dialect consultant on Broadway, and Monich, who was a faculty member of The Juilliard Theater Center, developed this tape to provide examples of good speech. This twenty-four page book and the tape comprise a set to be used together.

Speech and Silence: The Language of Drama. This workshop is conducted by the Artistic Director of the Shakespearean Theatre at the Folger. Director Emily Mann discusses her work on *The Glass Menagerie.* It is part of The Annenberg/CPB Multimedia Collection. Information is available by calling 1-800-LEARNER.

CHAPTER

Acting

Framework

Webster's Collegiate Dictionary *defines acting as "the art or practice of representing a character on a stage or before cameras." An actor must learn to study and interpret plays and learn to combine body language, voice, and diction to create a believable character.*

This chapter focuses on the discipline of acting. Like earlier chapters, the emphasis is on the need to analyze and develop techniques for portraying character, delivering lines, and mastering body language. While recognizing that actors can, to a degree, take on certain emotions, instructional emphasis is placed on the learned skills of acting, movement, speech, and interpretation.

In this chapter all previous work in improvisation, pantomime, voice, and diction will come together as students begin to assume dramatic roles.

The image of the actor making repeated curtain calls to thunderous applause is possibly what motivated many of your students to take a course in drama. Your challenge will be to preserve and cultivate student enthusiasm for acting and the vision of the curtain call, while demanding hard work and a mastery of basic acting skills.

Teaching Note

Activities found in the **Review Workshop** at the end of the chapter often require some planning or preliminary work by students. Be sure to check these activities, and make sure students have adequate time in which to complete them.

Instructional Objectives

- To become familiar with the special terminology of acting in order to work comfortably and efficiently onstage
- To create well-researched, convincing characterizations by studying plays and learning to score roles, score scripts, and build character sketches
- To develop a balanced approach to characterization using emotional or subjective acting, technical or objective acting, or a combination of these
- To successfully combine the sixteen keys to characterization with common onstage gestures, positions, movements, and stage business to portray a character

Vocabulary

emotional *or* subjective acting the playing of a role in such a way that the actor weeps, suffers, or struggles emotionally

technical *or* objective acting use of learned skills of acting, movement, speech, and interpretation to create roles; no emotional response is used

leading roles the main characters in a play

protagonist the main character in a play

antagonist the person or force working against the protagonist in a play

supporting roles those characters who act as contrasts to others; characters with whom other characters, usually the protagonist, are compared

straight parts roles in which the actor and the character are similar

character parts roles in which actors portray traits that differ from their own to produce a desired character

characterization putting together all facets of a character to bring life and interest to that character

primary source the observation of a person's posture, movements, habits, voice inflections, and mannerisms in order to build character

secondary sources books that help in developing characterization

body language communication that uses gestures, posture, and facial expressions instead of words

master gesture a distinctive action that is repeated and serves as a clue to a character's personality, such as a peculiar laugh or walk

inflection modulation, variety in pitch

subtext the meaning "between the lines" that an actor must draw from the script

substitution the use by an actor of a personal experience to relate to the experience of a character within a play

improvising the impromptu portrayal of a character or scene without any rehearsal or preparation

paraphrasing restating lines in one's own words

Ancillaries

Forms, Models, and Activities Blackline Masters, pages 11–20

Chapter Tests, pages 4, 5, 6

Scenes and Monologues: From Euripides to August Wilson

Transparencies 3, 4

Motivating Activity

This activity will introduce students to acting by having them portray and identify basic traits of characterization, including body language and voice. It will also demonstrate that students already have experiences and observations that they can draw on to add to their character portrayals.

Choose seven students to portray the seven dwarfs from Walt Disney's *Snow White and the Seven Dwarfs*. Do not tell the rest of the class which dwarf each student is portraying, but list on the board the dwarfs' names: Doc, Grumpy, Dopey, Sneezy, Sleepy, Bashful, and Happy.

Allow the students portraying dwarfs a few minutes to prepare a short scene in which they are making dinner for Snow White. As students are preparing their scene, explain to the rest of the class that they must identify each dwarf. After the scene is finished and the class has identified the dwarfs, discuss the characteristic traits of the dwarfs that lead to the identification. Emphasize the importance of body language and delivery of lines in indicating character.

Explain to students that even though this is a very basic characterization, it still demonstrates the experience and knowledge they already possess and can bring to the stage. Assure students that in this chapter they will learn even more ways to portray characters.

TEACH

Application Activities, page 101

Activity 1 If necessary, move desks and chairs aside to create a stage large enough for students to move comfortably. Masking tape or chalk can be used to mark the boundaries of the stage. If necessary, mark off the nine areas of the stage and walk students through them.

Actors should concentrate not only on their stage positions but also on how they arrive at those positions, making each movement contribute to the scene. The audience, positioned in front of the stage area, should be critical of the movements. They should be able to tell which character should be the center of attention and to explain which movements or gestures by other characters may have diverted that attention.

Activity 2 Provide students with enough time to develop their characters. They may need to refer to pages 143–145 for tips about creating a successful comedy. As students act, they should use voice techniques to accentuate their characters. Their body language will convey their emotions. A selection of props will help students get into their roles.

Activity 3 The director should help the actor find the meaning within the character and the emotions behind the monologue. The actor should take a few moments to understand the character. The two should discuss gestures and stage movements that will convey the emotions.

▶ Additional Application Activity

Have nine students stand in the nine acting areas. Give a small bean bag or a similar object to one of the students. As you or a student call out a stage position, such as downstage center, upstage right, and so on, the student holding the bean bag tosses it to the student standing in that acting area. Rotate students in and out of the various areas. With practice, students should learn to respond automatically to the directions.

Application Activity, page 105

You might prefer to make this a class activity. If so, rent or obtain a videotape and show it to the entire class. The analysis can then take the form of a class discussion. If you are able to obtain several appropriate videos, you might elect to divide the class into groups to view the movies of their choice and work together on the analysis.

▶ Additional Application Activity

Have students identify an actor they feel has been repeatedly typecast. Ask the following question: Do certain actors always seem to portray sinister villains, comic sidekicks, or romantic leads? Have students discuss the difference between typecasting and casting by type.

Application Activity, page 108

Rent or obtain a video and watch it as a class activity. Ask students to focus their attention on one actor's characterization. Have students work in small groups to discuss and prepare a single character sketch. Tell students that they should be prepared to defend their analyses. Compare the sketches of each group for areas of agreement and disagreement. For the discussion of the second question, have students review the character sketches for information about the place and period of the production. Emphasize the importance of including the setting in a character sketch.

Extension Rent or obtain videos of two or more performances of the same work featuring different actors in the leading roles. Watch the videos as a class. Ask students to focus on differences in characterization. Lead a class discussion on the differences in characterization. Did the students prefer one characterization to another? What did they learn about the character by comparing the different traits the actors chose to emphasize in their interpretations?

EXERCISES: Script Scoring, page 112

Before you begin these exercises, write the following sentences from **A Treasury of Scenes and Monologues** on the board.

- The truth is rarely pure and never simple.
- How independent can I become if I live right across the street from you?
- You did this all to deceive me, just for deception?
- You're the strangest girl I ever did see!
- Well, if you want to know, Cecily happens to be my aunt.

Begin by having students look at the script scoring symbols on page 111. Read each of these sentences aloud and have the class discuss the best way to score the sentence. Try scoring the sentences for different meanings in delivery. This should familiarize students with the symbols, making the script scoring exercise easier.

▶ Additional Exercise

Play a recording of the same passage from a Shakespearean play performed by two different actors. Ask students to concentrate on the differences in delivery as they listen to the two recordings. Have students discuss how the actors differed in their delivery and then discuss how each delivery might have been scored.

Application Activity, page 112

Before assigning this activity, make copies of the monologues you would like the students to work on and distribute the copies to the class. Advise students that they probably will not use all the symbols available to them when scoring a script. You might opt to have a few pairs of students read from their scripts. Have a class discussion on the differences in scoring and delivering. Allow students some latitude in using the symbols in the text or their own personal set of scoring symbols.

Application Activity, page 120

It is important for students to choose a character from a play that they have never seen performed. This will ensure that they do not simply use a primary source that reminds them of the actor they have seen playing the role. Insist that students list the traits under the headings suggested on page 120 or similar headings that you approve before they complete the lists. Encourage students to experiment with several primary sources, and, if necessary, have students use a combination of two or three sources. Make sure the listed attributes of the primary sources fit the chosen characters.

Application Activities, page 123

Activity 1 Clear a space in the classroom large enough to serve as the bus. To be sure that the bus does not increase in size to accommodate additional passengers as they board the bus, mark off the perimeters of the bus with tape or chalk. Tell students that they must remain inside the bus during the activity. Give some students "extra" roles as passengers on the bus. Then assign other students the roles listed in the activity. You might want to divide the class in half and have one half of the class complete the activity while the other half observes. If possible, have the two groups rehearse in areas where they cannot see each other, so the students in the second group have a clear plan before they see the first group perform. Evaluate each student on his or her ability to express the character's personality in contrast to the other characters on the bus.

Extension Some additional situations include the following:

- A swaggering military officer accustomed to giving orders that are executed promptly and without question

- A sly jewel thief who is able to slither through dark, tight places without being detected

- A titled aristocrat known for his meticulous attention to maintaining an impeccable appearance

Activity 2 After each student has acted out the character crossing the street, ask the other students to identify the lead. If they do not identify the lead the student was attempting to project, suggest ways the student could make the lead clearer to the audience. Tell students they should be prepared to discuss the leads they have chosen for their characters.

Extension Some additional situations include the following:

- A baseball player known for his base-stealing ability

- An absent-minded mathematician who can solve complicated equations without a calculator but sometimes forgets where he or she is going

- An impatient workaholic who hates to waste time that could be put to better use

EXERCISES: *Entrances and Exits or Movement, page 125*

Review the chart on page 125 before doing these exercises. It might be helpful to review the reasons for these rules, namely that certain patterns of movement and body positions allow actors to face the audience without blocking other actors. Clear an area in the classroom and mark off a space to serve as the stage. Use masking tape or chalk to mark the stage entrances and the stage exits. Ask students to watch carefully as one student enters and exits the stage. Ask them to note especially the proper use of the upstage foot for entering the stage and the upstage arm for gestures. Students should also note the *S* crossing pattern. After each student has completed the activity, ask the other students to assess the entrances and exits using the chart on page 125.

Extension The following situation can be used to extend the exercise:

> A woman and her child are seated on a sofa facing the audience. Her husband opens a door and enters stage right. He says, "I thought this day would never end!" and then crosses the stage and sits in a chair upstage left. After a few minutes, the woman gets up and exits through a door downstage left.

Application Activities, page 127

Before trying these activities, discuss with students the dramatic situations reflected in each line. Ask them what emotion each line reveals. Ask students how the suggested stage positions enhance the presentation of the emotions they have identified. Also, ask students what kind of relationship the suggested positions establish between the actor and the audience and among the actors on the stage. Then have a few students perform the activity while their classmates watch. Assess student performances based on the execution of the given stage technique and on the presentation of the identified emotions.

Extension Some additional situations include the following:

- While listening to a politician make a speech full of campaign promises, one actor in the audience says, "I've heard all this before." [cheat out]

- A group of jurors mill around a jury deliberation room. One juror abruptly announces, "All right! All right! I'll vote guilty, too." [turn the scene in]

EXERCISES: *Inflection, page 133*

Have students take turns reading the lines aloud. After the reading, ask them what emotion each line reveals.

Extension Have students say the following lines, using several different inflections. Have other students identify the different emotions expressed by the inflections used.

- It was you!

- What's the use?

- I have made up my mind. This is how we're going to do it.

- Surely, you're not going out in this weather.
- I'm sorry, but I just can't allow you to copy my notes.

▶ **Additional Inflection Exercises**

Have students attempt to convey the meaning of a line, using nonsense words or gibberish and inflection. For example, students might say, "Blab, blab, blab, blab, blab" so as to mean "Get out of my way." Practice using inflection to convey meaning by reading Lewis Carroll's poem "Jabberwocky."

Application Activities, page 136

Activity 1 Have students skim pages 181 through 218, reviewing the scenes from different plays. Students should choose to work with one of the contemporary plays because of the more familiar speech patterns. Before students begin writing the subtext for each character, suggest that they carefully read the complete scene to understand the characters' thoughts within the context of the total scene. Remind students that learning to think as a character thinks will help them deliver lines more effectively. Base the assessment of students' work on their ability to interpret the subtext. Elicit discussion from students as to how the second reading differed from the first and how these differences made the second reading more meaningful.

Activity 2 You might wish to have individual students deliver the lines while standing at the back of the classroom or behind a moveable bulletin board or screen. This focuses attention on the vocal aspect of the delivery, and students will not be able to rely on facial expressions to show the sarcasm implied in the subtexts. Focus especially on the final four lines in which the words are identical, but the subtext changes. Analyze closely the vocal changes that occur with each new subtext. This exercise provides an opportunity for students to experience the contrast between what is said and what is meant. Evaluate the students' ability to express the given emotion without the aid of facial expressions or body language.

▶ **Additional Application Activity**

Ask students to work in pairs to prepare a short scene using the following dialogue:

First Character:	I beg your pardon.
Second Character:	No problem.
First Character:	Do you mind?
Second Character:	Not at all.
First Character:	I think you have made a mistake.
Second Character:	Are you certain?
First Character:	Well of course. How foolish of me.

Students may not alter, drop, or add any lines. They must, however, develop a story that fits the dialogue and then write the subtext to show what each character thinks but does not say. If possible, clear a small space in the classroom and allow students to use simple props.

EXERCISES: Acting Techniques, page 140

Exercise 1 You might want to have the class discuss the different characters and decide on the best way to portray the emotions of each. Have the students who opted for the substitution technique describe the similar experience they would use to help capture the appropriate emotion. Have students who chose the improvisation technique explain their choice by demonstrating that they know the characters' motivations.

Exercise 2 After hearing one or more students read the original script, you might have the class write what they think the other voice is saying. Then have the reader supply the unheard voice for the script. Compare what students thought the unheard voice was saying and what the reader actually intended.

EXERCISES: Delivering Lines, page 142

Exercise 1 Remind students that the way in which they speak a person's name reveals how they feel about that person. Ask individual students to demonstrate how they might pronounce a person's name if they were extremely happy to see someone. How would the pronunciation vary if they were angry with that person?

Exercise 2 You might prefer to make paraphrasing the speech a class activity. First, read the entire excerpt to the class. Then have students break the excerpt down line by line, paraphrasing each line in their own words. Finally, combine the line-for-line paraphrase into a contemporary translation. After the paraphrased version is complete, you might want to have several students read both the original and the new versions. Discuss the differences in delivery.

Exercise 3 Before they read these sentences, have students work in pairs to decide what the key words are in each passage. You might wish to have one person in each pair read aloud each sentence with the initial sound word and the partner read the same sentence without the sound word. This exercise can demonstrate how the sound word can make it easier to change the vocal pitch without changing the meaning of the key words.

FYI

An unknown actor became famous in one of the most unusual schemes in American theater history. Edwin Forrest offered a prize of $500 for the best tragedy about a Native American written by an American playwright. The winning play was titled *Metamora,* by John Augustus Stone of Concord, Massachusetts. Forrest cast himself in the starring role and publicized the play by claiming it to be the first play by an American, about an American, and starring an American. While there may be some doubts about this claim, there is no doubt that his scheme worked. Edwin Forrest became the first celebrity of the American stage.

Application Activities, page 146

Before students begin, remind them that facial expressions and body language are important and that the breathing techniques for both laughter and crying are much the same. Allow time for students to first review and practice the breathing as taught on pages 144 and 145 and then to prepare emotionally for these readings. Students might apply the technique of substitution, described on page 137, by recalling a sad or funny event as a means of capturing the emotional response required by the activities. Possibly have each student concentrate on one each of the crying and laughing activities. Base assessment of performances on the believability of the laughter and tears.

EXERCISES: *Dialect, page 150*

Allow time for students to review the pronunciation guidelines on pages 148 and 149 before reading the lines. Some students might want to write out the dialect using their own phonetic system. Tape-recording and then playing back the students' voices as they read lines can also be helpful. Hearing one's own voice makes it easier to improve speaking a new dialect.

Extension Have two or more students who have mastered one of the dialects improvise a full scene, concentrating on dialogue rather than actions.

ASSESS

Chapter Review, page 156

Summary and Key Ideas Sample Responses

1. Directors often give beginning actors the same advice that Shakespeare expressed in Act III, Scene 2 of Hamlet. Refer to page 98 of the text for the original passage.

- Speak the lines of the author as written, distinctly and fluently, with an understanding of their meaning.
- Do not use elaborate and artificial gestures. Keep energy in reserve in order to build to an emotional climax smoothly and effectively.
- Do not resort to far-fetched action or noise simply to please unintelligent and unappreciative onlookers.

2. Konstantin Stanislavski, a Russian-born actor and director, created "The Method," the most discussed and influential acting theory today. Actors use Stanislavski's "magic if" to analyze both their own and their character's inner natures. The actors ask themselves what they would do if the events in the play were actually happening to them.

3. A character sketch should include summaries of the character's biography, mental traits, emotional traits, behavior, motivations, and physical traits, as well as information on the character's purpose and function in the play.

4. Both role scoring and script scoring are techniques that help actors become familiar with the characters they are portraying. In role scoring, the actor answers a series of questions about the character, including the following:

    • What rhythm might you associate with your character?

    • What is your character's master gesture?

    • What are your character's major wants and desires?

    To score a script an actor makes notes on the script, marking the pauses, pitch levels, emphasis, speed of delivery, phrasing, pronunciation, character revelation, movement, stage business, and any special function a given line or direction might have within the context of the play.

5. Students may choose any five of the sixteen keys to characterization. Refer to pages 113 through 119 for a complete discussion of each key.

6. A cross is movement from one stage position to another. It is usually followed by a countercross, which is a movement in the opposite direction by another actor, to maintain the balance of the stage picture.

7. There are thirteen recommendations for stage movement listed in the chart on page 125. Students should select three from each category.

8. Three rules for eating onstage:

    • Do not eat or drink any more than is necessary.

    • Do not deliver lines with food in your mouth unless the script calls for it.

    • Learn how to get rid of food that is in your mouth.

9. Some important techniques for playing comedy:

    • Lift the end of a punch line and leave it hanging, or play it "flat," or deadpan.

    • Clinch the punch line with a facial or bodily reaction.

    • Learn to feed a line to a fellow performer so that he or she can catch it in midair and clinch the laugh on the following laugh line.

    • Study the most effective way of topping a particular line.

Discussing Ideas

1. The discussion should focus on the clear distinction between the two approaches. In the emotional or subjective approach, an actor attempts to actually take on the emotion of the character. In the technical or objective approach, an actor relies on an analysis of the character's personality and on the learned skills needed to portray the emotion.

    In applying each approach to the mother/child situation in the question, students should indicate that an actor using the subjective approach might imagine herself in the actual situation or a similar situation and experience the suffering the mother might feel. Students should also recognize that an actor using an objective approach would focus on the gestures, body movements, and similar outward demonstrations of the emotion and would attempt to realistically portray that emotion onstage.

    You might wish to enlarge the discussion to include an assessment of the strengths and weaknesses of each approach in this or other dramatic situations.

2. Be sure students are able to explain the difference between the leading roles of protagonist and antagonist and a supporting role such as the foil. Students should not confuse the types of roles with straight or character parts. Leading and supporting roles can be either straight parts or character parts.

    When discussing the importance of roles, students should recognize that the protagonist and antagonist embody the basic conflict of the play while the supporting roles often offer a comparison or contrast to the leading roles. Be sure students understand, however, that supporting roles can be equally challenging for an actor and just as important for the success of the play.

3. You might have students work in groups of three or four. Each group should decide on a role and choose the characterization keys that would be the most helpful in developing the character. Each group can then report their choice of role and keys. For a productive class discussion, encourage individuals to challenge other groups by questioning the keys to characterization that were chosen.

4. The discussion about acting on arena and thrust stages should include some of the following key considerations:

- Actors must be conscious of the surrounding spectators who must be able to see and hear everything.
- Very few pointing of lines and accenting of key words must combine with a few clear-cut gestures that are effective from every angle.
- Actors must enter and exit without a curtain.
- Lines must be spoken so as to be heard even when the actor turns away.

Review Workshop, page 157

Independent Activities

Observation Clear a small area in the classroom for students to do their imitations. If simple props are necessary, have students be responsible for their own. You might allow time for students to practice in private. Encourage the class to be especially attentive to the minute gestures that will indicate the person being portrayed. When students recognize certain characteristics of the star being imitated, have them raise their hands before they state their guesses. In assessing each student's success, pay attention to subtle elements of the imitation.

Externalization As with the previous activity, it is best to clear a small space in the classroom before beginning. When each student

has acted out the scene, encourage other class members to identify the lead gesture, guess the action verb, and tell what they think is happening. Then ask students to assess the performances of one another by offering positive comments. You may want to include other action words such as repel, ignore, threaten, escape, and examine.

Cooperative Learning Activities

Concentration Suggest that students begin with a small imaginary mirror, focusing on just facial expressions, and then progress to a full-length imaginary mirror that captures all body movements. Allow ample time for students to rehearse. Assess the performances on the basis of concentration and synchronization of movement.

Stage Position and Movement Allow students ample time to develop their scenes. After each scene is performed, encourage the class to participate in a critique of the stage movements. A successful scene will incorporate crisp, pointed dialogue coupled with appropriate stage movements.

Across the Curriculum Activities

History If possible, students should do some research into the background of the character they choose. To prepare for this activity, either bring appropriate books from the library or allow time for students to work in the library. Have students avoid a historical character, such as Abraham Lincoln, who has been portrayed frequently in movies and plays. Students might tend to imitate a performance they have seen rather than develop their own characterization. Evaluate the character sketches for their thoroughness and accuracy of the character's personality.

Foreign Language You might want to vary the role of the resident of the foreign country. Suggest that the resident can be tolerant and patient, timid and reserved, or equally obnoxious as the tourist. Evaluate each student's characterization and use of dialect. If necessary, allow students time to think through a script and practice a particular dialect.

Final Activity

Have each student choose a character from a familiar play. It might be from one of the selections in **A Treasury of Scenes and Monologues** in the text or a play studied in a literature class. Then have students study their characters and create detailed character sketches following the format on page 107. After analyzing the characters and applying some objective acting techniques, each student should assume the role of his or her character and allow the rest of the class to conduct an interview. The student might first introduce himself or herself to the class in character and then sit, stand, pace, or engage in whatever posture seems appropriate to the character. As the class asks questions, the student should answer as the character would.

After answering questions for a predetermined amount of time, discuss with the class which answers or actions most enhanced the characterization. Also encourage the class to note anything that seemed out of character.

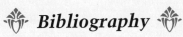

Bibliography

Books

Adler, Stella. *The Technique of Acting*. New York, NY: Bantam Books, 1988. Adler, a legend in the theater, presents a comprehensive and practical guide to her acclaimed acting techniques. The foreword is by Marlon Brando.

Barker, Clive. *Theatre Games: A New Approach to Drama Training*, 4th ed. New York, NY: Drama Book Specialists, 1977. Barker details how to play theater games through which acting skills develop. The games are arranged in order of complexity and illustrated with photographs and diagrams.

Benedetti, Robert L. *The Actor at Work*. Englewood Cliffs, NJ: Prentice Hall, 1986. The author uses the drama and role-playing of real life as the basis for acting. The foreword is by Ted Danson.

Boleslavsky, Richard. *Acting: The First Six Lessons*. New York, NY: Theatre Arts Books, 1975. Boleslavsky draws upon his experiences as an actor and director with the Moscow Art Theatre to take the beginning drama student through the basics of acting. The format of the book is a dialogue between teacher and student.

Brestoff, Richard. *The Great Acting Teachers and Their Methods*. Lyme, NH: Smith & Kraus, 1995. This book offers a critical look at masterful teachers of acting.

Brook, Peter. *There Are No Secrets: Thoughts on Acting and Theatre*. London, England: Methuen, 1993. The author provides an interesting look at the business of acting and the acting business.

Bruder, Melissa, et al. *A Practical Handbook for the Actor*. New York, NY: Vintage Books, 1986. Written by six students who attended a summer acting workshop given by David Mamet, this book gives advice about "truthful" acting and the analysis of scenes to make them relevant to the actor's life.

Cole, Toby, and Helen Chinoy. *Actors on Acting*. New York, NY: Crown, 1980. This collection of comments by actors about acting practices includes over one hundred selections that date from the sixth century B.C. to 1970. Separate national sections combine to form a concise history of the actors.

Crawford, Jerry L. *Acting: In Person and in Style*, 3d ed. Dubuque, IA: William C. Brown Publishers, 1983. Crawford covers acting styles from classical antiquity to Absurd theater with a blend of scholarship and practicality. Concrete advice and exercises for each style are also offered.

Franklin, Miriam A., and James G. Dixon. *Rehearsal: The Principles and Practice of Acting for the Stage*, 6th ed. New York, NY: Prentice Hall, 1983. This widely used textbook offers comprehensive and detailed coverage of the rehearsal process.

Gielgud, John, and John Miller. *Acting Shakespeare*. New York, NY: Scribner,

1992. In this book, one of the great Shakespearean actors of the twentieth century shares his approach to Shakespearean acting, interpretation, phrasing, and delivery.

Glenn, Stanley. *The Complete Actor.* Boston, MA: Allyn & Bacon, 1977. This practical acting guide is divided into five parts: The Actor as Creator, The Actor as Interpreter and Technician, Greek Theater, Shakespearean Tragedy, and Comedy.

Hagen, Uta. *A Challenge for the Actor.* New York, NY: Scribner, 1991. A giant of the New York stage, Hagen divides her book into four parts: The Actor, The Human Techniques, The Exercises, and The Role. The last section contains advice addressed to teachers of acting, suggesting improvisation for young students rather than staged and memorized performance.

Hagen, Uta, and Haskel Frankel. *Respect for Acting.* New York, NY: Macmillan, 1973. A highly respected actress and teacher, Hagen's approach to teaching is sensible and thorough.

Jeffri, Joan, ed. *The Actor Speaks: Actors Discuss Their Experiences and Careers.* Westport, CT: Greenwood Press, 1994. This book offers the advice of several established actors to anyone considering the theater as a career.

Jesse, Anita. *Let the Part Play You: A Practical Approach to the Actor's Creative Process,* 3d ed. Burbank, CA: Wolf Creek Press,1994. This book focuses on the business of building an actor's confidence by offering down-to-earth exercises and advice that respects the magic of acting.

Jilinsky, Andrius. *The Joy of Acting: A Primer for Actors.* New York, NY: Peter Lang, 1990. This text-manual presents carefully selected exercises that progress from simple to difficult.

Levin, Irina, and Igor Levin. *Working on the Play and the Role: The Stanislavski Method for Analyzing the Characters in a Drama.* Chicago, IL: Ivan R. Dee, 1992. The Levins break the text of *The Cherry Orchard* into individual "events" and lead the reader through an analysis of each situation, exploring the motivations and feelings of the characters. This method, once understood, is meant to be applied to any play.

Lewis, Robert. *Advice to the Players.* New York, NY: Harper & Row, 1980. Lewis founded the Actor's Studio with Elia Kazan and Cheryl Crawford in 1947. Lewis presents a program of study for the actor, including detailed exercises to strengthen technique.

Miller, Allan. *A Passion for Acting: Exploring the Creative Process.* New York, NY: Back Stage Books, 1992. Barbra Streisand was just fifteen when Miller started training her as an actor. This book includes many Streisand anecdotes as well as an innovative set of acting exercises. Topics include inspiration, relaxation, sense and emotional memories, character work, auditions, and rehearsals.

Moore, Sonia. *The Stanislavski System: The Professional Training of an Actor.* New York, NY: Penguin Books, 1984. This is a clearly written guide to the Stanislavskian method of acting, which endeavors to put individuals in touch with themselves and to increase their sensitivity. This guide includes detailed explanations of emotional memory, physical actions onstage, imagination, concentration, tempo-rhythm, and how to build a convincing character.

Morris, Eric. *Being & Doing: A Workbook for Actors.* Los Angeles, CA: Whitehouse/ Spelling Publications, 1981. This manual focuses on solving common acting problems. Morris seeks to engender "truthful" acting based on real-life experiences.

Morris, Eric, and Joan Hotchkis. *No Acting Please.* Los Angeles, CA: Whitehouse/ Spelling Publications, 1979. This book helps actors get in touch with a deeper self. There are sections on topics such as sense memory, ego preparation, and vulnerability relating to other actors. Excerpts from Hotchkis's journal, which record her own acting process and feelings, are included. The preface is by Jack Nicholson.

Owen, Mack. *The Stages of Acting: A Practical Approach for Beginning Actors.* New York, NY: Harper Collins Publishers, 1993. This book presents an acting course for beginners and intermediate acting students.

Poisson, Camille L. *Theater and the Adolescent Actor: Building a Successful School Program.* Hamden, CT: Archon Books, 1994. This book was inspired from Poisson's experience as a secondary school drama teacher, a master teacher, and a teacher-trainer at the Emerson College Theater Department. It includes a guide for creating and maintaining a high school drama program, functioning effectively in a public school environment, and meeting the needs of adolescents both as students and performers.

Rockwood, Jerome. *The Craftsmen of Dionysus: An Approach to Acting.* New York, NY: Applause Books, 1992. Rockwood describes the skills and attitudes required by good actors. This is a nurturing book that emphasizes the necessity of students cultivating discipline.

Shurtleff, Michael. *Audition: Everything an Actor Needs to Know to Get the Part.* New York, NY: Walker & Co., 1978. This book prepares actors for auditions by describing possible situations and predicaments and suggesting ways to deal with each circumstance effectively. The advice can apply, by extension, to anyone preparing for a job interview. The foreword is by Bob Fosse.

Spolin, Viola. *Theater Games for Rehearsal: A Director's Handbook.* Evanston, IL: Northwest University Press, 1985. This comprehensive rehearsal guide describes, among many other things, the technique of sidecoaching during a rehearsal.

Stanislavski, Konstantin. *An Actor Prepares.* New York, NY: Theatre Arts Books, 1936. This classic text describes Stanislavski's basic acting method.

———. *An Actor's Handbook.* New York, NY: Theatre Arts Books, 1963. This book is a compendium of alphabetically arranged comments on theater by Stanislavski.

———. *Building a Character.* New York, NY: Theatre Arts Books, 1977. A sequel to his earlier book, *An Actor Prepares*, the author covers physical characterization, speech, voice, movement, gestures, tempo, and rhythm in this book.

———. *Creating a Role.* New York, NY: Theatre Arts Books, 1980. This volume documents the end of Stanislavsky's life work. Three plays are discussed in detail: *Much Woe from Wit, Othello,* and *The Inspector General.*

———. *My Life in Art.* New York, NY: Theatre Arts Books, 1952. This history of Stanislavsky's childhood in Moscow describes his failure as an actor and continues through the establishment of his celebrated acting school.

Suzman, Janet. *Acting with Shakespeare: The Comedies.* New York, NY: Applause, 1995. This is a practical book for anyone attempting to stage Shakespeare's comedies.

Whelan, Jeremy. *Instant Acting: A Revolutionary Acting, Rehearsal & Audition Method for Beginners to Professionals.* Cincinnati, OH: Betterway Books, 1994. Whelan's basic technique is simple: Tape a reading of the scene, and then immediately act it out to the playback without lip movement. His methods help resolve the battle between instinct and technique. There are many exercises, and some focus on modifying inhibitions.

Zarilli, Phillip B., ed. *Acting (Re)Considered: Theories and Practices.* London, England; New York, NY: Routledge, 1995. This is a wide-ranging collection of theories on acting. Zarilli is a professor of theatre and drama at the University of Wisconsin-Madison and has been the director of the Asian/Experimental Theatre Program since 1980. In that program he uses Asian martial arts in training actors.

Videotapes and Films

All the World's a Stage. 1975. This film follows the training of three actors at the Juilliard School's Drama Division from audition and acceptance through their training. 16mm film, color; 20 minutes.

The Dresser. 1983. Peter Yates directs this version of Ronald Harwood's play about an old stage actor and his loyal valet in wartime England. The cast includes Albert Finney and Tom Courtenay. Video, color; 118 minutes.

A Few Good Men. 1992. Jack Nicholson, Tom Cruise, and Demi Moore star in this film version of the Broadway play. Daring to challenge the Marine Corps' code of conduct, two young military lawyers take an explosive legal case. Video, color; 138 minutes.

The Gin Game. 1984. This is a live, onstage performance featuring Jessica Tandy and Hume Cronyn, the original stars of this award-winning play. This two-character play delves into the relationship of two senior citizens. Video, color; 82 minutes.

The Glass Menagerie. 1987. This version stars Joanne Woodward and John Malkovich and is directed by Paul Newman. Available through Schlessinger Video Productions 1-800-843-3620. Video, color; 134 minutes.

The Great White Hope. 1970. An emotional character study of the first African American heavyweight champion, Jack Johnson, it features a classic performance by James Earl Jones. Video, color; 101 minutes.

Hamlet. 1948. Laurence Olivier won the 1948 Oscar for best actor for his performance in this film. Video, black and white; 150 minutes.

Hedda. 1975. Glenda Jackson co-stars with other Royal Shakespeare Company actors in this Trevor Nunn adaptation of Ibsen's *Hedda Gabler.* Video, color; 103 minutes.

Henry V. 1944. Laurence Olivier stars in, directs, and produces this version. Video, black and white; 137 minutes.

Henry V. 1989. This Kenneth Branagh version of Shakespeare's play includes an all-star cast. Video, color; 138 minutes.

The Little Foxes. 1941. Bette Davis stars in this version of Lillian Hellman's play about an amoral family and corruption in the South. Video, black and white; 116 minutes.

Long Day's Journey into Night: 30th Anniversary Edition. 1962. This film adaptation of O'Neill's play with Katharine Hepburn and Jason Robards is directed by Sidney Lumet. It is available through Critic's Choice Video 1-800-367-7765. 2 videos, black and white; 180 minutes.

Look Back in Anger. 1989. This adaptation of John Osborne's play was made for British television and stars Kenneth Branagh and Emma Thompson. Video, color; 114 minutes.

Marat/Sade. 1966. The Royal Shakespeare Company performs Peter Weiss's play in this film adaptation by Peter Brook. The action unfolds in a mental asylum, where the infamous Marquis de Sade leads his fellow inmates in a re-enactment of the bloody assassination of Jean-Paul Marat during the French Revolution. It is listed in The Video Catalog 1-800-733-2232. Video, color; 115 minutes.

On Golden Pond. 1981. A film written by Ernest Thompson, it stars Henry Fonda, Katharine Hepburn, and Jane Fonda. Video, color; 109 minutes.

Only When I Laugh. 1981. This is Neil Simon's adaptation of his play *The Gingerbread Lady.* Marsha Mason and Kristy McNichol play the principal roles. Video, color; 121 minutes.

The Piano Lesson. 1995. Charles S. Dutton performs his Broadway role of Boy Willie in this Pulitzer Prize-winning play by August Wilson directed by Lloyd Richards. Hallmark Hall of Fame. It is listed in The Video Catalog 1-800-733-2232. Video, color; 99 minutes.

Playing the Part: Characters and Actors in Drama. The Annenberg/CPB Multimedia Collection. Several interpretations of *Hamlet* are shown followed by an interview with Shakespearean actor John Vickery. Available by calling 1-800-LEARNER. Video, color; 30 minutes.

Playing Shakespeare. Princeton, NJ: Films for the Humanities, 1983. This series was produced by International London Weekend Television. It consists of discussions and dramatizations of various themes in Shakespeare's works. It is narrated by John Barton and includes performances by members of the Royal Shakespeare Company. These films are available for purchase or rental, in videotape or 16mm film, from Films for the Humanities, Inc., P.O. Box 2053, Princeton, NJ 08543.

The Rainmaker. 1956. Burt Lancaster and Katharine Hepburn play the principal roles in this movie adaptation of N. Richard Nash's play. Video, color; 121 minutes.

Richard III. 1955. Laurence Olivier directs and stars in this movie. The cast includes Ralph Richardson, John Gielgud, and Claire Bloom. Video, black and white; 161 minutes.

Stanislavski. Princeton, NJ: Films for the Humanities, 1972. This film details how "truth in art" was developed as a system. It includes actual film footage of Stanislavski's memorable roles, famous stagings, and dramatic scenes from Moscow Art Theater productions, as well as period photographs and excerpts from the director's notebook. 16mm film, black and white; 29 minutes.

Steel Magnolias. 1989. This story about how a group of Southern women weather difficult times in their lives features Julia Roberts, Sally Field, Shirley MacLaine, and Olympia Dukakis in the principal roles. Video, color; 118 minutes.

A Streetcar Named Desire. 1951. Warner Home Video. This Academy Award-winning film version of Tennessee Williams's play stars Marlon Brando and Vivien Leigh. It is available from Baker and Taylor Video 1-800-775-1100. Video, black and white; 122 minutes.

The Taming of the Shrew. 1967. Elizabeth Taylor and Richard Burton star in this version directed by Franco Zeffrelli. Video, color; 126 minutes.

Tartuffe. This is a French version of Molière's classic. It includes English subtitles. It is listed in Viewfinder's Catalog of Uncommon Video 1-800-342-3342. Video, color; 140 minutes.

Tartuffe. 1984. This Royal Shakespeare Company's version stars Anthony Sher. It is listed in Viewfinder's Catalog of Uncommon Video 1-800-342-3342. Video, color; 110 minutes.

The Teahouse of the August Moon. 1956. Marlon Brando and Glen Ford star in this comic story of the U.S. Army's attempts to Americanize a tiny Okinawan village. Video color; 124 minutes.

True West. 1983. This Sam Sheperd play features John Malkovich as a recluse who returns from the desert. It is listed in Viewfinder's Catalog of Uncommon Video 1-800-342-3342. Video, color; 110 minutes.

Uncle Vanya. 1962. This production was filmed at the Chichester Drama Festival in England with Laurence Olivier, Joan Plowright, Rosemary Harris, Michael Redgrave, and Sybil Thorndike. It is listed in Viewfinder's Catalog of Uncommon Video 1-800-342-3342. Video, color; 110 minutes.

Vanya on 42nd Street. 1994. This is an experimental film of a production of Chekhov's play. It is performed in an abandoned Manhattan theater by actors in contemporary clothes. Video, color; 119 minutes.

Who's Afraid of Virginia Woolf? 1966. Directed by Mike Nichols, this film version of Edward Albee's play features Richard Burton and Elizabeth Taylor. Video, black and white; 129 minutes.

Journal

Plays. Boston, MA: Plays, Inc. This drama magazine is designed for young people and includes a complete supply of royalty-free dramatic material for schools.

Internet

Acting Workshop On-Line. This site features online acting courses, tips for actors, question-and-answer forums, links to other acting sites, and much more. The Internet address is http://www.execpc.com/ ~blankda/acting2.html

The Actors' Page. This Internet site lists résumés and provides links to other resources for actors. The Internet address is http://www.serve.com/dgweb32/

Theaterplex. This Internet site features reviews of current shows and exclusive interviews with theater people such as Neil Simon, Jessica Lange, Eric Bogosian, Kenneth Branagh, Spalding Gray, Gregory Hines, David Mamet, Anna Deveare Smith, and Terrence McNally. The Internet address is http://www.gigaplex.com/theater/index.htm

TheatrGROUP: "Method" Acting Procedures. TheatrGROUP is a theater company that provides Stanislavski's "method" acting training on-site. The training is divided into thirteen different procedures including relaxation, concentration, "magic if," substitution, and more. The Internet address is http://www.theatrgroup.com/Method/

We're Making *Macbeth:* Teaching Shakespeare to Children. This site provides a step-by-step guide illustrating how one theater group taught *Macbeth* to children (includes examples and photos). The Internet address is http://www. dolphin.org/erik/nethernet/altskspr.html

SUMMARY AND KEY IDEAS

With Sample Responses

Have students decide what the proper theater etiquette should be in the following situations. Require students to defend their answers.

1. You find a prop has been left in the wings during a performance. As a stagehand, you want to be helpful. Should you pick it up and try to find the actor who has apparently left it behind? Why or why not?

   No, you should never move a prop. Actors often leave a prop in the wings, or someplace where they can pick it up when they need it.

2. The hairstyle and makeup you have been provided are not at all flattering. You look silly and feel embarrassed. Should you speak to the person in charge of makeup to work out a hairstyle and makeup that you both find satisfactory?

> ## Teaching Note
>
> Have students create posters encouraging good theater etiquette. These posters can be directed at the cast, the crew, or the audience. Place the posters in the classroom or backstage to serve as reminders of proper theater behavior.

   Subordinate yourself to the performance by accepting your role and the hairstyle and makeup. If you have difficulty determining the purpose of the design or the overall effect the director is trying to achieve, speak to the director.

3. A cast party is scheduled after the last performance of a successful production. You feel you owe your parents and friends a great deal for their support. Should you ask them to join you at the cast party?

   Cast parties are reserved only for those who worked on the show. This is a time for celebrating the special bond that is formed between the cast and crew.

DISCUSSING IDEAS

1. Review the guidelines of theater etiquette for actors. Give reasons these guidelines

are so important to follow. Try to create more guidelines by reflecting on your own experience in the theater.

Students should emphasize in their discussion the effect that not following these guidelines will have. The discussion should focus on the importance of the entire cast following the guidelines in order for a production to run smoothly.

2. Discuss the effect the following behaviors would have on performance.

   - One of the principals is constantly late for rehearsals, making the other members of the cast and crew wait as long as thirty minutes for rehearsal to begin.

   - A member of the crew is openly critical of another crew member.

   - On the night of the first performance, several members of the cast cannot resist peeking through the curtains to wave at family members.

By continually being late for rehearsal, a member of the cast places an additional burden on the others and suggests a disregard for the importance of the play and the efforts of others. Open criticism of a member of the cast or crew erodes confidence and destroys the esprit de corps essential for a successful effort. It is important to establish a certain artistic distance from the audience. This allows actors to mentally get into character and the crew to concentrate on the task at hand. Attempting to communicate with the audience personally prior to or during a performance makes establishing that artistic distance very difficult.

ACTIVITY

Have students investigate rules that some theaters have adopted for audiences. For example, many theaters now prohibit the use of any recording or photographic devices, especially flash equipment. Others will not seat late arrivals until the first intermission.

Part Two

A Treasury of Scenes and Monologues

Scenes and Monologues   **48**

Readers Theater   **50**

Framework

The play is the backbone of drama. Drama as we know it exists within the confines of, and because of, the play. It is the arena in which actors implement the skills they develop through study and practice.

A Treasury of Scenes and Monologues contains a wide assortment of play cuttings taken from contemporary as well as classic plays. These excerpts have been chosen to give drama students exposure to many different kinds of plays and playwrights. There are scenes that have roles for a man and a woman, for two women, for two men, and for mixed groups; additionally, there are monologues for women and for men. Thus, A Treasury of Scenes and Monologues offers your students the opportunity to perform in a great variety of dramatic situations.

A Treasury of Scenes and Monologues

Instructional Objective

- To implement and develop acting skills by performing in a variety of scenes and monologues

Ancillaries

Resource Lists and Bibliographies

Scenes and Monologues: From Euripides to August Wilson

TEACH

Scenes

1. You might wish to provide the directors with a synopsis of the play to help them understand the plot, characters, and conflicts. The director should be diplomatic and fair-minded when choosing the cast and should provide the actors with critiques that contain concrete suggestions for improvement. After the director has assigned roles, review the concepts of characterization (pp. 105–119) and subtext (p. 134) to help the cast get into their roles.

2. To assist students in understanding the time period and culture of their play, you might provide samples of other works by the playwright; a few key historic events of the time period; or paintings, photos, or literature from that period. These can serve as starters for the students' own research. Before students draft their essays, remind them that strong essays contain specific details.

3. Students should discuss the costumes and scenery that will help the audience feel the authenticity of the era and culture. Set aside time for students to create key props that will add to the presentation. If students have difficulty with the dialect, provide aural examples.

Monologues

1. After students have chosen their monologues, provide them with time to write a character sketch. Ask students to consider the character's social position, the time period, and other elements that mold character. Help students identify the key emotion that elicits the monologue and gestures that can help convey that emotion.

2. If students write answering monologues, ask them to identify scenes in the original that reveal this character's personality. Any answering monologue must be true to character. If students have chosen a different voice for the monologue, they should also be true to character. After the student delivers the monologue, ask the class to identify the main emotion conveyed and the gestures, lines, or vocal qualities that communicated this emotion. Further discussion could include additional ways to convey the emotion. Include a second performance based on these suggestions.

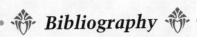

CLOSE

🌼 *Bibliography* 🌼

Books

Alterman, Glenn. *2 Minutes and Under: Original Character Monologues for Actors.* Newbury, VT: Smith and Kraus, 1993.

Beard, Jocelyn A., ed. *The Best Stage Scenes of 1994.* Lyme, NY: Smith and Kraus, Inc., 1994.

————. ed. *The Best Stage Scenes of 1993.* Lyme, NY: Smith and Kraus, Inc., 1993.

————. ed. *Scenes from Classic Plays 468 B.C. to 1980 A.D.* Lyme, NH: Smith and Kraus, 1993.

Bert, Norman A., and Deb Bert, eds. *Play It Again! More One-Act Plays for Acting Students.* Colorado Springs, CO: Meriwether Publishing, 1993.

Blunt, Jerry, ed. *An Audition Handbook of Great Speeches.* Woodstock, IL: The Dramatic Publishing Co., 1990.

Earley, M., and P. Keil, eds. *The Modern Monologue: Men.* Routledge, NY: Theatre Arts Books, 1993.

Haring-Smith, Tori, ed. *Monologues for Women by Women.* Portsmouth, NH: Heinemann, 1994.

Hooks, Ed, ed. *The Ultimate Scene and Monologue Sourcebook: An Actor's Guide to Over 1000 Monologues and Dialogues from More Than 300 Contemporary Plays.* New York, NY: Back Stage Books, 1994.

Horvath, J., L. Mueller, and J. Temchin, eds. *Duo! The Best Scenes for the 90's for Two.* New York, NY: Applause, 1994.

King, Woodie, Jr., ed. *Voices of Color: 50 Scenes and Monologues by African American Playwrights.* New York, NY: Applause, 1994.

Luby, Dianne, ed. *Words of Women: Monologues and Advice for Actresses.* London, England: Samuel French, 1994.

Novak, Elaine Adams, ed. *Styles of Acting: A Scenebook for Aspiring Actors.* Englewood Cliffs, NJ: Prentice Hall, 1985.

Osborn, M. Elizabeth. *The Way We Live Now: American Plays and the AIDS Crisis.* New York, NY: Theatre Communications Group, 1990.

Rudnicki, Stefan, ed. *The Actor's Book of Classical Scenes.* New York, NY: Penguin Books, 1992.

San Francisco Mime Troupe. *By Popular Demand: Plays and Other Works.* San Francisco, CA: The Troupe, 1980.

Slaight, Craig, and Jack Sharrar, eds. *Great Scenes for Young Actors from the Stage.* Newbury, VT: Smith and Kraus, 1991.

Readers Theater, *pages 247–250*

SUMMARY AND KEY IDEAS

With Sample Responses

1. What is the difference between a play review and a dramatic reading?

   A play review includes more extensive commentary than a dramatic reading. In a play review the performer presents selected scenes along with a discussion of the author and the literary value of the play. In a dramatic reading, the play is usually presented in condensed form, with at most a short introduction and brief narrative connections. One form of dramatic reading, called a monodrama, involves the reader "becoming" a single character or the author.

Teaching Note

Literature that students encounter in English class can be a rich source of readers theater material. Help students develop criteria for evaluating pieces of literature for use as readers theater.

2. Name three types of group readings and the differences among them.

   (1) In a choral reading a group of actors serve as a chorus or as a narrator.
   (2) In chamber theater a non-dramatic work is turned into a script. Often stage directions and narrative phrases are read.
   (3) In combination reading and performing, actors pantomime the action of the lines read by the reading actors.

DISCUSSING IDEAS

1. What must one consider when choosing and adapting a selection for readers theater?

   Discussion should touch on the following points:

   • *Selections should appeal to the interests of the audience and draw on the performers' strengths.*

   • *Selections should emphasize plot more than description.*

   • *When condensing a play, be sure the plot still progresses smoothly. Include connecting narratives if necessary.*

   • *When preparing a play review, select passages that are interesting in themselves and that exemplify the author's style.*

2. What might actors gain from participating in readers theater?

   Discussion should touch on the following points: Readers theater provides an opportunity for actors to focus on interpretation and on the skills of voice, diction, and vocal interpretation. By preparing play reviews, actors learn about playwrights' personal styles and their roles in theater history. Dramatic readings help actors learn about the relationships among characters in a play, since the performer plays more than one role and therefore controls the interaction among the characters. Group readings require precise timing, making intense interaction among performers necessary.

3. What special considerations do group readings require?

   Discussion should touch on the following points: For a group reading, the selected play must be cut carefully so that the main thrust of the plot is clear. Group readings sometimes require a narrator. Also, the best means of presenting the material—choral reading, chamber theater, or combination reading and performing—must be decided.

ACTIVITY

Divide the class into three groups. Select one of Aesop's fables or another children's story or poem. Using the same piece of work for each group of students, ask one group to perform a choral reading, another group to prepare the work as chamber theater, and one group to present a combination reading and performing. After the performances, ask students what they learned from the activity. Is the selection more suitable to one form of readers theater than to another? What did the students learn about the selection by watching the other performances? What did they learn about the selection by adapting it for performance?

Part Three

Appreciating the Drama

CHAPTER 5
The Structure of Drama   52

CHAPTER 6
Varieties of Drama   60

CHAPTER 7
The History of Drama   70

◈ Puppet Theater   80

CHAPTER 5

The Structure of Drama

Framework

Greek philosopher Aristotle outlined what he believed to be the key elements of drama in his work Poetics. For many years dramatists followed Aristotle's outline when creating drama by including and elaborating on the key elements he identified. Some modern dramatists, however, depart from Aristotle's ideas by changing the structure and the purpose of the play. Although some dramatic traditions have been changed, many of Aristotle's key elements are still considered to be essential in good drama, namely exposition, plot, character, and theme.

After briefly contrasting tradition and innovation in drama, this chapter teaches students the narrative essentials of drama, enabling them to develop a sense of a play's structure, or its overall plan of development. The activities in this chapter give students the opportunity to work with the four narrative essentials of drama, requiring them to identify the use of these elements in dramatic presentations and asking them to use the narrative essentials in their own work.

To understand a play's structure, one must recognize the essential narrative elements and their functions in the play. As students gain confidence in identifying these elements, they will grow to appreciate and more fully understand the plays they read, watch, and perform.

Teaching Note

Activities found in the **Review Workshop** at the end of the chapter often require some planning or preliminary work by students. Be sure to check these activities, and make sure students have adequate time in which to complete them.

Instructional Objectives

- To understand and identify the narrative essentials of drama: exposition, plot, characters, and theme
- To recognize the classic elements of drama as described by Aristotle and to differentiate them from certain modern variations
- To recognize the six basic parts of plot structure and to understand their functions in a play

Vocabulary

protagonist the main character in a play

exposition the information put before an audience that gives the *where, when, why,* and *who* facts of a play

atmosphere the environment of the play created by staging and lighting

mood the emotional feeling of a play

preliminary situation a clearly defined explanation of the events in the lives of the leading characters before the start of a play's action

plot (noun) the series of related events that take place in a play; (verb) to plan stage business, as to plot the action; to plan a speech by working out the phrasing, emphasis, and inflections

antagonist the person or the force working against the protagonist in a play

denouement an element of the plot that is the solution of a mystery or an explanation of the outcome

soliloquy a speech delivered by an actor alone onstage that reveals the character's innermost thoughts

theme the basic idea of a play

moral the lesson or the principle contained within or taught by a play

dialogue the lines of a play spoken by characters

action that which happens onstage to hold the audience's attention

situation a problem or challenge a character or characters must face

Ancillaries

Forms, Models, and Activities Blackline Masters, page 21

Chapter Test, page 7

Scenes and Monologues: From Euripides to August Wilson

Transparency 5

Motivating Activity

Choose a fairy tale, a play, or a story with which the class is familiar. On the board, write the names of the characters and the main theme, as well as some parts of the story that represent stages of the plot structure. For example, if you choose "Cinderella," write the following on the board:

- Cinderella, the prince, the fairy godmother, the wicked stepsisters and stepmother
- The fairy godmother arrives and helps Cinderella prepare for the ball.
- An invitation to the ball arrives.
- Cinderella is found to be the owner of the glass slipper.
- Patience, modesty, and humility will be rewarded.
- Cinderella attends the ball, meets the prince, and rushes home at midnight.
- Cinderella and the prince get married.
- The stepsisters go to the ball, leaving Cinderella behind.
- The prince finds the glass slipper and begins his search for the owner.
- Cinderella and the prince live happily ever after.

Have students identify the characters and theme. Then ask them to identify the elements of the plot and to put them in order. As students do so, introduce and identify these plot elements: the initial incident (the invitation); the rising action (the stepsisters go to the ball, the fairy godmother arrives, Cinderella attends the ball, the prince finds the glass slipper); the climax (Cinderella is found to be the owner of the glass slipper); the falling action (the prince marries Cinderella); and the conclusion (they live happily ever after).

❈ TEACH ❈

Application Activity, page 257

Before students begin this activity, you might provide copies of the first two scenes from one of Shakespeare's more familiar plays, such as *Othello* or *Hamlet*. Encourage students to list all of the main characters in the play or all the people in the scene. They should also identify the time and the place as precisely as possible. Most importantly, students should be able to recognize the conflicts, problems, or issues that are at the heart of the plot or conflict.

FYI

Playwright Sam Shepard is known for constantly making notes about anything and everything he observes. He writes his moment-by-moment thoughts and impressions on loose-leaf pages, in spiral notebooks, on scraps of paper, and even on napkins. Then he uses these notes as he writes his plays. He says that fitting his notes into the dramatic structure of a play gives him a structured way to look back at his experiences. "When it comes right down to it," Shepard has said, "what you're really listening to in a writer is . . . his ability to face himself."

Application Activities, page 261

Activity 1 You might want to create a handout of a blank chart that presents the stages in plot development (see **Forms, Models, and Activities Blackline Masters** page 21). Responses should address all of the stages in plot structure outlined on page 258.

Extension You can have students create another plot structure chart for a story of their own. For this activity, they need not write an entire story; they should only outline the development of a plot for their story idea.

Activity 2 If students find Polti's terminology difficult to associate with dramatic situations in modern plays and films, provide synonyms for some of Polti's terms. For example, *supplication (requesting, petitioning), abduction (kidnapping), enmity (hatred), slaying (killing),* and *erroneous (mistaken).* Remember, these thirty-six situations are generally accepted as being complete and inclusive of every dramatic situation.

Extension Discuss some popular plays and movies to determine if one dramatic situation seems to occur more often than others. If the discussion yields a situation that is more widely used than others, discuss with students why they think that is so.

Application Activity, page 264

Encourage students to choose a main character from a work they know very well. Explain that students need not choose a complex or tragic character. In fact, simple, two-dimensional figures, such as Scrooge or another especially disagreeable or deceitful character, might work particularly well.

After each student has prepared his or her character, write a list of the characters on the board and then allow the class time to develop questions for each character. Good questions might involve asking about the character's attitude toward other characters or events in the play. Students might ask why the character said or did certain things. More challenging questions will involve asking the character about events outside of the play. For example, someone might ask Scrooge, "What do you think about the minimum wage and a four-day work week?" Evaluate students both on their ability to accurately assume the character and on their ability to frame appropriate questions for the character being interviewed.

● Chapter Review, page 266

Summary and Key Ideas Sample Responses

1. The four narrative essentials of a play are exposition, plot, characters, and theme. Exposition is the information put before an audience that reveals the *where, when, why,* and *who* of the play. Plot is a series of related events that take place before the audience, involving the development and the resolution of the major conflict. Characters are the people in the play. Theme is the basic idea of a play, which the author dramatizes through the conflicts of characters. These narrative essentials are communicated through the dialogue and action of the drama.

2. Aristotle first expressed the principles of traditional drama in his discussion of tragedy, *Poetics*. He said the key elements of a play were plot, character, diction, reasoning, sound, and spectacle.

3. Modern plays might differ in structure from traditional plays. Instead of containing three or five acts, modern plays might consist of two parts or several scenes with a single intermission or no intermission at all. Modern plays increasingly use an open stage, such as the arena and the thrust stages, which eliminate the principle of aesthetic distance. The type of stage can affect the style a playwright uses when creating drama.

4. Atmosphere is the environment of the play. The atmosphere helps bring out the feelings that create the mood, or the emotional feeling of the play.

5. Following the preliminary situation are the initial incident, the rising action, the climax, the falling action, and the conclusion. The denouement is considered another part of plot structure that includes everything after the climax.

6. A playwright might develop a character through his or her actions. A character might also be developed through dialogue, or the lines of the play, or through soliloquies, speeches in which actors talk alone or think aloud. Playwrights often use a combination of these methods of development.

7. The theme is the basic idea of a play, which the author dramatizes through the conflicts of characters. A moral, on the other hand, is a lesson or principle contained within a play or taught by a play.

Discussing Ideas

1. This activity might be more productive if done as a classroom activity. If each student analyzes the same play, discussion will be more unified than if each student discusses a different play. Whether done in class or at home, be certain that students select a television play rather than a television sitcom. Sitcoms frequently have fixed elements of plot, character, and situation that need not be reestablished with each episode. Before analyzing the movie or play, urge students to pay close attention to how the preliminary situation is revealed.

   The discussion should identify the exposition *(when, where, why,* and *who),* the characters, the plot, and the theme. During the discussion, students might identify the protagonist and note the devices used to reveal the protagonist and other important characters, such as actions or dialogue. Students might discuss how the plot is developed, discuss what the mood and atmosphere of the movie or television play are, and then explain how the theme or moral is revealed.

2. Discussion should include some of the following aspects. In *Waiting for Godot,* which is divided into two acts, the second act seems to repeat the first. There is a total or near-total absence of action; the landscape is flat and bare; and the characters are identified in the list of characters one way but call each other something else. Distress and boredom convey the endlessness of waiting for a Godot (or god) who never comes; thus, there is no real conclusion.

The Chairs contains disjointed dialogue and an abstract theme. The main characters converse with invisible guests, contradict one another, and become the directors and spectators of their own drama. At the end of the play, an Orator, who is supposed to deliver a message, faces rows of empty chairs and is mute.

3. Students might select a play or movie with a moral, since this is often more obvious than theme. Before the discussion, help students differentiate between theme and moral by reminding them that a moral is a lesson, while a theme is a basic idea that recurs throughout the work. Discussion might be prompted by turning the focus to ways in which the main character and the events of the plot serve to embody the theme.

Extension Encourage students to identify another play or literary selection that reflects the same or a similar theme. Focus discussion on which work contains the more powerful dramatization of the theme.

Review Workshop, page 267

Independent Activity

A Day in the Life Emphasize to students that their minidrama does not need to reflect a profound universal truth. It can be something quite simple and ordinary, such as learning something new about a friend or realizing something important about a parent. If students have difficulty getting started, you might suggest that they try to recall a day when they learned something about themselves or about human nature. Then have students work backward to the climactic moment in the experience. Assess students' understanding of the four narrative essentials and of the stages in plot development.

Cooperative Learning Activity

Analyzing a Nontraditional Play This activity provides an opportunity for students to focus on the conscious manipulation of traditional dramatic elements and structure. When evaluating student responses, be sure students have accurately identified the exposition of the play and have looked closely at the use of dialogue, action, and situation as a means of developing characters. Most importantly, probe students' thoughts on the ways in which the playwright has manipulated the plot structure or has deviated from traditional plot structure.

Extension Encourage students to discuss the benefits of "breaking the rules," as Albee did in *The Sandbox* or as another playwright might have done in a nontraditional play. You might prompt analysis with these questions:

- Do you find this nontraditional play more interesting or fun to watch than a traditional one?

- Do you think you will remember this play longer, or do you think it has had a greater impact on you than traditional plays you have read or seen?

- Do you find nontraditional plays confusing? How does that add to or interfere with your pleasure in reading or viewing the play?

- Are some nontraditional techniques merely an attempt to surprise and shock rather than a serious attempt to improve the dramatic experience? If you think so, give an example.

- What present nontraditional techniques might become a permanent part of drama? Which are probably only passing fads?

Across the Curriculum Activity

Literature Evaluate students on their ability to identify the four narrative essentials and on their ability to recognize the differences between a play and a work of fiction. For example, students might explain that if the short story is to be presented as a play, much of the narrative and expository writing must be rewritten as dialogue to hold the audience's attention.

Final Activity

Have students choose a historical event as the initial incident for a minidrama. For example, students might select the surrender at Appomattox Court House, the Boston Tea Party, or the attack on Pearl Harbor as an initial incident. Ask students to place a character in that setting and write a monologue for the character that subtly reveals the preliminary situation; the *where, when, why,* and *who;* the dramatic conflict; and the theme of the minidrama. For example, the character might be a pacifist hearing of the Pearl Harbor attack or King George III hearing of the Boston Tea Party.

Have volunteers read their monologues while the rest of the class listens for clues to the preliminary situation, elements of the exposition, the dramatic conflict, and the theme. Discuss how these elements are used and if they are used effectively.

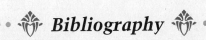

❧ *Bibliography* ❧

Books

Ball, David. *Backwards & Forwards: A Technical Manual.* Carbondale and Edwardsville, IL: Southern Illinois University Press, 1983. This is a guide to reading plays. Ball developed his method while working at the Guthrie Theater. The author supplies strategies for discovering a playwright's intentions and uses *Hamlet* to illustrate his methodology.

Bentley, Eric. *The Life of the Drama.* New York, NY: Applause, 1964. Bentley has written a scholarly book that breaks a play into plot, character, dialogue, thought, and enactment. Part two discusses the following genres: melodrama, farce, tragedy, comedy, and tragicomedy.

Brater, Enoch, ed. *Feminine Focus: The New Women Playwrights.* New York, NY: Oxford University Press, 1989. Brater presents a critical analysis of plays written by women.

Brockett, Oscar G. *The Theatre: An Introduction,* 3d ed. New York, NY: Holt, Rinehart & Winston, 1974. This is one of the most widely used college textbooks in America, covering all the basic topics.

Brook, Peter. *The Open Door: Thoughts on Acting and Theatre.* New York, NY: Parthenon Books, 1993. This collection of writing comes from an important theater critic.

Brown-Guillory, Elizabeth. *Their Place on the Stage: Black Women Playwrights in America.* New York, NY: Praeger, 1990. The author analyzes plays by Alice Childress, Lorraine Hansberry, and Ntozake Shange. She traces the development of African American theater with its roots in African theatrics to the present, giving the reader a feminist perspective.

Bryer, Jackson R., ed. *The Playwright's Art: Conversations with Contemporary American Dramatists.* New Brunswick, NJ: Rutgers University Press, 1995. Bryer gives his readers firsthand accounts of what prompts several modern playwrights to write.

Cassady, Marshall. *Characters in Action: A Guide to Playwriting.* Lanham, MD: University Press of America, 1984. In this handbook on writing plays, the author emphasizes character development as the key to dramatic structure.

Catron, Louis E. *The Elements of Playwriting.* New York, NY: Macmillan, 1993. Catron, playwriting professor at the College of William and Mary, presents a guide to constructing dramatic material based on the essential elements, such as characterization and plot.

———.*Writing, Producing, and Selling Your Play: The Complete Guide for the Beginning and Advanced Playwright.* Englewood Cliffs, NJ: Prentice Hall, 1984. Catron gives concrete guidelines for writing plays, emphasizing craft and structure rather than theory.

Cohen, Edward M. *Working on a New Play: A Play Development Handbook for Actors, Directors, Designers & Playwrights.*

Englewood Cliffs, NJ: Prentice Hall, 1988. Cohen attempts to explain how a play is developed through numerous drafts and also to guide readers away from bad advice. Cohen is the Associate Director of the Jewish Repertory Theatre. Chapters include The Living Room Stage, The Open Reading, Actors and Readings, and The Rehearsal Process. This book is aimed at the professional playwright.

Cole, Toby, ed. *Playwrights on Playwriting: the Meaning and Making of Modern Drama from Ibsen to Ionesco.* New York, NY: Hill and Wang, 1960. This is an introduction to the ideas of modern and the modernistic theater. In the first part, numerous playwrights express their beliefs and hopes. In the second part, these playwrights talk about specific plays.

Funke, Lewis. *Playwrights Talk About Writing: 12 Interviews by Lewis Funke.* Chicago, IL: Dramatic Publishing Company, 1975. In this book, twelve innovative and successful playwrights discuss their writing, work habits, training, and attitudes with Funke, who was the Drama Editor of the *New York Times* for many years.

Murray, Edward. *Varieties of Dramatic Structure: A Study of Theory and Practice.* Lanham, MD: University Press of America, 1990. This is a critical and scholarly book.

Pereira, Kim. *August Wilson and the African American Odyssey.* Urbana, Chicago, IL: University of Illinois Press, 1995. Pereira offers a critical study of four of Wilson's plays: *Ma Rainey's Black Bottom, Fences, Joe Turner's Come and Gone,* and *The Piano Lesson.* Pereira shows how Wilson uses the themes of separation, migration, and reunion to depict the physical and psychological journeys of African Americans in the twentieth century.

Peterson, Bernard L., Jr. *Contemporary Black American Playwrights and Their Plays: A Biographical Directory and Dramatic Index.* New York, NY: Greenwood Press, 1988. The encyclopedic format of this book documents more than seven hundred African American dramatists, screenwriters, radio and television script writers, musical theater collaborators, and other originators of theatrical works, who worked from 1950 to 1987.

Polti, Georges. *Thirty-Six Dramatic Situations,* trans. Lucille Ray. Boston, MA: The Writer, Inc., 1977. This approach to dramaturgy is based on thirty-six situations such as madness, remorse, and mistaken jealousy.

Sweet, Jeffrey. *The Dramatist's Toolkit: The Craft of the Working Playwright.* Portsmouth, NH: Heinemann, 1993. In this concrete and logical approach to the craft, there are helpful tips such as beginning a script with a bang, punching up a faltering scene, writing streamlined exposition, and deepening characterization. Sweet aims his comments at the professional writer.

Wilkinson, Jane, ed. *Talking with African Writers: Interviews with African Poets, Playwrights and Novelists.* Portsmouth, NH: Heinemann, 1992. This book casts a broad net and interviews writers of nondramatic material. Nevertheless, many concerns are shared among the writers and the playwrights represented here.

Videotapes and Films

The Belle of Amherst. Julie Harris plays Emily Dickinson in this adaptation of the Broadway production. It is listed in The Video Catalog 1-800-733-2232. PBS Home Video, color; 90 minutes.

The Diary of Anne Frank. 1959. Starring in this Academy Award-winning film are Millie Perkins and Shelley Winters. It is listed in Critic's Choice Video 1-800-367-7765. Video, black and white; 156 minutes.

Driving Miss Daisy. 1989. Jessica Tandy and Morgan Freeman star in this film adaptation of Alfred Uhry's stage play about aging and friendship. This movie won four Oscars: Best Screenplay, Best Makeup, Best Actress, and Best Picture. Video, color; 99 minutes.

Emerging Playwrights. New York State Department of Education, 1980. This video contains thirteen film interviews with contemporary playwrights and directors, including Lanford Wilson, Jonathan Reynolds, Peter Copani, David Mamet, Albert Innaurato, John Guare, and Chris Durang. Video; 30 minutes.

A Frame for Meaning: Theme in Drama. Dramatist David H. Hwang discusses *M. Butterfly,* and other scholars discuss *Hamlet.* This resource is available through the Annenberg/CPB Multimedia Collection 1-800-LEARNER.

The Glass Menagerie. 1987. This film version starring Joanne Woodward and John Malkovich is directed by Paul Newman. It is listed in Schlessinger Video Productions 1-800-843-3620. Video, color; 134 minutes.

Image of Reality: The Elements of Drama. This video contains excerpts from August Wilson's plays, an interview with the author, and a discussion of the origin, structure, and purpose of drama. It is available through the Annenberg/CPB Multimedia Collection 1-800-LEARNER. Video, color; 30 minutes.

Patterns of Action: Plot and Conflict in Drama. This video contains excerpts from a dramatization of *Oedipus Rex* and a discussion by A.R. Gurney Jr. about the plot and inherent conflicts of the play. It is available through the Annenberg/CPB Multimedia Collection 1-800-LEARNER. Video, color; 30 minutes.

The Piano Lesson. 1995. Charles S. Dutton reprises his Broadway role of Boy Willie in this Pulitzer-Prize-winning play by August Wilson directed by Lloyd Richards. This play was also a Hallmark Hall of Fame production. It is listed in The Video Catalog 1-800-733-2232. Video, color; 99 minutes.

Six Degrees of Separation. 1993. MGM/UA Home Video. Featuring Stockard Channing and Will Smith, this film is based on Guare's stage play in which a charismatic hustler passes himself off as Sidney Poitier's son. This video is available from Baker and Taylor Video 1-800-775-1100. Video, color; 111 minutes.

A Soldier's Story. 1984. RCA/Columbia Pictures Home Video. This is Norman Jewison's film version of Charles Fuller's Pulitzer-Prize-winning play starring Howard Rollins. Video, color; 101 minutes.

The Time of Your Life. 1948. This is an adaptation of William Saroyan's prize-winning play starring James Cagney. Video, black and white; 109 minutes.

The Vision Quest: Myth and Symbolism in Drama. This contains Alaskan playwright David Hunsaker's dramatization of Eskimo myth and Eskimo productions of Greek tragedies. It is available through the Annenberg/CPB Multimedia Collection 1-800-LEARNER.

Cassettes and Recordings

The Negro Writer in America. James Baldwin, Lorraine Hansberry, Langston Hughes, Alfred Kazin, and Emile Capouya participate in a discussion on African American writers. It is listed in The Audio Forum 1-800-243-1234. Audiocassette; 46 minutes.

Internet

The Dramatic Exchange. This World Wide Web site is dedicated to archiving and distributing scripts. It provides a place for playwrights to "publish" and distribute their plays, a place for producers to find new plays to produce, and a place for those interested in drama to browse. The Internet address is http://www.dramex.org/

Screenwriters' and Playwrights' Home Page. Information about theater-related items can be found at this Internet address: http://www.teleport.com/~cdeemer/scrwriter.html

Theaterplex. This Internet site features reviews of current shows and exclusive interviews with theater people, such as Neil Simon, Eric Bogosian, Kenneth Branagh, Spalding Gray, Gregory Hines, David Mamet, Anna Deveare Smith, and Terrence McNally. The Internet address is http://www.gigaplex.com/theater/index.htm

Diana Cantu Reviews Theatre and Culture. Diana Cantu's latest theater reviews can be obtained on this Internet address: http://www.thegroup.net/diana.htm

CD-ROM

Play Ops: 500+ Opportunities for Playwrights. This software program offers script-writing help to the professional playwright. The CD-ROM is produced by Datafox and can be obtained from Applause Books, New York, NY (212) 595-4735.

6

Varieties of Drama

Framework

Drama encompasses a wide variety of styles and types. To simplify the information for beginning drama students, an effort is made to categorize much of drama into two broad categories: tragedy and comedy. A tragedy, by definition, is a play that depicts a human as the victim of fate, creating a feeling of inevitability throughout the play. Comedy was originally considered to be any work that had a happy ending. Comedy, however, is now classified into two categories: high and low. There are many types of drama, however, that contain an element of both tragedy and comedy and cannot be easily placed into either of these two categories. All types of drama can also be identified by style, which is defined by the way in which a play is written, produced, and performed.

In this chapter students will learn how the various styles and types of drama affect the structure of a play. Students will follow the development of the different styles of drama from Greek theater to the avant-garde of the twentieth century and encounter the elements of each form. Through their exploration of the varieties and styles of drama, students will increase their understanding and awareness of the theater. As they learn more about the types, styles, and devices used in drama, students will be able to recognize these elements as they read, watch, and perform plays. By recognizing the style and type of a play, students will have a context for interpretation, which, in turn, will increase their overall understanding of the play.

Teaching Note

Activities found in the **Review Workshop** at the end of the chapter often require some planning or preliminary work by students. Be sure to check these activities, and make sure students have adequate time in which to complete them.

Instructional Objectives

- To identify the essential characteristics of tragedy and comedy
- To distinguish among different types of comedy and identify the seven most common devices playwrights use to provoke laughter
- To understand styles and trends in contemporary theater in order to better interpret dramatic works

Vocabulary

tragedy a play in which the protagonist fails to achieve desired goals or is overcome by opposing forces

pathos an element in drama that arouses feelings of pity and compassion in an audience

hamartia an error in judgment or a shortcoming on the part of a tragic protagonist

catharsis a purging or cleansing that comes as a result of emotional release

comedy a play that treats characters and situations in a humorous way and has a happy ending

low comedy a play that is quite physical, sometimes vulgar, and highly exaggerated in style and performance

farce a kind of comedy involving clowning, practical jokes, and improbable characters and situations

screen scene farcical scenes in which some of the actors hide from the other actors onstage yet are still able to hear and comment on the onstage dialogue

aside a line spoken directly to the audience

burlesque a form of low comedy that mocks a broad topic

parody a type of low comedy that mocks a certain work by imitating the author's style for comic effect

caricature an exaggeration of a certain feature of a character or a literary work

high comedy a play that includes comedy of manners and satire and uses clever lines, word plays, and allusions

comedy of manners a play that shows the humorous traits of a particular segment of society, usually the upper class

satire a humorous attack on accepted conventions of society, holding up human vices and follies to ridicule

fantasy a play that deals with unrealistic and fantastic characters

romantic comedy a play that features plots focusing on love affairs, written in the style of romanticism

sentimental comedy a play that is marked by an emotional and ideal presentation of life; a reaction to Restoration drama

melodrama a serious play that arouses intense emotion and usually has a happy ending

play of ideas a play that deals with a social problem or ethical issue, sometimes presenting a solution

theatrical conventions a special or traditional way of doing things onstage

representational a play performed as if the audience were watching the action through an imaginary fourth wall

presentational a play in which the audience is recognized as an audience and the play as a play; consequently, the actors may speak directly to the audience

allegory a form of storytelling that teaches moral concepts

Ancillaries

Forms, Models, and Activities Blackline Masters, pages 22–24

Chapter Tests, pages 8, 9

Scenes and Monologues: From Euripides to August Wilson

Transparency 6

Motivating Activity

Explain to the class that actors must first know the type and style of a play in order to understand the characters they will portray. Use the following activity to demonstrate that a single plot line can be presented as different types of drama, depending on the interpretation of the action and the characters.

Divide the class into two groups and explain that each group will develop a scene from "The Hare and the Tortoise." If necessary, retell the story:

> The tortoise and the hare argued about who was swifter, and they agreed to run a race. The hare sprinted out well ahead of the tortoise. Seeing how slow his adversary was, the hare became so confident that he relaxed and even lay down for a nap by the roadside. Meanwhile, the tortoise plodded on without stopping, passed the hare asleep on the road, and got to the finish line first.

Provide direction to the groups before they begin to work. Tell one group that the play is a tragedy. Explain that the hare has always earned the respect of other animals for his speed. However, his pride keeps him from achieving his goal, thus he loses the community's respect.

Tell the other group that the play is a comedy. Explain that the turtle is a slow, funny, bumbling character, who achieves recognition for a great achievement despite his lack of speed. In the end, the turtle wins the respect of all.

After the performances, help students recognize that plot alone does not determine the meaning of a play. Explain that in this chapter students will learn a variety of ways to interpret and classify plays.

TEACH

Application Activities, page 274

Activity 1 If you make this a class activity, give the questions to the students before you show them the play, and have them jot down answers as they watch. After students have viewed the video, have them work in groups to compare and contrast their answers. Students should provide words or actions from the play as support for their answers. In a follow-up discussion, help students identify the elements of tragedy in each play.

Activity 2 There are many ideas in Anouilh's description. To make the description easier to understand, divide it into separate ideas. After viewing the video of the play, ask students to examine each idea closely, state whether they agree or disagree with it, and use details from the play to support their positions. For example, students could consider one of these statements:

- "Tragedy is clean, it is firm, it is flawless. It has nothing to do with melodrama—with wicked villains, persecuted maidens, avengers, gleams of hope, and eleventh-hour repentances."

- "In a tragedy, nothing is in doubt and everyone's destiny is known. That makes for tranquillity. Tragedy is restful; and the reason is that hope, that foul, deceitful thing, has no part in it. There isn't any hope. You're trapped."

- "The whole sky has fallen on you, and all you can do about it is to shout. Now don't mistake me: I said 'shout': I did not say groan, whimper, complain."

Extension Have students look for similarities and differences between Anouilh's modern definition of tragedy and Aristotle's classic definition. Some students might propose that Anouilh's definition is a logical extension of the classical definition, while other students might focus on the differences between the two. Encourage students to defend their conclusions with evidence from the text.

Activity 3 To lead students into this activity, discuss key topics from or elements of the playwright's era. Then help students understand how those topics or elements may be worked into the play. If a playwright has written about an earlier era, research both eras and see whether concerns from each are worked into the play. Students should be able to identify which elements from the play created the sense of emotional timelessness. It may be helpful to remind them that a tragedy possesses the element of inevitability.

Extension Have the class write a new ending for *Romeo and Juliet* and discuss how it affects the play. For example, suppose a messenger is rushing to Romeo with the news that Juliet only appears to be dead, but the messenger arrives an instant too late. Is the story still a tragedy? Discussion should contrast the plot manipulation of melodrama with the inevitability of genuine tragedy.

Application Activities, page 275

Activity 1 Whether the students read or watch the play, anticipate that they might not be able to identify all seven parts of the definition in certain plays or films. If you choose a form of low comedy, for example, there might not be evidence of intellectual or mental stimuli, but explain to students that the comedy did not play on their emotions as tragedy does. Evaluate students on how well they understand the fundamental differences between tragedy and comedy.

Extension Depending on your students, you might want to offer an alternative approach to this activity: Split the class into seven groups and assign each group one part of the definition of comedy. While they watch or read the comedy in class, each group should find evidence for its assigned topic. Afterwards, have the groups come together as a class to share their observations. Consider combining this activity with the activity appearing on page 279.

Activity 2 Students will need time to research the history of the comedy if the era differs from that of the tragedy they researched. They should be able to explain how comedic elements are often tied to the place and time. They may recognize that "classic" comedies also contain characters with which the audience can identify. If students seem to have difficulty pinpointing what makes the comedy funny, ask them to examine character, situation, and dialogue.

The final report should have a recognizable thesis statement in the introduction. Supporting paragraphs should provide specific details, and the conclusion should wrap up the ideas.

Additional Activity Ask students to consider whether historical period and culture are more important in a comedy or in a tragedy. After they have shared several ideas, divide the class so that half the students are on the *pro comedy* side and the other are on the *pro tragedy* side. The sides can then debate the issue.

Application Activity, page 279

If you choose to show a videotape in class, you might prefer to have the class work as a group to generate a discussion. Have each student create a two-column chart: one column to list the seven causes of laughter and one to list examples of each from the comedy. When students are finished watching, have them discuss specific examples of each of the seven causes of laughter.

If you choose to have students read a comedy, you should choose one play for the entire class to use and obtain a copy. Again, have students use a list of the seven causes of laughter while they read. They can attempt to predict where the laughs will occur and to identify the technique used to generate the laughter.

Extension To enhance the activity, show the video after students have read the play. This way they can check their predictions as they watch.

Whether students read or watch the comedy or both, evaluate them on their understanding of the causes of laughter as well as their ability to recognize these causes in a play.

▶ *Additional Application Activities*

- Divide the class into seven groups. Write the seven common causes of laughter on individual index cards and have each group pick one card. Have students brainstorm comic vignettes that exemplify the cause of laughter that their group chose. (For example, a hulking wrestler in a ballet class might exemplify incongruity.) Groups can simply record their vignettes on paper or they can act out their vignettes in front of the class.

- Point out that many television sitcoms are filmed in a studio without an audience. To simulate an audience, previously recorded laughter, commonly called "canned" laughter, is added to the soundtrack. Record a television sitcom that uses canned laughter in its soundtrack. Show it to students and have them critique its use in the program. Suggest that students look especially for ways in which the laughter emphasizes exaggeration, incongruity, anticipation, recognition, and relief.

Application Activity, page 282

Whether you show a video in class or have students read a play at home, you might have the entire class analyze the same play. This makes it easier for you to evaluate each student and also gives you the option of having a unified class discussion. Assess the success of this activity by how accurately students identify examples of comedy, rather than by how many examples they identify. You might prefer to make this a whole-group activity in which students make independent lists but then come together to compare their results and discuss any differences.

▶ **Additional Application Activities**

- Display the photograph on page 280. Ask students to explain how the costumes and facial expressions enhance the low comedy of the play being performed.

FYI

Many varieties of theater do not endure; they are passing fads. One such passing form was the medicine show, which was popular in rural America in the late nineteenth and early twentieth century. Traveling companies such as the Hamlin Wizard Oil Company prospered by putting on free variety shows and then selling "medicines" and other inexpensive items to the assembled audience. Another variety of American theater, vaudeville, was popular from the 1880s to the early 1930s. Vaudeville was a series of acts by magicians, singers, jugglers, comics, animals, and others. At about the same time, the British enjoyed variety shows known as music hall. Although similar forms of theater date back to the 1600s, music hall began in 1852 when Charles Morton built the Canterbury Music Hall in London. Music was the main attraction, and the shows were overseen by a master of ceremonies called the chairman. Eventually, the focus of music hall shifted toward comics and more spectacular acts. American vaudeville and British music hall both faded rapidly after radio and film became popular.

- Have students turn down the sound on their televisions and watch a gifted physical comedian, such as Ellen Degeneres or Jim Carrey. Without sound, the actor's use of body language and expression are emphasized. After students have watched the comedians, have small groups create silent comic scenes of their own. These scenes do not have to be from any particular play; they should just be scenes that contain comedic actions, such as asides, screen scenes, or the mouth-agape freeze.

Application Activity, page 287

Before introducing this activity, consider the different ways that you can ask students to respond. For example, if you want to keep the activity simple, you can have students provide oral or written explanations. For a greater challenge, you can have students improvise scenes that present the dramatic situation in one of the suggested forms (social drama, psychological drama, monodrama, a "whodunit," or an allegory). Evaluate students on their understanding of the type of drama they use to create a scene.

▶ **Additional Situations**

- Two friends who grew up together lose track of each other after high school. Years later, they meet in court. One is the prosecuting attorney, and the other is on trial.
- A nuclear power plant has developed a leak. Three members of the safety crew on duty must decide who will enter the plant to turn off the reactor. If it is not turned off within twenty minutes, an entire community will suffer serious and even fatal doses of radiation, but the person who turns off the reactor is certain to die of radiation exposure.

Application Activity, page 293

Students may need to follow the cues within the style descriptions to identify when the style began (e.g., naturalism grew out of realism, so students should refer to realism for a target year). You might help students begin their search by providing titles from the bibliography. Before students begin their research, remind them of proper note-taking techniques so that they can document their sources.

Chapter Review, page 294

Summary and Key Ideas Sample Responses

1. The protagonist in a tragedy is a significant person who is average or better. A character weakness or mistake in judgment carries the character inevitably toward an unhappy end in spite of her or his noble struggle. The protagonist in a comedy, however, is often a less-than-average person in some way, perhaps a romantic, a dreamer, or a rogue. The comic protagonist manages to overcome opposing forces or to achieve desired goals or both, arriving at a happy conclusion.

2. A tragedy elicits feelings of pity and compassion in the audience, resulting from an element in drama called pathos. When the protagonist falls to opposing forces at the end of a tragedy, the audience undergoes a catharsis.

3. The seven causes of laughter are as follows:
   - **Exaggeration** such as overstatement, understatement, and distorted physical or personality traits
   - **Incongruity** anything that seems out of place, out of time, or out of character
   - **Anticipation** or looking forward to a laugh, could be caused by a variety of situations, such as a running gag or a case of mistaken identity that will eventually be discovered
   - **Ambiguity** a type of humor based on double meanings, such as puns and word plays, that allow for more than one interpretation
   - **Recognition** or the discovery of hidden meanings or motivations; a realization sometimes accompanied by a double or even triple take
   - **Protection** laughter provoked by cruel, violent, and abusive acts because the audience knows the acts are not really happening and no one is really injured
   - **Relief** the release of pent-up emotions in the form of laughter

4. Students might list play of ideas, melodrama, romantic comedy, sentimental comedy, psychological drama, the "whodunit," allegory, and fantasy. Each of the types listed should include descriptions of the sad emotions they elicit and the "happy endings" they present.

5. Students should choose and describe three styles from the list of twentieth-century theater styles on pages 288–293.

Discussing Ideas

1. A good discussion will address the universality of tragic themes and the ability of the audience to identify with the tragic hero, a person who is above average but is brought down by a single character flaw or error in judgment. Students should also recognize that the outcome is never in doubt. This inevitability provokes compassion and pity. A good discussion will also include the fact that an audience feels a sense of release, or catharsis, when the tragedy ends.

2. Students should be able to cite examples of comedies that have become outdated because they depend on an understanding of contemporary people and events. Comedians who poke fun at politicians and celebrities often lose their appeal once the object of their humor has left the public eye. Similarly, discussion should include the fact that tragedy addresses issues of human nature such as ambition, trust, love, and human frailty that apply to all people in every time and place.

3. Student responses are likely to vary; however, the important element is that responses reflect an understanding of the types of comedy. In general, you can expect some examples of low comedy, such as the physical comedy of The Three Stooges, cat-and-mouse type cartoons, and some of the sillier stand-up comedians and sitcoms. Other forms of drama might be cited in more realistic sitcoms and in spin-offs from films or theater productions such as *The Odd Couple*. While comedies of manners might be less common on television, students might mention certain political satirists and stand-up comedians as examples of high comedy.

4. Students should recognize that the key difference lies in the fact that representational drama, sometimes called "fourth-wall theater," does not acknowledge the

existence of the audience, whereas presentational theater does. Students should be able to specify how this acknowledgment of the audience takes place in presentational theater, such as actors addressing the audience or even performing some actions in the audience.

5. Through discussion students should be able to infer that playwrights who create experimental drama might risk being misunderstood. Audiences that attend such dramas might find them difficult to understand. A good discussion would also cover why playwrights and audiences would be willing to take such risks. For example, such drama might be innovative, provocative, or inspiring.

Review Workshop, page 295

Independent Activity

Performance Art Before performances begin, you might have students submit their interpretations of the poems they chose. This will help you evaluate their performances more accurately. Remember that you are not evaluating students on their ability to interpret the poem but on their ability to convey their interpretation through performance art. This activity should be judged on the basis of originality and the student's ability to convey a central theme through a variety of dramatic elements. A good performance will have a sense of unity despite its disparate parts.

Cooperative Learning Activity

Stylization This activity gives students an opportunity to see the relationship between the content and the form of drama. As they plan language and costumes, students will have to decide what aspect of the scene they want to emphasize. If any students need additional support, you might provide them with a

professional example before they begin the activity. You might show students photographs or videotaped scenes from stylized adaptations of classic works, such as *West Side Story, The Wiz,* or *Kiss Me, Kate.* Then contrast them with scenes from the original plays: *Romeo and Juliet, The Wizard of Oz,* or *The Taming of the Shrew.*

Encourage the groups to begin by generating ideas before assigning tasks. This way, all students will have a chance to participate. Tasks include rewriting the script, selecting and creating costumes, and performing and directing the action.

▶ **Additional Activity** Have the students review the outline of *Romeo and Juliet* on page 258. Then ask them to suggest changes that would turn scenes into either low comedy or high comedy. Here are some examples:

- Juliet falls off the balcony (low comedy/ burlesque)
- After Juliet takes the potion, she staggers about the room, clutches her throat, and thrashes about for a prolonged time (low comedy/melodrama)
- The Montagues and Capulets can't resist tasting the poison because it appears to be a fine wine and so they all die (high comedy/ satire)

After the discussion, divide the students into two groups. Assign a level of comedy to each group. Then have the groups create and perform comic versions of scenes from *Romeo and Juliet.*

Across the Curriculum Activity

History Students should demonstrate an understanding of what makes each theme or person distinctive. If students choose themes, they should select material from various historical periods. If they choose people, they should select a person whose identity can be conveyed through simple words and actions. After their presentations, students should explain why they made their particular choices.

Final Activity

Divide the class into groups of at least four students, and have each group write and perform the story "The Three Little Pigs," using a style they have learned in this chapter as a basis. Each group is to present the play in a recognizable type, such as a farce, a melodrama, or some other form. For example, students might consider a play of ideas focusing on the problems of the homeless. Encourage students to be creative and to have fun.

Before students begin, have groups confer to be sure that they have selected different styles. Then allow each group time to reflect on the characteristics of the style they selected and to create and rehearse the story.

After the performances, engage the class in a discussion. Encourage students to try to answer the following questions:

- What elements of each style were most obvious?
- What characteristics of comedy or tragedy were used?
- What are some other ways that this play could have been performed?

Bibliography

Books

Bentley, Eric, ed. *The Theory of the Modern Stage.* New York, NY: Penguin Books, 1976. Bentley takes a scholarly look at the makers of modern theater including: Artaud, Brecht, Pirandello, Shaw, and Zola. The second part provides six essays, which add up to a historical overview of the period.

Braun, Edward. *The Theatre of Meyerhold: Revolution on the Modern Stage.* New York, NY: Drama Book Specialists, 1979. The author gives a critical analysis of a major theatrical figure and his work.

Brockett, Oscar G., *Perspectives on Contemporary Theatre.* Baton Rouge, LA: Louisiana State University, 1971. Brockett gives an overview of major trends. He demonstrates that much of modern theater is rooted in Western traditions and discusses how changes in values are reflected in theater.

————. *The Theatre: An Introduction.* 4th ed. New York, NY: Holt, Rinehart & Winston, 1979. Brockett surveys the historical development of Western dramatic literature and the art and craft of theater. This is a standard reference book and textbook, containing numerous illustrations.

Brook, Peter. *The Empty Space.* New York, NY: Atheneum, 1982. The English director discusses his techniques and theories in this book. He divides all theater into four groups—Deadly, Holy, Rough, and Immediate—and describes each category.

Brustein, Robert. *Seasons of Discontent: Dramatic Opinions 1959-65.* New York, NY: Simon and Schuster, 1967. This book is an analytical record of seven critical years in American cultural history by a leader in the theater community.

Davis, R.G. *The San Francisco Mime Troupe: The First Ten Years.* Palo Alto, CA: Ramparts Press, 1975. This is a history of the counterculture mime group as seen through the eyes of a participant.

Esslin, Martin. *The Theatre of the Absurd,* 3rd ed. New York, NY: Penguin Books, 1983. Esslin's book explores, explains, and catalogues the important creators and works in this intriguing genre.

Green, Susan. *Bread & Puppet: Stories of Struggle & Faith from Central America.* Burlington, VT: Green Valley Film and Art, Inc., 1985. This book tells an emotional story and is filled with photographs of enormous puppets and engaged audiences. Green documents a mixture of enormous puppets, beauty, conscience, and political action. Bread & Puppet is a group of political actors working for justice and peace.

Huerta, Jorge A. *Chicano Theater: Themes and Forms.* Ypsilanti, MI: Bilingual Press/Editorial Bilingue, 1982. This book documents El Teatro Campesino and much more from the Chicano tradition.

Komparu, Kunio. *The Noh Theater: Principles and Perspectives.* New York, NY and Tokyo: John Weatherhill, Inc., 1983. This is the first book written in English to give a comprehensive and thorough explanation and analysis of the principles of Noh Theater. The author is a Noh actor.

Van Erven, Eugene. *The Playful Revolution: Theatre and Liberation in Asia.* Bloomington, IN: Indiana University Press, 1992. This groundbreaking book reports on the Theater of Liberation movements in the Philippines, South Korea, India, Pakistan, Indonesia, and Thailand.

Videotapes and Films

Antony and Cleopatra. 1981. A Bard Productions Ltd. release, Timothy Dalton and Lynn Redgrave star in this filmed stage production of Shakespeare's tragedy. Video, color; 183 minutes.

Arsenic and Old Lace. 1944. This classic stars Cary Grant and is directed by Frank Capra. Adair and Alexander repeat their Broadway roles. It is listed in Critic's Choice Video 1-800-367-7765. Video, black and white or color; 118 minutes.

Cyrano de Bergerac. 1984. Derek Jacobi and the Royal Shakespeare Company perform in this classic. It is available through Schlessinger Video Productions 1-800-843-3620. Video, color; 176 minutes.

Cyrano de Bergerac. 1989. Gerard Depardieu stars in this French version with English subtitles. It is available through Schlessinger Video Productions 1-800-843-3620. Video, color; 135 minutes.

Death of a Salesman. 1985. This is a TV version starring Dustin Hoffman. It is available through Schlessinger Video Productions 1-800-843-3620. Video, color; 135 minutes.

The Dumb Waiter. 1987. John Travolta and Tom Conti star in this TV adaptation of Harold Pinter's absurdist drama. Video, color; 60 minutes.

A Funny Thing Happened on the Way to the Forum. 1966. Zero Mostel recreates his Tony-winning role in this screen version of the Broadway musical hit. Video, color; 100 minutes.

I Remember Mama. 1948. Irene Dunne and Barbara Bel Geddes star in this film version of John van Druten's play. It is the story of a Norwegian immigrant family struggling to survive in early twentieth-century San Francisco. It is listed in Critic's Choice Video 1-800-367-7765. Video, black and white; 134 minutes.

The Inspector General. This 1954 film version is listed in The Audio Forum 1-800-243-1234. Video, black and white.

The Life and Adventures of Nicholas Nickleby. This story by Charles Dickens is dramatized by the Royal Shakespeare Company. It is listed in The Video Catalog 1-800-733-2232. 9 videos, color; 9 hours.

Macbeth. 1948. Orson Welles directs and stars in this atmospheric version of Shakespeare's play in which the actors speak with Scottish accents. Video, black and white; 89 minutes.

Major Barbara. 1941. This British screen version of George Bernard Shaw's classic play includes the cast of Rex Harrison, Emlyn Williams, and Sybil Thorndike. It is listed in The Video Catalog 1-800-733-2232. Video, black and white; 135 minutes.

The Miracle Worker. 1962. Anne Bancroft and Patty Duke re-create their Broadway performances in this production. Video, black and white; 107 minutes.

No Time for Sergeants. 1955. Andy Griffith plays Will Stockdale in this version written for television by Ira Levin. Video, black and white; 60 minutes.

Oedipus Rex. 1957. In this version directed by Sir Tyrone Guthrie, actors wear masks as worn in traditional Greek tragedy. It is available through Schlessinger Video Productions 1-800-843-3620. Video, black and white; 90 minutes.

A Raisin in the Sun. 1961. RCA/Columbia Pictures Home Video. Sidney Poitier leads the cast in this story of a black family at odds about ways to spend a $10,000 insurance settlement. Video, black and white; 128 minutes.

Rosencrantz and Guildenstern Are Dead. 1990. In this version Tom Stoppard directs Gary Oldman and Tim Roth in their verbal adventures. Video, color; 118 minutes.

Roxanne. 1987. Columbia TriStar Home Video. Steve Martin and Daryl Hannah star in a modern-day *Cyrano de Bergerac.* Video, color; 107 minutes.

The School for Scandal. 1965. Joan Plowright stars in this film version. It is available through Schlessinger Video Productions 1-800-843-3620. Video, color; 100 minutes.

The Search for Signs of Intelligent Life in the Universe. 1991. One in a series of five cassettes from *The Lily Tomlin Video Collection,* this video features the Tony award-winning one-woman show written by Jane Wagner and re-created by Lily Tomlin. This video is listed in The Video Catalog 1-800-733-2232.

Styles of the Noh Theater. Norwood Institute for Advanced Studies in the Theatre Arts, 1976. Sadayo Kita, master performer of the sixteenth generation, demonstrates the delicate and intricate elegance of the Noh drama. The film includes a discussion of the drama's aesthetic origin in Zen Buddhism and also includes the performance of a Noh play. 16mm film, color; 17 minutes.

A Streetcar Named Desire. 1951. Warner Home Video. Elia Kazan's Academy Award-winning film version of Tennessee Williams's play stars Marlon Brando and Vivien Leigh. It is available from Baker and Taylor Video 1-800-775-1100. Video, black and white; 122 minutes.

The Taming of the Shrew. 1967. Elizabeth Taylor and Richard Burton star in this version, which is directed by Franco Zeffirelli. Video, color; 126 minutes.

Tartuffe. Gerard Depardieu stars in this French version of Molière's classic, including English subtitles. It is listed in Viewfinder's Catalog of Uncommon Video 1-800-342-3342. Video, color; 140 minutes.

The Teahouse of the August Moon. 1956. Marlon Brando and Glen Ford star in this story of the U.S. Army's attempts to Americanize a tiny Okinawan village. Video, color; 124 minutes.

Who's Afraid of Virginia Woolf? 1966. Directed by Mike Nichols, Richard Burton and Elizabeth Taylor star in this film version of Edward Albee's play. Video, black and white; 129 minutes.

Whose Life Is It Anyway? 1981. Richard Dreyfuss takes the leading role in this movie, which is directed by John Badham. Video, color; 118 minutes.

Journals

Asian Theatre Journal. Honolulu, HI: University of Hawaii Press. This journal focuses on performance arts of Asia.

Latin American Theatre Review. Lawrence, KS: University of Kansas. This journal contains interviews, history, international news, profiles, and features about leading theater companies and innovators in the field.

MID (Modern International Drama). Binghamton: State University of NY at Binghamton. This journal publishes previously untranslated contemporary plays.

Performing Arts Journal. Baltimore: Johns Hopkins University Press. This journal contains international coverage of contemporary theater, dance, music, and drama.

U.S. Outdoor Drama. Chapel Hill, Institute of Outdoor Drama. This is a newsletter about all aspects of outdoor drama.

Internet

African American Theatre. Through features such as artist biographies, play overviews, and theater education, this site explores the history of and investigates current movements in African American theater. The Internet address is http://www.bridgesweb.com/african_american.html

Association for Hispanic Classical Theater. This site is dedicated to maintaining and promoting interest in Spanish Golden Age *comedia.* Both Spanish and English versions of comedia plays are available for downloading at no cost. The Internet address is http://www.coh.arizona.edu/spanish/comedia/default.html

Children's Theatre Resource Page. The editors of this web page claim that the page is geared for adults but that it is certainly suitable for children. It offers history, examples, and other information concerning Children's Theater. The Internet address is http://faculty-web.at.nwu.edu/theater/tya/

The Puppetry Home Page. This site contains many informative puppetry resources under headings such as technique, construction, puppeteers, tour schedules, and related issues. The Internet address is http://www.sagecraft.com/puppetry/

CHAPTER 7

History of Drama

Framework

The history of drama is tightly intertwined with the history of humanity. Drama is a means for people to creatively express the effects of the events occurring around them. Beginning with ritual chants and dramatic recounts of the adventures of war and the hunt, drama has been an imitation of life, depicting the worst and the best of human experience. As drama evolved, many forms and styles of theater emerged, each reflecting the time period in which it was written: Sophocles' Antigone, Shakespeare's Hamlet, Ibsen's A Doll's House, and contemporary works, such as Wilson's The Piano Lesson.

This chapter helps students develop an understanding of how drama developed over time, and of how the history of drama is related to the history of humanity. Beginning with its earliest forms—retelling tales and ritualized singing and dancing—tracing drama as it developed through the Greek, Roman, Medieval, Renaissance, and Restoration periods, and finally concluding with its development in Europe, Asia, and the United States, this chapter focuses on significant periods in the evolution of drama. Being able to put a play in its historical context helps students more fully appreciate and understand it.

Relating the development of drama to students' knowledge of history can enrich the study of this chapter. An awareness of prevailing political and social climates can deepen the understanding of the drama of a given period. Encourage students to make historical connections whenever possible.

Teaching Note

Activities found in the **Review Workshop** at the end of the chapter often require some planning or preliminary work by students. Be sure to check these activities, and make sure students have adequate time in which to complete them.

Instructional Objectives

- To achieve an understanding of the evolution of the theater from its earliest days to the present
- To recognize the interplay between theater history and world history
- To identify great playwrights, their most influential works, and their contributions to the development of the theater

Vocabulary

trilogy   a set of three related plays

closet drama   a play meant to be read rather than acted

Saint play   a play based on the life of a saint

Mystery play   a play based on biblical history

Passion Play   a play concerned with the last week in the life of Christ. It has been performed every ten years in Oberammergau, Germany, since 1760.

mansions   a series of acting stations that represented biblical locations (The Saint and Mystery plays were performed with mansions.)

cycle   a series of short plays depicting religious history from creation through doomsday, performed by medieval guilds in the late fourteenth century

folk drama   plays originating during the Middle Ages that were presented outdoors during planting time, harvest time, and other secular holidays

Morality play   a play dealing with right and wrong, usually in the form of an allegory

Moral Interlude   a short version of a Morality play that usually includes more humorous incidents

commedia dell'arte   professional improvised comedy that developed in Italy during the Renaissance

raked   slanted or set at an angle. A raked stage inclines from the area closest to the audience to the rear of the stage.

Peking Opera   a form of Chinese drama that originated in the nineteenth century

No (Noh)   a six-hundred-year-old Japanese form of drama that is presented in three parts: *jo-ha-kyu*

Bunraku   Japanese drama that features puppets about four feet tall; also called Doll Theater

Kabuki   Japanese drama from the seventeenth century; combines aspects of both the *No* and *Bunraku* forms of drama

Ancillaries

Forms, Models, and Activities Blackline Masters, pages 25–31

Chapter Tests, pages 10, 11

Scenes and Monologues: From Euripides to August Wilson

Transparency 7

Motivating Activity

This activity will help students understand the historical context of drama by creating a large time line, which will be used throughout this chapter. In preparation for the activity, ask students to bring history or reference books to class. You will also need to provide a large piece of paper, probably from a roll.

Have students work in small groups or as individuals to list the significant historical events from a given time period, which you can assign, starting with ancient Greece and continuing through the present. Compile the lists on one side of a large time line, leaving room on the other side to list developments in drama as they are studied.

Put the time line on the wall or board while the chapter is being studied. Have students add information about drama, plays, and playwrights as they progress through the chapter. Emphasize the importance of events in world history and how they have affected the development of drama.

Application Activity, page 304

Students can begin their research by identifying key terms and elements from the time (e.g., from Greek drama the chorus as a means of explaining the situation and the term *skene*) and explaining how or why they were common to that time. Students should try to understand what role drama had in the society. Encourage students to look at several plays so that they have an informed picture.

FYI

The ancient Athenians ascribed greater importance to the theater than most people do today. In the city-state of Athens, citizens were expected to attend dramatic festivals. All native-born males were required to be in the chorus of a play once during their adolescent years. This requirement was considered to be part of the formal education of an Athenian citizen.

Authors who created the masterpieces of the era, including Aeschylus, Sophocles, Euripides, and Aristophanes, were considered leaders not only in drama but also of the society as a whole. A clue to this elevated status can be found in the Greek word for playwright, *didaskalos*, which was also the word for "teacher."

Extension If you include a question-and-answer session after the presentation, the presenter will gain practice in relaying information in an unrehearsed as well as a rehearsed manner. Remind students that it is allowable not to know an answer; however, make sure presenters know they will be responsible for finding the answer later. This is also a good way to teach the class to be active participants: prior to the presentation, they should prepare at least one question about the period. If it is not covered during the presentation, they will be able to ask their question later.

Application Activity, page 311

To make this a whole-group activity you might direct students to a single play, such as *Othello*, and instruct them to look only for the asides. Three asides in *Othello* can be found in Act II, Scene I. The first is delivered by Desdemona, the wife of Othello, and the second and third are spoken by Iago, the villain of the play. You might discuss with students that asides can give information about characters that advances the plot. Ask students to find asides, found later in *Othello* or in another play, that appear to be addressed, at least in part, to the groundlings. Evaluate students on their ability to find the asides and to isolate the part of each aside that seems to be directed to the groundlings.

Chapter Review, page 326

Summary and Key Ideas Sample Responses

1. Drama probably originated as a somewhat ritualized retelling of an adventure, victory, or other great event. The retelling probably took the form of pantomime or rhythmic chanting. The first record of drama was found on a carved stone. The record tells of Ikhernofret of Abydos's leading role in a three-day pageant that told the story of the resurrection of the god Osiris.

2. The chorus in a Greek tragedy served to explain the situation, to bring the audience up-to-date, and to make a commentary on the action from the point of view of established ideas. The chorus also sometimes engaged in dialogue with the actors.

3. Among the most famous authors of Greek tragedies are Aeschylus, the author of the Greek trilogy called the *Oresteia*; Sophocles, the author of *Oedipus Rex* and *Antigone*; and Euripides, the author of *The Trojan Women* and *Medea*. Other famous Greek authors include Aristophanes, author of *The Frogs, The Clouds,* and *Lysistrata*; and Menander, author of *Dyskolos*.

4. Saint and Mystery plays were the first types of Christian drama to be translated from the Latin used in the earlier church plays and liturgical chants. For the first time laymembers of the parishes were allowed to act in the dramas. Also, Saint and Mystery plays used mansions to portray Heaven, Pilate's house, Jerusalem, and Hell's mouth. In the fourteenth century, medieval trade unions took over the performances in England. Members of the trade unions used pageant wagons that moved through town as they performed a cycle of plays that depicted religious history from creation through doomsday.

5. The Renaissance was a period of transition from the medieval to the modern world in western Europe. During the Renaissance, interest in the classics was reborn and the belief in the potential for human perfection touched almost every aspect of life.

   During the Renaissance in Italy, theater architecture and stage equipment were developed, and sets with perspective and colored lighting were introduced. Opera and the commedia dell'arte developed in Italy during the Renaissance. Elsewhere in Europe, strolling players created melodramatic history plays, rowdy comedies, and romantic love stories that were the origins of the great dramas of later generations.

   The climax of Renaissance drama, however, occurred in Elizabethan England, where theater became a vital social force. The first English comedy, *Ralph Roister Doister*, was produced, as was the first English Tragedy, *Gorboduc*. Many notable and enduring plays, including those by Shakespeare, Marlowe, and Jonson, were also written during this time. The first English public playhouse, the Theatre, was built during this time period.

6. Among the stock characters of the commedia dell'arte were the upper-class types: the innamorati and innamoratae, beautifully dressed young lovers; Pantalone, a middle-aged or elderly man; and Dottore, an elderly gentleman who was sometimes the friend or rival of Pantalone. Male servant characters, called

zanni, were clever persuaders and schemers; among them were Brighella, Scapino, Pulcinella, Pedrolino, Capitano, and Scaramuccia. The female servant character was Fontesca, or Columbina, who was a clever and flirtatious serving maid.

7. The three Elizabethan dramatists whose plays never lost appeal are Christopher Marlowe, Ben Jonson, and William Shakespeare.

8. The essence of the *Nō* theater is an interweaving of words, dance, and music into the story. Typically, a god, a warrior, and a beautiful woman are involved in the story, and the drama concludes with a frenzied dance. All actors are male.

9. English dramatist Bernard Shaw, known for his satiric humor and fascinating characters, is the author of *Saint Joan, Candida, Man and Superman, Caesar and Cleopatra, Pygmalion, Androcles and the Lion*, and *Arms and the Man*.

   Cervantes contributed to the mounting interest in theater in Renaissance Spain.

   American playwright Eugene O'Neill wrote tragedies dealing with issues ranging from interpersonal relationships to faith; among these are *The Emperor Jones, The Iceman Cometh, The Hairy Ape*, and *Long Day's Journey into Night*.

   Goethe is the author of *Faust*. He and Friedrich von Schiller developed an approach to theater and acting that influenced actors and playwrights far beyond their German homeland.

   Henrik Ibsen of Norway is sometimes called the father of modern drama and the father of realism. He wrote *A Doll's House, Ghosts, Hedda Gabler, An Enemy of the People*, and *The Master Builder*.

   Elizabethan dramatist Christopher Marlowe introduced the first use of blank (unrhymed) verse; his plays include *Tamburlaine the Great, The Jew of Malta, Edward II*, and *Doctor Faustus*.

   American playwright Arthur Miller, the author of moral and political tragedies, wrote *The Crucible* and *All My Sons*. In 1949 he won the Pulitzer Prize and Drama Circle Award for *Death of a Salesman*.

Discussing Ideas

1. Although answers will vary, reasons should be based on historical information. For example, if students choose early Greece, the discussion should cover the thrill of dramatic contests, the use of clever mechanical devices, the outdoor theaters, and the importance of drama in society at that time.

2. Discussion might include these points: Shakespeare understood the theater from both sides of the stage: he knew what it was like to develop a plot, give it a dramatic structure, and bring it to life. As an actor, he probably had a sense of audience response, which might have helped him understand and develop the themes that unify a play, giving his writing coherence and universality.

3. Before beginning the discussion, have students refer to page 296 for the entire quote. Discussion should touch on the quote's suggestion that everyone plays a part in the world, and that people are involved in many personal dramas in their lives. The stage for each person's life is the historical and cultural setting in which the person lives.

Review Workshop, page 327

Independent Activities

Twentieth-Century Morality Play If you prefer to make this a group activity, divide the class into small groups and have each group decide which fable to portray. Ask each group to discuss the moral of the fable before developing the play. It might be helpful if students first decide which virtue or quality the characters in the fable personify. After each group performs, have the remaining students discuss the lesson taught by the play. Assess performances on the representation of virtues and qualities by the main characters and by the clarity of the lesson taught.

Shakespearean Interpretation As students search for a monologue, remind them that several shorter speeches can be combined to form a monologue as long as the topic is related. Also, explain to students that a monologue should be emotional, not simply informational; a long speech that gives information is a soliloquy, not a monologue. You might wish to direct students to the following characters for interesting monologues: King Lear, Hamlet, Othello, Julius Caesar, Kate, Portia, and Juliet. Before students perform their monologues, you might help them review their answers to the role-scoring questions. This will give you a basis to evaluate students' portrayal of their characters. Assess performances on the ability of an actor to portray the character as he or she scored the role. After the performances, discuss the character analyses and use this discussion as a basis for determining the reasons for the longevity of Shakespeare's characters.

Cooperative Learning Activity

Tragic Greek Myths Students might need to visit a library to research various myths. Two possibilities for this activity are the myth of Prometheus and the myth of Pandora. After students have chosen their myths, suggest that groups brainstorm the best ways to use a chorus to enhance the dramatization of the myths they have chosen. Remind students that they can use the chorus in the following ways: to comment on the action; to explain the situation; and to interact in the dialogue. Evaluate group performances on the use of the chorus for forwarding the plot or adding to the moral of the story. Commend creative resolutions of the conflict in the tragedy.

Alternative Myth A Roman myth (told only by the Latin poet Ovid) that would lend itself well to a retelling with a chorus is the story of Arachne. Proud Arachne thinks she is so skillful and quick a weaver that she accepts a challenge to compete against the goddess of weaving, Minerva. Neither wins, but Minerva is so angered by Arachne's pride that she turns her into a spider, thereby condemning her to weave forever.

Across the Curriculum Activity

History After students have chosen their topics and begun their research, ask them to share their topics and initial findings with the class. If students still have a broad topic, provide them with suggestions to narrow the topic. If students do not seem to be finding information, encourage the rest of the class to brainstorm questions about the topic or terms or playwrights from the era. In a wrap-up discussion, ask students how the theater of the time related to daily life.

Later, divide the class into groups. Members should discuss their findings in greater depth and should begin making connections as to whether drama seems to be mere entertainment or a reflection of life. Encourage students to provide specific examples and to accept opinions counter to their own. In an effective argument, the arguer sees both sides of the issue but diffuses the opinion of the opposition. Ask students if they see ways to diffuse the opposition with their own topics.

CLOSE

Final Activity

Find a variety of scenes and monologues from various plays throughout history. You might select a Greek tragedy; a Restoration play; a Shakespearean play; another Renaissance drama; a recent musical; a work from Shaw, Ibsen, or O'Neill; and a work from Beckett, Pinter, or Ionesco. Copy these scenes or monologues, removing anything that might identify their title, date, or author, such as a familiar character's name.

Divide the class into small groups and give each group an excerpt. Ask students to determine the period in which the piece was written and, if possible, to suggest a country or area of origin. Tell students to pay particular attention to the language and content of the play, and also to the dramatic devices used. Ask them to supply reasons from the play for the conclusions they draw about time and place. Each group can then read the scene or monologue aloud, present its conclusions, and invite discussion from the rest of the class before having the actual facts revealed.

Bibliography

Books

Bentley, Eric, ed. *The Theory of the Modern Stage*. New York, NY: Penguin Books, 1976. This basic text and reference book has been updated and now includes sections on Asian and African theater.

Brockett, Oscar G. *History of the Theatre*. Boston, MA: Allyn Bacon, Inc., 1995. This newly updated reference and textbook includes extensive sections on Africa and Asia.

Fo, Dario. *The Tricks of the Trade*, trans. Joe Farrell. London, England: Methuen Drama, 1991. This book is about the special combination of acting, political philosophy, and history that is witnessed in Dario Fo's work. This could be considered essential reading for those interested in political theater.

Howard, Annabelle. *Classroom Classics Series*. Littleton, MA: Sundance Publishers & Distributors, 1993. These interdisciplinary instructional materials based on classic plays were written by a teacher for middle schools and high schools. Titles are *Antigone, The Government Inspector, The Grouch, Julius Caesar, Life Is a Dream, Macbeth, Metamora,* and *A Midsummer Night's Dream*. Each title includes student and director scripts, workbooks, and a board game called *Break a Leg!*

Kanellos, Nicholas. *A History of Hispanic Theatre in the United States: Origins to 1940*. Austin, TX: University of Texas Press, 1990. Kanellos tells of a time when Hispanic theater flourished in America, and he explains much Hispanic theatrical tradition.

Kennedy, Scott. *In Search of African Theatre.* New York, NY: Charles Scribner's Sons, 1973. This book concentrates on drama in traditional African societies. Beautiful black and white photographs appear throughout the book.

May, Robin. *History of the Theater.* Edison, NJ: Chartwell Books, Inc. 1986. Impressively illustrated, this book traces the history of theater from ancient Egypt to the 1980s.

Peterson, Bernard L., Jr. *Early Black American Playwrights and Dramatic Writers: A Biographical Directory and Catalog of Plays, Films, and Broadcasting Scripts.* New York, NY: Greenwood Press, 1990. This book is a valuable research effort in an important area of drama history.

Reid, Aileen. *Theatre Posters.* New York, NY: Smithmark Publishers, Inc.,1993. Photographs, drawings, and reproductions range from the early letter press in 1779 to *Miss Saigon* in 1988 in this illustrated history of theater posters.

Warren, Lee. *The Theater of Africa: An Introduction.* Englewood Cliffs, NJ: Prentice Hall, 1975. This is a text representing the major theatrical traditions of the African continent.

Wilson, Garff B. *Three Hundred Years of American Drama and Theatre: From "Ye Bare and Ye Cubb" to "A Chorus Line."* Englewood Cliffs, NJ: Prentice Hall, 1982. This history of theater includes "imaginary visits" to the theaters of each era.

Videotapes and Films

All My Sons. 1986. This video is a TV version of the play by Arthur Miller. Video, color; 122 minutes.

The BBC's Complete Dramatic Works of William Shakespeare. These videos are available through Schlessinger Video Productions 1-800-843-3620. 19 videos, color; 110-200 minutes each.

Black Theatre Movement from A Raisin in the Sun *to the Present.* 1979. In this film African American theater is traced from the 1959 presentation of *A Raisin in the Sun* to plays and musicals in the late 1970s. It includes interviews with performers, writers, and directors and film footage of performances. 16mm film, color; 130 minutes.

Desire Under the Elms. 1958. Burl Ives, Sophia Loren, and Anthony Perkins star in this version of Eugene O'Neill's play. Video, black and white; 114 minutes.

Doctor Faustus. 1968. This is a version starring Richard Burton and Elizabeth Taylor. It is available through Schlessinger Video Productions 1-800-843-3620. Video, color; 93 minutes.

A Doll's House. 1973. Jane Fonda stars in Joseph Losey's film of Ibsen's play. It is listed in Viewfinder's Catalog of Uncommon Video 1-800-342-3342. Video, color; 106 minutes.

A Doll's House. 1989. The cast of this film includes Claire Bloom, Anthony Hopkins, Ralph Richardson, Denholm Elliott, and Dame Edith Evans. It is listed in The Video Catalog 1-800-733-2232. Video, color; 105 minutes.

Drama: Play Performances. Chicago, IL: Films Incorporated, Public Media, 1978. This film includes excerpts from performances and a discussion of their relevance in the evolution of drama. Excerpts are from the following plays: *Peer Gynt, The Wild Duck, Three Sisters, The Ghost Sonata, Oedipus Tyrannus, Macbeth, Woyzeck, St. Joan, The Venetian Twins, The Way of the World, Ubi Roi, Sizwe Bansi Is Dead, Six Characters in Search of an Author,* and *Miss Julie.* For more information, write to Films Incorporated, Public Media, 5545 Ravenswood Avenue, Chicago, IL 60640.

The Emperor Jones. 1933. Eugene O'Neill chose Paul Robeson to play the lead in this screen version of his play. It is listed in The Video Catalog 1-800-733-2232. Video, black and white; 72 minutes.

Eugene O'Neill: Journey into Genius. Matthew Modine plays the young O'Neill in this presentation. It is listed in Viewfinder's Catalog of Uncommon Video 1-800-342-3342. Video, color; 60 minutes.

Hamlet. 1948. Laurence Olivier won an Oscar for best actor and for producer of best picture in 1948. He also directed this movie. Video, black and white; 150 minutes.

Hedda. 1975. Trevor Nunn is the screenwriter and director of this adaptation of Ibsen's *Hedda Gabler.* Glenda Jackson costars with other Royal Shakespeare Company actors. Video, color; 103 minutes.

Henry V. 1944. Laurence Olivier stars, directs, and produces this version of the play. Video, black and white; 137 minutes.

Henry V. 1989. This video is Kenneth Branagh's version of Shakespeare's play. Video, color; 138 minutes.

History of the Drama Series. Princeton, NJ: Films for the Humanities, produced by Howard Mantel, 1976. The titles of this series include the following: *The Birth of Modern Theater; Classical Comedy; The Comedy of Manners; Contemporary Theatre; Modern American Drama; The Rise of Greek Tragedy; Shakespeare and His Stage; The Theater of Social Problems;* and *Theatre of the Absurd.* Films are available for purchase or rental, in videotape or 16mm film, averaging 60 minutes, from Films for the Humanities, Inc., P.O. Box 2053, Princeton, NJ 08543.

King Lear. 1984. Laurence Olivier plays Lear in this version. Video, color; 158 minutes.

A Life in the Theatre. 1993. Gregory Mosher's 1993 television production of David Mamet's play stars Jack Lemmon and Matthew Broderick. It is listed in Viewfinder's Catalog of Uncommon Video 1-800-342-3342. Video, color; 94 minutes.

Lost in Yonkers. 1993. Neil Simon wrote the screenplay for this adaptation of his play, winner of both Pulitzer Prize and Tony Award. Video, color; 110 minutes.

Macbeth. 1948. Orson Welles directs and stars in this atmospheric version of Shakespeare's play in which the actors speak with Scottish accents. Video, black and white; 89 minutes.

Macbeth. 1971. This Roman Polanski film version is a violent interpretation of the play in which Jon Finch plays Macbeth and Francesca Annis plays Lady Macbeth. A Pacific Arts and PBS Home Video. Video, color; 139 minutes.

Major Barbara. 1941. Rex Harrison, Emlyn Williams, and Sybil Thorndike star in this British screen version of George Bernard Shaw's classic play. It is listed in The Video Catalog 1-800-733-2232. Video, black and white; 135 minutes.

M. Butterfly. 1993. Jeremy Irons stars in this adaptation of the Tony-winning Broadway play by David H. Hwang. It is listed in The Video Catalog 1-800-733-2232. Video, color; 101 minutes.

"MASTER HAROLD". . .and the Boys. 1984. This version of Athol Fugard's play stars Matthew Broderick and Zakes Mokai. It is listed in Viewfinder's Catalog of Uncommon Video 1-800-342-3342. Video, color; 90 minutes.

Medea. Maria Callas gives her only non-operatic film performance in this Italian version of *Medea* directed by Pier Paolo Passolini, including subtitles in English. It is listed in Viewfinder's Catalog of Uncommon Video 1-800-342-3342.

Our Town. 1940. Thornton Wilder's classic about small-town America is directed by Sam Wood and stars Frank Craven, William Holden, Martha Scott, and Thomas Mitchell. Video, black and white; 90 minutes.

The Piano Lesson. 1995. Charles S. Dutton performs his Broadway role of Boy Willie in this Pulitzer-Prize-winning play by August Wilson directed by Lloyd Richards. Hallmark Hall of Fame. It is listed in The Video Catalog 1-800-733-2232. Video, color; 99 minutes.

A Raisin in the Sun. 1961. RCA/Columbia Pictures Home Video. Sidney Poitier leads the cast in this story of an African American family at odds about ways to spend a $10,000 insurance settlement. Video, black and white; 128 minutes.

Richard III. 1955. Laurence Olivier plays Richard and also directs this movie. The cast includes Ralph Richardson, John Gielgud, and Claire Bloom. Video, black and white; 161 minutes.

Romeo and Juliet. 1968. In this version, Franco Zeffirelli directs Olivia Hussey and Leonard Whiting, both teenagers at the time of filming. Video, color; 138 minutes.

Shakespeare's Greatest Plays. There are three collections in this series:
Shakespearean Drama: King Lear, Macbeth and Othello. 6 videos, color; 9 hours.
Shakespeare and Intrigue: The Tempest, King Richard II, and The Merry Wives of Windsor. 5 videos, color; 7 hours 30 minutes.
Shakespeare and Love: Romeo and Juliet, Antony and Cleopatra, and The Taming of the Shrew. 5 videos, color; 8 hours. These collections are listed in The Video Catalog 1-800-733-2232.

The Taming of the Shrew. 1967. Elizabeth Taylor and Richard Burton star in this version directed by Franco Zeffirelli. Video, color; 126 minutes.

Uncle Vanya. 1962. This production is filmed at the Chichester Drama Festival in England and stars Laurence Olivier, Joan Plowright, Rosemary Harris, Michael Redgrave, and Sybil Thorndike. It is listed in Viewfinder's Catalog of Uncommon Video 1-800-342-3342. Video, color; 110 minutes.

Internet

Didaskalia. This site explores the latest developments in ancient Greek and Roman drama, dance, and music as they are performed today. The Internet address is http://www.warwick.ac.uk/didaskalia/didaskalia.html

English Actors at the Turn of the Twentieth Century. This site offers a collection of pictures of more than forty turn-of-the-century British actors in costume. The Internet address is http://www.siue.edu/COSTUMES/actors/pics.html

The History of Costume. This site explores the early history of costume in cultures such as Persia, Judah, and ancient Greece and Rome. The Internet address is http://www.siue.edu/COSTUMES/history.html

Kabuki for Everyone. This site offers a well-rounded introduction to Kabuki Theater, including videos of Kabuki productions, sound clips of Kabuki music, articles on the history of Kabuki Theater, and a step by-step video of one actor's transformation through makeup into a woman for a Kabuki production. The Internet address is http://www.fix.co.jp/kabuki/

Theatre Paths. This is an Internet site that gives a theater history course on-line. The Internet address is http://arts.usf.edu/theater/paths.html

The@tropolis. This site offers exposure to theater throughout the world, including histories, current events, and links for seven major parts of the globe. The Internet address is http://www.geocities.com/Athens/Acropolis/4445/

Webspeare. This site functions as an informational Shakespeare resource for high school students and their teachers, including study guides, links, and online texts. The Internet address is http://idt.net/~kcn/webspeare.htm

CD-ROM

The Crucible. This is a CD-ROM produced for Mac and Windows. This software package provides the full text of the play, a one-hour video interview with Arthur Miller, and background information on the Puritan and McCarthy eras, as well as interviews with directors, set designers, and actors, including Dustin Hoffman. It is available from Viking Penguin 1-800-526-0275.

Macbeth. Mac/Win (Hybrid). This CD-ROM offers different ways to think about this text, such as an analysis, textual reference tools, edited text, the full performance in video, and a karaoke feature. It is available from EDUCORP Multimedia 1-800-843-9497.

The Shakespeare Collection. Mac/Win. Published by Zane. This CD-ROM series explores the work, life, and times of Shakespeare. It is available from EDUCORP Multimedia 1-800-843-9497.

Timetable of History Series: Arts and Entertainment. 1993-94 edition. This CD-ROM contains 4,300 historical events with maps, animations, quotes, and historical videos from the CBS news archives, and it offers search capabilities. It is available from Schlessinger Video Productions 1-800-843-3620.

Multimedia

Beckett Directs Beckett: A Trilogy. It is listed in The Video Catalog 1-800-733-2232. The following tragicomic plays of Samuel Beckett are directed by the playwright himself:
Volume I: Waiting for Godot. Video, 2 cassettes; 137 minutes.
Volume II: Krapp's Last Tape. Video, 1 cassette; 46 minutes.
Volume III: Endgame. Video, 2 cassettes; 96 minutes.

Early English Theater. Princeton, NJ: Films for the Humanities, produced by Stephen Mantell, 1981. A discussion and history of Mystery and Morality plays and Elizabethan drama before Shakespeare are contained in these filmstrips. Teacher's guide, two 35mm filmstrips of 95 frames each, two audiocassettes; 30 minutes.

Romeo and Juliet: Center Stage. An eighty-five-minute performance video shows students from Springfield Central, Massachusetts, performing Romeo and Juliet under the direction of Shakespeare & Company. The twenty-five-minute video follows the students through their preparation for the performance. Extensive rehearsal footage and comments by the student actors are linked to the CD-ROM and to the classroom activities described in the Teacher's Guide. Sunburst offers a free five-minute video showcasing this product. Published by Sunburst 1-800-321-7511 for grades 7-12. This is a multimedia package containing one CD-ROM, two videos, and a Teacher's Guide.

Puppet Theater, pages 328–330

SUMMARY AND KEY IDEAS

With Sample Responses

1. Name the three types of puppets used most frequently in American theater and television, and briefly describe each type.

   • **Hand Puppets,** *the simplest form of puppet, often consist of a cloth tube into which the hand is inserted. Simple eyes, nose, ears, and similar features can be added using buttons or other simple items.*

   • **Rod Puppets** *are generally constructed from more rigid materials such as wood or plastic. They are controlled from below by wire rods or thin strips of wood.*

   • **Marionettes** *are similar to rod puppets. However, they often have jointed bodies and are controlled from above by black or clear nylon strings.*

2. What should puppeteers attempt to conceal from the audience during a performance?

   When using hand puppets, the puppeteer should attempt to conceal the juncture of the arm and the puppet. This is usually done by covering the arm with a black sleeve. With rod puppets and marionettes, care should be taken to conceal the rods and strings controlling the puppets. Small, thin strips of wood or wire are usually preferred for rod puppets, while black or clear nylon string is generally used with marionettes.

DISCUSSING IDEAS

1. Discuss this statement: "It is the versatility of puppetry that affords the student of drama great challenges and great opportunities."

   Discussion should touch on the following points: Diversity is possible because of the broad range of characters and costumes. Puppets can be simple sock-like creatures or highly costumed characters with specific facial and body features.

Examples from television and classic Japanese puppet theater serve to illustrate the diversity of this art form and its broad audience appeal. The challenge lies in being able to merge oneself with an inanimate object to create a single performer. The opportunity lies in the mask the puppet provides for the performer. Behind this mask the inexperienced performer can feel safe to experiment and "let go."

2. Discuss the advantages and disadvantages of each of the three principal types of puppets.

   • **Hand Puppets**

   Advantages
   Easy to make
   Expressive

   Disadvantages
   Limited body movements
   Tend to be limited to humorous characterizations

   • **Rod Puppets**

   Advantages
   Realistic
   Allows for numerous character types

   Disadvantages
   Difficult to manipulate
   Difficult to construct

   • **Marionettes**

   Advantages
   Realistic
   Joints allow many types of movement

   Disadvantages
   Difficult to manipulate
   Often require several puppeteers

ACTIVITY

Have students work in groups of two or three to create one or more hand puppets and use them in a performance. The performance can be based on an original script or on an existing story or play. Encourage creativity in the design of the puppets by suggesting the use of unusual material for sleeves and features.

Part Four

Producing the Drama

CHAPTER 8
Producing the Play — 82

CHAPTER 9
Producing the Musical Play — 90

CHAPTER 10
Stage Settings — 100

CHAPTER 11
Lighting and Sound — 108

CHAPTER 12
Costuming — 116

CHAPTER 13
Makeup — 124

❖ How to Judge a Play — 131

CHAPTER

8 *Producing the Play*

Framework

The many tasks and responsibilities involved in producing a play require the participation of many people. From the grips to the properties chief to the director to the cast, all staff members play vital parts in a production. The production staff, including the artistic staff and the behind-the-scenes staff, is responsible for costumes, sets, lighting, ticket sales, budget, publicity, direction, and much more.

By providing information about the various aspects of production, this chapter stresses the importance of the production staff. The various steps required to produce a play, from the selection of the play to the dress rehearsals, are explained and placed in a production schedule that gives students a full picture of the elements needed to bring a production together.

After studying this chapter, students should appreciate the fact that theater is not an activity for a single type of person; in fact, with the wide range of skills utilized in theater, almost anyone can find some aspect in which he or she can find enjoyment.

Teaching Note

Activities found in the **Review Workshop** at the end of the chapter often require some planning or preliminary work by students. Be sure to check these activities, and make sure students have adequate time in which to complete them.

Instructional Objectives

- To understand the business of producing a play, including the responsibilities of each staff member
- To learn how to stage a play by dividing tasks into manageable parts, preparing a schedule, and delegating responsibilities
- To understand auditions and casting from the perspectives of both a performer and a director
- To distinguish among the different types of rehearsals: blocking, working, polishing, technical, and dress

Vocabulary

producer the person who finds the financial investors, hires the director and production staff, sets the budget, and pays the bills for a theatrical production

director the person in charge of molding all aspects of production—the acting, scenery, costumes, makeup, lighting, and so on—into a unified whole

assistant director the person who acts as the liaison between the director and the cast and crew and who takes charge of the rehearsal when the director is absent

prompter the person who keeps the director's promptbook and makes notes on cues, signals, and so on

scenic designer a person who designs settings and sometimes costumes, makeup, and lighting

technical director a person who executes the designs of the scenic artist with the help of a crew

stage manager the person who is completely in charge backstage during the rehearsals and performances

grip a stagehand who moves scenery

properties chief the person who is in charge of getting the furniture and props, storing them, arranging them on the set, preparing the prop table, and giving the actors the props they need

business manager the person responsible for the financial arrangements of a production

publicity manager the person who handles the advertising and promotion of a play in the press, the radio, and other media

house manager the person responsible for distribution of programs, seating of the audience, and training the ushers

promptbook a script marked with directions and cues for use by the prompter

audition a tryout for a position in a play

reading rehearsal a rehearsal at which the play is read by the director or by members of the cast

blocking rehearsal a rehearsal at which the movement and groupings on the stage are practiced

working rehearsal a rehearsal at which interpretation of the play is developed and words and actions are put together

polishing rehearsal the final rehearsal at which all parts of the play are brought together so that flaws can be worked out

technical rehearsal a rehearsal at which lighting, scenery, and props are used so that changes go smoothly

dress rehearsal an uninterrupted rehearsal with costumes and props; the final rehearsal before performance

Ancillaries

Forms, Models, and Activities Blackline Masters, pages 32–42

Resource Lists and Bibliographies

Chapter Tests, pages 12, 13

Scenes and Monologues: From Euripides to August Wilson

Transparencies 8–13

Motivating Activity

A dramatic production does not depend solely on the actors; many other people are necessary to bring a play to life. This activity will provide a means of drawing students' attention to some of those people.

Show students a few minutes of a film. As students watch the film, have them list as many settings, costumes, lighting effects, sound effects, and actions as possible. Remind them that props, clothing, and furniture should be included. After they have watched the film and listed their observations, write these headings on the board: *Settings, Costumes, Lighting Effects, Sound Effects, Actions.* Then have students combine their lists on the board under the correct headings. Explain that many people were responsible for designing the sets, creating the costumes and makeup, creating the lighting, and arranging the furniture and props. Other people typed scripts, shot film, and paid the bills. Then play the credits and have students contrast the number of actors with the number of people listed in the production credits.

TEACH

Application Activities, page 339

Activity 1 Students can work in small groups to generate the chart. They may benefit from using a Venn diagram to see how much some jobs overlap. When groups have completed the charts, the members should each pick a position they think they could do. More than one person may choose the same position. Working alone, each member should list personal traits or skills that match this position. Then, in the group, each member should read his or her list. Members can brainstorm skills or traits that the speaker may have overlooked.

Extension Create a situation in which the students must either combine some positions or eliminate them entirely. Discuss which positions could be combined and how. What would happen to the play if a position were eliminated? Ask students to brainstorm other positions (and their corresponding duties) to add to the existing list.

Activity 2 Divide students into small groups. Have each group select two positions on the artistic staff. Then have the group brainstorm the responsibilities of each position and the qualities that the ideal applicant should possess. After this preliminary work, groups should be ready to create their ads. An effective ad should concisely state the job requirements and the qualities desired in an applicant.

▶ Additional Application Activity

Have pairs of students create brief skits that depict a job interview between a director and a person applying for a position on the artistic staff. Encourage students to have fun with these skits. For example, one applicant might be totally unsuited for the job but might be unwilling to face this fact. Another applicant might have the wrong impression of what the job entails.

Application Activities, page 343

Activity 1 One way to begin this activity is to have students list the stage manager's responsibilities and then imagine problems in each area of responsibility. Answers should include reasonable solutions to proposed problems.

Activity 2 Divide students into small groups. Have each group choose a play and decide on the best way to promote it. Oral presentations might include performing a short scene or a combination of selected lines from the play to pique the interest of the public. Since most groups will not have access to photographs of the production, visual presentations might consist of sketches or written lines from the play. Commend creativity in the advertisements.

▶ Additional Application Activity

Have students form small groups. Then have each group decide on a method of demonstrating the responsibilities of one of the following people: stage manager, publicity manager, business manager, properties chief, and house manager. Students might present this information using written or verbal explanations, charts, or diagrams. Students might opt to present a short skit to illustrate the duties of one of these positions.

Application Activities, page 348

Activity 1 Remind students that they should pay particular attention to the actors' abilities and the school's facilities and financial resources. If there are several schools or a community theater in the area, students should research which plays have been performed in the last five years. Groups that are leaning towards an expensive production should brainstorm ideas of how to raise additional funds. Groups leaning towards a musical should make sure that actors have the singing ability and that band or orchestra members are willing to participate.

During the class presentations, each group should sell its play. Encourage students to be creative in their presentations (e.g., members might dress up in rough costumes, bring props, bring photos of the play, or draw up a budget). After each presentation, give students time to capture a few ideas in writing. After the last presentation they can then discuss the presentations in general and choose the best play.

Activity 2 If the performance is available on videotape, play it for the class. If more than one version is available, choose two, and play a few minutes from each scene. Either method will help students visualize the time period and the appropriate visual elements. Encourage students to use these tapes as a starting point only, and to put their own distinctive mark on the production. You might even request that students break into groups, with each group focusing on a particular technical or visual element (lights, sound, scenery, costumes, or makeup).

▶ Additional Application Activity

Divide the class into groups of five or six students, and ask each group to select a play that would appeal to students in their school. Remind them to consider the actors' abilities and the school's facilities and financial resources during the process of choosing a play. Provide enough time for each group to consider several different plays. Afterward, discuss the different possibilities and reasons for choosing these plays. Have the class determine the best play for the particular audience and place.

Application Activities, page 352

Activity 1 Before students begin, you might hold a group discussion about the qualities directors look for in an actor. The discussion should include vocal expression, naturalness, appropriateness for the role, and gesture and posture. Encourage students to choose a variety of selections. You might take the role of the casting director since you probably have more knowledge of the images that different roles require. Base student evaluation on the qualities listed above.

Activity 2 Before students begin this activity, you might suggest that they list their skills, their experience, and their interests. You can retain the students' lists for a time when a class or school production is scheduled, or for use during the Review Workshop.

▶ Additional Application Activity

Have students read the director's comments portion of the tryout information form on page 350. Then have them use those categories, as well as others that they choose, to create self-evaluation forms. Have students evaluate their own strengths and weaknesses in each category. Have them include brief descriptions of the types of roles for which they would probably be considered. Then have them list the types of roles for which they would like to be considered. Evaluating themselves critically will help students begin to develop realistic goals

FYI

Although the focus of a production is usually on the actors, the acting is often the tip of the iceberg in a production. Often more work, money, and planning go into the stage settings, costumes, props, and other behind-the-scenes tasks. For example, *Miss Saigon*, a love story set in South Vietnam near the end of the Vietnam War, requires an 18-foot-high, 600-pound statue of communist leader Ho Chi Minh, a working, full-size replica of a 1959 Cadillac, and a full-size, computer-controlled helicopter. In addition, it uses 375 costumes, 206 props, 45 weapons, 470 lighting instruments, 8 fog and smoke machines, and 300 pounds of dry ice for each performance. There is a total of 218 people involved in organizing, operating, and staging all of these props, special effects, and set pieces. Nineteen trucks are required to move the show.

Application Activity, page 367

Provide students with ample time to choose their monologues. After monologues are chosen, you might divide students into small groups and suggest that they conduct a reading rehearsal so they can practice interpreting their particular selections. After they have conducted the reading rehearsals, allow students time to practice individually at home. Finally, have each student present his or her selection in front of the class as if it were a polishing rehearsal. Interaction between the actor and the classmates offering critiques should be positive and pleasant, much like a true polishing rehearsal. Assess student performances based on interpretation and delivery, including inflections, rhythm, and gestures. Also, assess students on their positive and helpful comments for each actor.

Application Activity, page 370

To make this a classroom debate, divide the class into two groups, one that thinks a dress rehearsal is necessary and one that does not. Give each group time to brainstorm a list of arguments for their positions before the classroom debate. Assess students on the validity of the arguments given and the thought put into the arguments.

Extension Have the class discuss or debate one or both of the following statements: (1) An audience should always be in attendance for dress rehearsals. (2) A dress rehearsal must never be interrupted.

 ASSESS

Chapter Review, Page 372

Summary and Key Ideas Sample Responses

1. For a complete discussion of the responsibilities of the production staff, see pages 334–342 of the Student Edition.

    * The prompter takes notes in the promptbook, and provides cues and lines if an actor hesitates or skips a line.

    * The technical director executes the designs of the scenic designer. With the assistance of a crew, the technical director builds sets, paints drops, creates costumes, and hangs lights.

    * The stage manager, who takes charge backstage, makes cue sheets for lights, sound, curtains, and set and prop changes. This person also times rehearsals and performances and handles any emergencies.

    * The properties chief acquires all furniture and props and makes sure they are all available and in good working order. This person is also responsible for storing props, preparing a prop table, and making sure actors have props when they need them.

    * The business manager is responsible for the financial arrangements of a production. The job responsibilities include keeping track of expenses, paying bills, handling funds, ensuring all contributors are acknowledged in the program, taking charge of printing and selling tickets, supervising advertising sales, and trying to achieve a profit.

    * The publicity manager creates the advertisements for a production and promotes the production in the media.

    * The house manager makes sure that the audience is comfortable, the ushers are trained and equipped, the admission and intermissions run smoothly, and the ticket stubs are saved for the business manager.

2. A master production schedule ensures that no steps are skipped and that time is planned for every step in a production.

3. The promptbook is considered "the backbone of a production" because it contains not only the entire script but also sketches, notes, and important cues. In addition, the names, addresses, and phone numbers of everyone involved in the production are included in the promptbook.

4. For a complete discussion of types of auditions, see pages 349–352 of the Student Edition.

    * Anyone can try out for an open audition.

- A closed audition is limited to only professional union actors or only certain students.

- Applicants can use rehearsed material for a prepared audition.

- An applicant must read unfamiliar material for a cold reading.

- For an improvisational audition, actors must improvise scenes around assigned characters and situations.

- For a textual tryout, applicants read material from printed sources.

5. A résumé should contain all the information a casting director might want, such as name, address, phone number, voice range, experience, training, and education. A résumé for an acting role should also include a type classification and a glossy headshot. A budget should include all sources of income and all the projected expenses for the entire production.

6. For a complete discussion of each type of rehearsal, see pages 356–370 of the Student Edition.

- A blocking rehearsal is designed to work out movement and stage groupings.

- At a working rehearsal, interpretation is developed and words and actions are put together as actors develop their characters.

- In a polishing rehearsal, all lines should be memorized and actions set, and the rhythm of the play and the action should be fine-tuned.

- A technical rehearsal allows problems with lights, curtains, scenery, and props to be solved.

- A dress rehearsal is an uninterrupted performance complete with costumes and props. It is also the time when publicity photos are usually taken.

7. Curtain calls should be rehearsed because they provide the audience with the last impression of a play.

Discussing Ideas

1. A good discussion will include an assessment of school facilities, such as auditorium and stage space, available financing, and lighting equipment, as well as an awareness of acting and production talent. The discussion should also reflect an

awareness of how limitations might be overcome or sidestepped.

2. Students should realize that facilities are only secondary to a performance; they are not a substitute for creativity. Help students recognize that limitations might actually foster creativity and thus help in producing a lively, engaging performance.

3. A discussion of the director's role should focus on that person's foresight. Discussion should focus on a director's ability to visualize actors as the characters they will become after much rehearsal, not as the individuals they are in reality. This foresight is important because throughout rehearsals the director tries to shape the actors to fit this image.

Review Workshop, page 373

Independent Activity

Writing a Résumé If students choose to write the résumé about themselves, have them refer to the lists of their skills, experience, and interests created for the Application Activities on page 352. Résumés should be judged on content, neatness, and organization. Point out to students that a résumé is important because it is an actor's first introduction to a potential employer.

Help Wanted Ad If possible, provide models of interesting Help Wanted ads from local or regional newspapers. Explain to students that effective ads have two characteristics: (1) They are eye-catching , capturing readers' attention. (2) They provide all of the important details about a job's requirements in a concise manner. When evaluating students' advertisements, keep in mind that a good ad will exhibit both factors.

Cooperative Learning Activity

Promptbook This activity provides an opportunity for students to visualize an actual production after reading a printed script. Creating the promptbook shows them how to record their artistic ideas for a play. Obtain photocopies of several plays from which each group can choose. As students compare promptbooks, you might have them discuss the differences in notations, reflecting on how different cues would change the interpretation of the play. Promptbooks should have comprehensive cues that assist the flow of the play.

Across the Curriculum Activity

Math This activity allows students to understand the type of financial planning that is involved in a theatrical production and also to discover the practical application of math skills. If possible, have students determine the actual expenses of such items as custodial fees, costume rental, printing, and advertising. (Sources can be found in the **Suppliers List** in the **Teacher's Resource Binder**.) Also, they will need to take the number of seats in the auditorium into account to estimate the selling price of tickets. You will need to allow time for students to gather estimates. You might prefer to have students work in small groups for this activity.

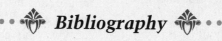

CLOSE

Final Activity

For this activity, plan for the class to see a university, community, or professional theater production. If possible, try to see the production in rehearsal. Ask students to pay particular attention to the work of the behind-the-scenes crews. If you are able to attend a rehearsal, have students pay attention to the director's comments and the production staff's responses.

After you have seen the performance or rehearsal, lead a class discussion on the aspects of production that students noticed, including props, sets, stage directions, lighting, and the interaction among the cast and crews.

Encourage students who are seriously interested in the theater business to volunteer with local theater companies. Many community theaters need and appreciate volunteers.

Bibliography

Books

Cole, Toby, and Helen Chinoy. *Directors on Directing: A Sourcebook of the Modern Theatre.* Indianapolis, IN: Bobbs-Merrill, 1980. This is a collection of personal insights into the art of directing.

Dean, Alexander, and Lawrence Carra. *Fundamentals of Play Directing.* New York, NY: Holt, Rinehart & Winston, 1980. This is a how-to book for the inexperienced director, including advice on blocking, working with actors, and other fundamentals.

Dilker, Barbara. *Stage Management Forms and Formats.* New York, NY: Drama Book Publishers, 1982. A collection of more than 100 ready-to-use forms appears in this book. The accompanying text explains the purpose of each form, and completed samples illustrate some variations of use.

James, Thurston. *The What, Where, When of Theater Props.* Cincinnati, OH: Betterway Books, 1992. This reference book describes and illustrates a vast array of theater props and places them in historical context. It is useful for production staff and for writers working with a particular period.

Kelly, Thomas A. *The Back Stage Guide to Stage Management.* New York, NY: Back Stage Books, 1991. Kelly covers the entire process from pre-production planning to opening night. The author also describes successful ways to run auditions and rehearsals, create promptbooks, write cue sheets, and remain calm while accomplishing all the tasks.

Mitter, Shomit. *Systems of Rehearsal: Stanislavsky, Brecht, Grotowski, and Peter Brook.* New York, NY: Routledge, 1992. A sophisticated comparison of successful styles of rehearsing are described in detail by Mitter.

Stern, Lawrence. *Stage Management.* Boston, MA: Allyn & Bacon, 1995. This is a practical guide based on personal experience.

Time-saving tips and guidelines for the well-managed theater are described, and many illustrations are included.

● Wolfe, Welby B. *Materials of the Scene: An Introduction to Technical Theatre.* New York, NY: Harper & Row, 1977. Wolfe logically explains basic principles and practical directions for the beginner. The text is illustrated with precise drawings.

Videotapes and Films

Borrowed Faces. 1980. McGraw-Hill Films. In this film, the audition and casting process of the Colorado Shakespeare Festival is viewed from the perspective of director and actors. Individual actors are followed from pre-audition, casting, and rehearsal through performance. 16mm film, color; 29 minutes.

Signature: Marsha Norman. The viewer follows Norman backstage as she works with actors, designers, composers, and producers. It is available through Annenberg/CPB Multimedia Collection 1-800-LEARNER. Video, color; 60 minutes.

Journals

● *AATE Newsletter.* American Alliance for Theatre & Education, Theatre Dept., Arizona State University, Tempe, AZ 85287-3411. This newsletter offers current information about grants, jobs, and events for educators and theater artists who work for or with youth.

Backstage. New York, NY: BPI Communications. This is a weekly newspaper for those interested in professional theater.

Drama-Theatre Teacher. Tempe, AZ: American Alliance for Theatre and Education. This journal includes articles on theater education with an emphasis on classroom instruction for pre-school through twelfth grade.

Dramatics. Cincinnati, OH: Educational Theatre Association. This journal offers information devoted to the practice of theater arts in secondary schools.

Educational Theatre News. Whittier, Southern California Educational Theatre Association. This newsletter covers secondary, youth, community, and college theater activities in the United States and abroad.

● *Theater Week.* New York, NY: That New Magazine, Inc. This magazine covers Broadway and regional theater. Back issues are available.

Youth Theatre Journal. Tempe, AZ: American Alliance for Theatre and Education. This journal covers all aspects of theater for young audiences and for theater education.

Internet

ArtsEdge. This is an Internet site linking arts and education through technology. It is maintained by the Kennedy Center's Education Department. The Internet address is http://artsedge.kennedy-center.org

ArtsNet. This is an Internet site designed to provide clear access to a multitude of arts resources. It is an alphabetical and comprehensive listing of arts information sources. It is maintained by the Carnegie Mellon University. The Internet address is http://www.artsnet.org

Arts Wire. This is a service mark of the New York Foundation for the Arts, and it provides on-line communications for the arts. There is a weekly digest of arts news in which many cultural resources are described. The Internet address is http://www.artswire.org

The On Broadway World Wide Web Information Page. This resource provides information on Broadway plays and musicals. The Internet address is http://artsnet.heinz.cmu.edu:80/OnBroadway/

Playbill Online. This is an Internet site with the following categories of theater information and services: Feature Articles, Theatre Industry Nitty Gritty, Join the Playbill On-line Theatre Club, Theatre Listings, Multimedia Center, Who's Who, Celebrities, Recordings, Books, Jobs, Newsletters, Quizzes, Awards, Travel Packages, and Talk to Us. The Internet address is http://www1.playbill.com/

Multimedia

Speech and Silence: The Language of Drama. This workshop is conducted by the Artistic Director of the Shakespearean Theatre at the Folger. Director Emily Mann discusses her work on *The Glass Menagerie.* It is available through Annenberg/CPB Multimedia Collection 1-800-LEARNER.

Producing the Musical Play

Framework

Musical theater dates back to the first operas, which were performed in Italy during the Renaissance. Since then, musical theater has been produced in many different forms; operettas, comic operas, musical revues, musical comedies, and musical plays are common forms of musical theater today.

This chapter introduces students to the various kinds of musical theater and the special demands and potential problems musical theater presents for a cast and crew. Students will also learn that by very carefully choosing and meticulously planning a production, the staff can avoid many potential problems.

In many ways, the musical is unique. Musical theater has its own terminology, its own problems, and its own special rewards. By introducing students to these aspects of musical theater, they will have a better understanding of musical theater, both as performers and observers.

Teaching Note

Activities found in the **Review Workshop** at the end of the chapter often require some planning or preliminary work by students. Be sure to check these activities, and make sure students have adequate time in which to complete them.

Instructional Objectives

- To identify the different types of musical theater: opera, operetta, comic opera, musical revue, musical comedy, and musical play
- To become familiar with the special terminology of musical theater
- To learn staffing needs, performance techniques, and staging requirements for musical theater

Vocabulary

opera   a form of musical theater in which all conversations are sung

operetta   a form of musical theater in which the music is lighter than opera and conversation is spoken

comic opera   humorous or satirical operetta

musical revue   a production consisting of a series of independent song and dance scenes tied loosely together; often satirical

musical comedy   a form of musical theater, a combination of operetta and musical revue—loosely connected production numbers

musical play   a form of musical theater in which the emphasis is on real people in real situations

crossover   a short scene played in front of a shallow drop or curtain while scenery is being changed

change music   the music played between scenes while sets are being changed

spoof   a literary work that pokes fun at certain subjects or time periods

satire   a humorous attack on accepted conventions of society, holding up human vices and follies to ridicule

concept musical   a series of scenes loosely connected and focusing on a theatrical concept

hanging plot   a listing of all the flying scenery and what is on each piece, prepared by the technical director or the stage manager

storage plot   a diagram showing how scenic units are to be stored in the wing areas during a show

backlighting   the use of lighting instruments above and behind performers to accent the performers and set them apart from the background

reversible   a costume that is double-faced so that by reversing it the illusion of a different costume is created

coordinates   costumes that are separates, which are interchangeable, or sometimes reversible, such as ties, vests, and so on

combo   a small group of instrumentalists

Ancillaries

Forms, Models, and Activities Blackline
   Masters, page 43

Resource Lists and Bibliographies

Chapter Tests, pages 14, 15

Transparency 14

Motivating Activity

Most students have some association with music, whether through radio, television, or films. This activity will provide an opportunity for students to draw on this prior experience and apply it to a theatrical situation.

Assemble a collection of musical selections that represent a range of types of music: folk music, popular music, show tunes, and songs from films, for example. Play several selections, and ask students to name physical activities that have the same feelings or rhythms as the selections. For example, "Hi, Ho, Hi, Ho, It's Off to Work We Go" from Disney's *Snow White and the Seven Dwarfs* was sung as the seven dwarfs marched off to work in the morning.

Divide the class into three or four groups and explain that each group is to choose an activity to perform in time to one of the songs. Students can dance, lip-synch a live performance, or pantomime actions such as hammering or marching.

Play the selections, and allow students time to plan and practice their performances.

Before they begin, have them clear a place in the classroom that is large enough for whatever activities they have chosen. Then play the music again as each group takes its turn performing.

After the performances, discuss how music can suggest moods or actions as well as unify the activities of many different people.

🔀 TEACH 🔀

Application Activity, page 381

This activity is designed to teach students how to obtain the information they need to assess the nonproduction costs of a musical play. Provide the students with the addresses of various publishers listed in the **Resource Lists and Bibliographies** section of your **Teacher's Resource Binder.** Have each student or group of students write a letter to a publishing company requesting information about script and royalty charges for various musicals. Provide students with the information they will need to obtain an accurate response from the publisher, such as the number of seats in your auditorium, the approximate ticket price, and the length of rehearsal time. It might take some students longer to receive responses, so schedule a time at the end of the chapter for students to discuss their findings. If your school has produced musicals in the past, share the financial records with the class so the students will have an idea of what to expect.

Extension Have students estimate the number and types of actors needed for a particular musical play. How many, for example, must be able to sing? How many must be able to dance?

▶ *Additional Application Activity*

This activity will help familiarize students with musical play terminology. Have students work individually or in small groups to create crossword puzzles for the terms that appear on pages 377 and 378. Using a sheet of graph paper, have students write one long term in the center of a grid, allowing one letter per square. Then have them link other terms to the original term while staying within the confines of the grid. Next, students will number the words and write clues for them. Finally, they should create blank versions of their puzzles to exchange with their classmates.

Application Activity, page 387

To guide students into this activity, choose a musical play and bring in either a videotape or an audiotape/CD of the performance. Tell students that you will play the musical for ten to fifteen minutes, and that they should take notes on how the music and dance affect theme, character, setting, and action. Depending upon which musical and which scene you choose you may need to provide background information for students to understand the context. After the showing, elicit student discussion about their notes. Ask which style the musical represents and what elements helped them come to that conclusion.

Divide the class into small groups, which will each choose a straight play. Groups should take some time to discuss the plot, characters, and strengths of the play. Then, one student should serve as a note taker while the group brainstorms ideas about what makes the musical more or less expressive than the straight play. Since one member might list something as a con and another as a pro, each idea should be accompanied by a brief explanation. Members can conclude the activity by drafting a short group paper answering the question of whether multiple art forms distract an audience from the play's message. If members are not in agreement, they may break into subgroups to write their reports.

Application Activity, page 393

Students viewing a movie musical might assume that the sets and costumes are too elaborate for a school performance. You might, however, encourage students to think of ways that the musical can be adapted for school performances. Have the entire class analyze the same element of the musical or have each student analyze a different element. Create a ranking system to indicate the appropriateness of the musical play for your school. For example, use 1 to mean "very appropriate" and 5 to mean "completely inappropriate."

▶ Additional Application Activity

For this activity, students will first read the script of a musical and then watch a video of that musical being performed. Before choosing a musical for the class to analyze, be certain that you have access to both the script and a video performance of the musical. Have students first read the script of the musical (perhaps as a homework assignment), and then have them make decisions about how they would produce the play if they were directing it. Students should make notes on the following:

- sets (how many and what kind)
- costumes
- basic lighting ideas
- music (full orchestra or combo? *entr'acte?*)

Then show a video of the musical in class. Have students discuss how this production differed from the production they envisioned.

Focus the discussion on how the use of sets, costumes, lighting, and music can affect the audience's interpretation of a play. Explain that the director's vision of the final production also affects the audience's interpretation.

FYI

Stephen Sondheim, who wrote the lyrics for *West Side Story,* learned how to write a musical when he was only fifteen years old. Sondheim attended school with the son of Oscar Hammerstein, the playwright and lyricist of such masterpieces as *Oklahoma!* and *The Sound of Music.* The elder Hammerstein told Sondheim to work on his writing skills in four steps. First, take a play he admired and turn it into a musical. Then, take a play he did not like and turn that into a musical. Third, take some non-dramatic material, such as a short story or a novel, and create a musical based on it. Finally, write a completely original piece. Sondheim took the next six years—his college years—to write those four musicals. Five years later, Sondheim became famous as the lyric writer for *West Side Story.* With several masterpieces now to his credit—including *A Funny Thing Happened on the Way to the Forum, A Little Night Music, Sweeney Todd,* and *Sunday in the Park with George*—Sondheim says he learned most of what he knows about writing for musical theater by following Hammerstein's advice.

🌺 ASSESS 🌺

Chapter Review, page 394

Summary and Key Ideas Sample Responses

1. An opera is a form of musical theater in which all dialogue is sung.

   In an operetta, lines are both spoken and sung. Although the music of an operetta is lighter than it is in an opera, the music is still more prominent than the plot, the characters, or the acting.

   A comic opera is a humorous operetta.

   A musical comedy combines music and humor; however, realistic characters and clever dialogue distinguish it from a comic opera.

2. Staffing is more difficult for a musical play than for a regular production because of the larger number of specialized staff members that are needed. This additional staff includes a vocal director, an instrumental director, and a choreographer. Also, the abilities of the available actors must be considered. Actors must be able to act, dance, and sing, whereas in a regular production, acting is the main consideration.

3. When selecting a musical for production, the following must be considered:
- script and royalty fees compared to budget limits
- the available talent to produce, direct, and act in the show
- the musical, scenic, and lighting demands
- the time available for rehearsal
- appropriateness for both high school performers and audiences

The play itself should be one that both the performers and the audience will enjoy, and it should not have demands that a high school production cannot meet. For example, the play should not require elaborate special effects or mechanisms that are unavailable to most schools.

4. Three types of musical plays are spoofs, satires, and concept musicals.
- Spoofs make fun of certain ideas or time periods.
- Satires criticize human actions or social behaviors.
- Concept musicals build an entire musical around a single idea.

5. A complete list of performance principles can be found on pages 384–385 of the Student Edition. Key performance principles include the following:
- Singers should stress the first beat of each measure.
- Lyrics should be clear and understandable to the audience.
- Singers should imagine that the songs are coming out of their eyes in order to lift the sound.
- Performers should direct their attention to the audience during musical numbers.
- Every player should help keep the audience's attention on the key characters in every scene.
- Actors should remain in character, even when their actions seem unimportant.
- Actors should look active at all times, even if this means freezing in mid-gesture.
- The entire cast should try to enjoy themselves and should look as if they are, because enthusiasm is contagious.

6. Most musicals have more scene changes and take up more stage space than regular plays. Therefore, the director must plan the best way to manage all the scene changes and the extra lighting. In addition, costumes are usually bolder and more stylized. The music might also create problems because of the limited vocal range of the actors. Since acoustics can be a problem, the director must make sure that the music does not drown out the actors' voices and also that it does not overwhelm the audience.

Discussing Ideas

1. The discussion should reflect an understanding that actors, conductors, choreographers, and directors need to coordinate rehearsal times, work together to solve problems, and work together during rehearsals to make sure all the elements come together in a unified production.

2. A good discussion will bring out the fact that musicals have more people and movements than most other plays. Because of this, certain problems need to be addressed. For example, because the actors and chorus take up so much of the stage, the director must be sure that one does not block the other. In addition, the director must organize the entrances and exits of the large number of actors and chorus so as to avoid a traffic problem, while maintaining a dynamic sight line with the staging.

3. You might want to have students turn to pages 384 and 385 to review and discuss the principles as a class. You can assign this activity either as an independent or a group activity. If students only listen to performances, they will mainly concern themselves with the first three items. Students should specify which particular actions or examples demonstrate each principle.

4. Students should recognize that musical plays can be plagued by many of the same problems that can hamper any production. Some additional problems might include royalty fees; actors lacking a necessary skill, such as dancing; scheduling the numerous kinds of rehearsals; coordinating many moving bodies onstage at the same time; coordinating with the orchestra, the singers, or both; casting a spotlight on moving actors; as well as actors moving effectively in costume.

Review Workshop, page 395

Independent Activity

Comparing Adaptations Have students present evidence from the plays to support their comparisons. A good report will exhibit a well-prepared, thorough comparison. Students should also be prepared to explain their answers to the questions in the activity.

▶ **Additional Independent Activities**

• Have each student select a short story, a novel, or a TV show to adapt into a musical. Then, have them create titles for three songs that the musical might contain. Students should be able to provide evidence from their short stories, novels, or television shows to explain their choices of song titles.

• Have each student select a song from a musical and recite it rather than sing it. Encourage students to review the eight performance principles on page 384 before they begin. Explain that the recitative style can be just as effective as singing.

Cooperative Learning Activity

Rock Opera This activity gives students an opportunity to create a musical piece that reflects their own tastes in music. Accept a wide variety of interpretations for the songs that they choose, but encourage students to choose songs that are unified by at least one element or idea.

Extension If time allows, you might extend this activity by allowing students to perform a simplified version of their interpretation.

Across the Curriculum Activity

The Living Arts Help students narrow their topics—they can provide a clearer picture if they have a narrow topic. Refer them to the text so that they can find key terms that will help them conduct their research. Strategies such as brainstorming, outlining, freewriting, and clustering can help them generate or organize their ideas. If time permits, allow students to present their reports to the entire class. Otherwise, divide the class into several group, with presentations occurring among group members.

Final Activity

To give students an idea of how much fun it can be to perform a musical, have them work together to perform one song. Choose a high-energy song from a musical. It can be a familiar or an unfamiliar musical. (A song from the *Grease* sound track might be fun for students.) Look for a highly melodic or rhythmic selection, and have students memorize the words. Allow ample time for memorization.

When all of the students have learned the lyrics, have them sing along with the recorded version as if they were performing it onstage. This will involve at least two steps. First, the students need to decide what actions they will perform while they sing. Next, they will need to clear or create a space where they can perform the song. If possible, have them do this before a live audience, perhaps another class.

Books

Berkson, Robert. *Musical Theater Choreography.* New York, NY: Back Stage Books, 1990. Designed specifically for first-time choreographers, dancers, and directors, this book gives a step-by-step guide to staging dance sequences for musicals.

Filichia, Peter. *Let's Put On a Musical!* New York, NY: Avon Books, 1993. This book is a guide to amateur musical play production.

Gottfried, Martin. *Broadway Musicals.* New York, NY: Harry N. Abrams, Inc., 1979. Gottfried has documented the history and inner workings of Broadway musicals.

Green, Stanley. *Broadway Musicals,* 4th ed. Milwaukee, WI: H. Leonard Publishing Corp., 1994. This book explains how musical comedies of the 1920s and 1930s were followed by the musical play and how the concept musical eventually emerged. With almost four hundred pictures, many in full color, this book is both a theoretical and pictorial history of Broadway musicals.

Guernsey, Otis L., Jr. *Broadway Song and Story: Playwrights, Lyricists, Composers Discuss Their Hits.* New York, NY: Dodd, Mead, 1985. The author gives insights into the success, stress, and inspiration that contribute to launching a Broadway show.

Kaye, Deena, and James Lebrecht. *Sound and Music for the Theatre: The Art and Technique of Design.* New York, NY: Back Stage Books, 1992. The authors trace an entire process of sound design that draws upon music, live sound effects, and recorded material to shape a theatrical reality. Researching sources for recorded music and effects, developing a sound plot, and running equipment are also discussed.

Kimball, Robert, and Alfred Simon. *The Gershwins.* New York, NY: Atheneum, 1973. The authors have created a colorful tribute to the brothers George and Ira Gershwin. The tribute is a combination of scrapbook, journal, album, home movie, and pictorial biography. More than three hundred photographs are included.

Kislan, Richard. *The Musical: A Look at the American Musical Theater.* New York, NY: Applause Theatre Book Publishing, 1995. This is an entertaining book about musicals—their history, performers, authors, and composers. The author also describes the basic principles, materials, and techniques that are essential for a musical production—the book, lyrics, score, dance, and set design.

Mandelbaum, Ken. *"A Chorus Line" and the Musicals of Michael Bennett.* New York, NY: St. Martin's Press, 1989. The reader is taken behind the scenes to watch as the unique creative process that shaped *A Chorus Line* is revealed. Mandelbaum describes how the show affected its participants and why it is such a popular show.

Marsolais, Ken, Rodger McFarlane, and Tom Viola. *Broadway Day and Night: Backstage and Behind the Scenes.* New York, NY: Pocket Books, 1992. Emotional, nostalgic, and humorous essays with photos were commissioned for this book, and they give the reader a true insider's look at Broadway. The authors' royalties are paid directly to "Broadway Cares/Equity Fights AIDS." The introduction is by Angela Lansbury.

Mordden, Ethan. *Rodgers & Hammerstein.* New York, NY: Harry N. Abrams, Inc., 1992. This is both a comprehensive and celebratory book. The anecdotal text is accompanied by over two hundred illustrations.

Oliver, Donald. *How to Audition for the Musical Theatre: A Step-by-Step Guide to Effective Preparation.* Lyme, NH: A Smith and Kraus Book, 1995. From years of Broadway experience, Oliver gives practical advice to aspiring actors and other theater professionals.

Richards, Stanley. *Ten Great Musicals of the American Theatre.* Radnor, PA: Chilton Book Company, 1973. The complete books and lyrics for numerous musicals appear in this one volume. *Of Thee I Sing, Porgy and Bess, One Touch of Venus, Brigadoon, Kiss Me Kate, West Side Story, Fiddler on the Roof, 1776,* and *Company* are among those listed.

Silver, Fred. *Auditioning for the Musical Theatre.* New York, NY: Newmarket Press, 1988. Tactics and techniques for auditioning for the musical theater are written by a man who worked with many of the greats. Discussions about the differences between auditioning for a musical and auditioning for a play, choosing the right material, acting a song, wearing the correct clothing, and many more relevant topics are included.

Soeby, Lynn M. *Way Off Broadway: A Complete Guide to Producing Musicals with School and Community Groups.* Jefferson, NC: McFarland & Co., 1991. This is a guide for the producer who does not have millions of dollars to spend to produce a musical, but who nevertheless wants to create the most exciting show possible.

Sunderland, Margot, and Kenneth Pickering. *Choreographing the Stage Musical.* New York, NY: Theatre Arts Books/Routledge, 1990. This book offers advice for those uncertain about choreographing a show.

Young, David. *How to Direct a Musical: Broadway—Your Way!* New York, NY: Routledge, 1994. Special material for working with youth, teens, and physically challenged persons is included in Young's firsthand account of how to create a stage musical. Young addresses the first-time director, while advice to the more seasoned directors comes from Colleen Dewhurst, Anne Meara, and others. Excerpts from Dr. Young's diary reveal his reasoning behind certain of his artistic choices.

Videotapes and Films

Andrew Lloyd Webber: Encore. Fourteen songs from shows such as *Evita* and *The Phantom of the Opera* are included on this video. It is listed in The Video Catalog 1-800-733-2232. Video, color; 58 minutes.

Barnum. Michael Crawford stars as P.T. Barnum in this Cy Coleman musical filmed at the West End Theater in London. It is listed in Viewfinder's Catalog of Uncommon Video 1-800-342-3342.

The Best of Broadway Musicals. This video presents original cast members from various musicals that were taped live on the Ed Sullivan Show and interviews with Lerner and Loewe and Rodgers and Hammerstein. It is listed in The Video Catalog 1-800-733-2232. Video, color; 60 minutes.

Bye Bye Birdie. 1963. This film version of the musical stars Ann Margret, Janet Leigh, and Dick Van Dyke. It is listed in Critic's Choice Video 1-800-367-7765. Video, color; 112 minutes.

Carousel with Soundtrack. 1956. This is a film version of the Rodgers and Hammerstein classic musical. It is listed in The Video Catalog 1-800-733-2232. Video, black and white; 110 minutes.

42nd Street. Ginger Rogers stars in this 1933 Busby Berkeley musical. It is listed in Critic's Choice Video 1-800-367-7765. Video, black and white; 89 minutes.

A Funny Thing Happened on the Way to the Forum. 1966. Zero Mostel re-creates his Tony-winning role in this screen version of the Broadway musical hit. Video, color; 100 minutes.

Man of La Mancha. 1972. Peter O'Toole plays the seventeenth-century nobleman who imagines himself a knight of old. It is listed in Critic's Choice Video 1-800-367-7765. Video, color; 130 minutes.

The Mikado. 1939. This vintage film captures a performance by the D'Oyly Carte Opera and features the London Symphony Orchestra. It is listed in The Video Catalog 1-800-733-2232. Video, black and white; 93 minutes.

Les Misérables. 1935. This film version of Victor Hugo's book with Charles Laughton is not the musical version, but it might be of interest to anyone studying the musical or studying the art of adaptation. Video, black and white; 108 minutes.

Peter Pan. 1960. This original uncut version of the musical stars Mary Martin. It is listed in Critic's Choice Video 1-800-367-7765. Video, color; 110 minutes.

The Phantom of the Opera. David Staller and Elizabeth Walsh star in this musical performed live at the Hirschfield Theater in New York. It is listed in Critic's Choice Video 1 800 367 7765. Video, color; 93 minutes.

The Pirates of Penzance. 1983. This movie version of Joseph Papp's New York Shakespeare Festival production stars Kevin Kline and Linda Ronstadt. It is listed in Viewfinder's Catalog of Uncommon Video 1-800-342-3342. Video, color; 112 minutes.

The Sound of Music with Soundtrack. 1965. Julie Andrews performs in this classic musical. Video, color; 174 minutes.

State Fair. 1945. This is a film version of a Rodgers and Hammerstein classic. Video, color; 100 minutes.

Sweeney Todd: The Demon Barber of Fleet Street. 1936. Tod Slaughter stars in this British version of the musical by Stephen Sondheim. Video, color; 68 minutes.

That's Entertainment! MGM. MGM celebrates its history with scenes from memorable musicals. There are three videos in this series:
That's Entertainment! 1974. Video, color; 132 minutes.
That's Entertainment Part II! 1976. Video, color; 133 minutes.
That's Entertainment Part III! 1994. Video, color; 108 minutes.

Threepenny Opera. In this 1931 adaptation of Bertolt Brecht/Kurt Weill's play set in London, the bandit, Mack the Knife, marries Polly and starts a conflict between the beggars and the thieves. It is listed in The Audio Forum 1-800-243-1234. Video, black and white; 112 minutes.

Voices of Sarafina. New Yorker Films Video. The viewers are taken behind the scenes of the Tony-nominated Broadway hit that dramatizes the 1976 uprising of 15,000 South African schoolchildren. To obtain a Special Order from Baker and Taylor Entertainment, call (Western 1-800-775-3300; Eastern 1-800-775-2600). Video, color; 85 minutes.

West Side Story. 1961. This is a film version starring Natalie Wood. It is listed in Critic's Choice Video 1-800-367-7765. Video, color; 151 minutes.

Journals

Musical Show. New York, NY: Tams-Witmark Music Library. This magazine is devoted to the amateur presentation of Broadway musicals on the stage.

Theater Week. New York, NY: That New Magazine, Inc. This magazine covers Broadway and regional theater. Back issues are available.

Internet

Broadway and Musical Theater Sites. This site offers links to other musical theater sites, as well as to homepages of specific musical productions. The Internet address is http://artsnet.heinz.cmu.edu/Artsites/Broadway.html

The Gilbert and Sullivan Archive. This Internet site devoted to the operas and other works of William S. Gilbert and Arthur S. Sullivan includes a variety of related items, such as clip art, librettos, plot summaries, pictures of the original stars of Gilbert and Sullivan musicals, song scores, midi files (sound clips), and newsletter articles. New items are being added regularly. The Internet address is http://math.idbsu.edu/gas/GaS.html

The On Broadway World Wide Web Information Page. This Internet site provides information on Broadway plays and musicals. The Internet address is http://artsnet.heinz.cmu.edu:80/OnBroadway/

The Stephen Sondheim Stage. This Internet site is an on-line source for all information regarding Stephen Sondheim and his theatrical creations. The Internet address is http://www.sondheim.com/

Theatricopia. Musical Theater is the focus of this site, which offers informative categories such as awards, shows, lyrics, books, multimedia, composers, and general theater links. The Internet address is http://www.saintmarys.edu/~jhobgood/Jill/theatre.html

CD-ROM

Computer Music: An Interactive Documentary. CD-ROM. Mac/Win (Hybrid). Published by Digital Studios, this documentary from the CyberLearning Collection, produced in association with the University of California, Santa Cruz, fuses video, sound laboratory, and workbook to show the state of the high-tech world of computer music. It is available from EDUCORP Multimedia 1-800-843-9497.

Multimedia

The King and I with Soundtrack. 1956. This package includes a video of the Rodgers and Hammerstein classic, the original theatrical trailer and movietone newsreel, and an audiocassette of the soundtrack. It is listed in The Video Catalog 1-800-733-2232. Video, color; 139 minutes.

Oklahoma! with Soundtrack. The video features the Oscar-winning score by Rodgers and Hammerstein and choreography by Agnes DeMille. An audiocassette is included. It is listed in The Video Catalog 1-800-733-2232. Video; 152 minutes.

South Pacific with Soundtrack. 1958. This package includes a video of a classic Rodgers and Hammerstein World War II romance, the movietone newsreel, and an audiocassette of the soundtrack. It is listed in The Video Catalog 1-800-733-2232. Video, black and white; 164 minutes.

CHAPTER 10

Stage Settings

Framework

Not only do stage settings indicate time and location, they also provide the atmosphere and a context in which to place the characters of a play. There are many conventions of stage settings that suggest an illusion of reality in lieu of a true depiction of reality. These conventions comprise some of the practical considerations of presenting a play.

It is important for students to know how stage settings can affect the audience's interpretation of a play, and how the styles of stage settings have changed throughout history. It is also important for actors to possess a solid background in the fundamentals of set design in order to understand the reason so much planning is needed to create sets, and how stage settings help to project a particular interpretation of a play to the audience. This chapter introduces students to these basic concepts of stage settings.

With an emphasis on practical, how-to information, this chapter helps students make the transition from theory to practice. Beginning with an introduction to choices in scenery and set design, this chapter also explains set construction and stage safety. Students will learn to appreciate the importance of the sets and scenery they see onstage as well as learn how to create, erect, paint, and move sets and scenery.

Teaching Note

Activities found in the **Review Workshop** at the end of the chapter often require some planning or preliminary work by students. Be sure to check these activities, and make sure students have adequate time in which to complete them.

Instructional Objectives

- To understand the purpose and effect of scenery in a play
- To become familiar with the development of scenic design from the Renaissance to the present
- To identify types of sets and the basic principles of set design
- To learn how to produce sturdy, attractive sets and to move them safely

Vocabulary

box set a two-wall or three-wall set representing an interior of a room, often covered by a ceiling

unit set a basic stage setting from which several settings can be created

permanent set a set that remains the same throughout a play, regardless of change of locale

screens two-fold and three-fold flats used either as walls against a drapery background or to cover openings or furnishings when changing scenes

profile or cut-down set a set using two-dimensional pieces of scenery, such as hedges or bushes

prisms or *periaktoi* sets made up of three six-foot flats or two four-foot flats and one six-foot flat, shaped as equilateral or isosceles triangles mounted on a wheeled carriage that can be pivoted

curtain set the use of curtains as a backdrop for a play

unity situation in which all elements of the set form a perfect whole, centering on the main idea of the play

emphasis the focus of the audience's attention on some part of the stage

proportion stage setting that takes the human being as the unit of measurement

balance the visual symmetry of the stage

hue the purity of color

value the lightness or darkness of a color

tints light or pastel colors

shades dark or deep colors

intensity the brightness or dullness of color or light

saturation the brightness or dullness of a color

Ancillaries

Forms, Models, and Activities Blackline Masters, pages 44–50

Resource Lists and Bibliographies

Chapter Tests, pages 16, 17, 18

Transparencies 15–18

Motivating Activity

This activity will help students understand the importance of designing a set for the stage by contrasting a real room with a room designed as a set. The activity will address the considerations set designers must address, including the actors' ability to move about onstage and the audience's ability to see and hear.

Have each student sketch the furniture arrangement in his or her living room as if looking down on the room from above. Make sure that students note windows, doorways, and the direction in which the furniture is facing. Then tell them to imagine that their living rooms are to be the settings of plays. Have students create second sketches with the changes they would make to present their living rooms as theater sets, including the placement of furniture, windows, and doors. Also, have them note which wall would be the "fourth wall."

After both sketches are completed, have several students display their two sketches. Discuss the changes students made in the original room and the effectiveness of these changes. Did the sketches indicate where the actors will enter and exit? Is most of the furniture facing the audience? Will the audience be able to see the action and hear the dialogue onstage? Explain that a set must do more than depict a living room; it must be practical, allowing actors adequate space to perform and the audience full visual access to the action of the play.

As a final activity, students will have the opportunity to analyze and improve their sketches. As they progress through this chapter, encourage students to think about the changes they would like to make to their original stage setting sketches.

☒ TEACH ☒

Application Activity, page 402

Allow ample time for students to choose a scene. It is important that students choose familiar plays in order to select scenery that captures the overall mood and atmosphere intended by the author. Encourage students to read through the entire scene and to visualize the set before they begin writing. Urge them to include only those things that must be on the set according to the script, including rugs, lights, windows, and props. Remind students that these items are often mentioned in the stage directions or merely implied in the dialogue. Assess student responses by referring them to the chart on page 402, which details what effective scenery and design should do. Also note any elements of time, setting, character traits, and style suggested by the scenery students have chosen.

Extension If students have difficulty deciding on a play, allow them to select a work of literature that might be dramatized. Some possibilities might include an Edgar Allan Poe short story, a favorite science fiction selection, a myth, or a folktale.

Extension Once students have completed their lists and descriptions of scenery, have them make sketches of the sets that conform to the conventions listed on page 401.

Application Activity, page 415

Schedule a time when the class can visit the auditorium or theater. Divide the class into groups, and supply each group with yardsticks and tape measures. Encourage students to carry clipboards or notebooks for recording data. Have students organize the information they gather into charts. You might need to supply lighting information, since most of that equipment will be stored. When you evaluate the activity, make sure students have answered all the questions on the predesign

checklist. To stimulate the follow-up discussion, ask questions such as the following:

- Why does a scenic designer need to know about available storage space?
- How would a raked floor affect the choice of scenery?
- Why are exact measurements of the apron and flats important?

Keep these checklists for students to use in the Application Activity on page 436.

Application Activity, page 422

Have students create charts on graph paper. At the left of the chart, they can list the names of the main characters in a play of their choice. At the top of the chart, students can list several categories such as color, texture, time of day, and room in a house. By free-associating the characters with the various categories, the design choices might be made more easily. Students must now place characters in a scenic design. Encourage them to think about combining colors or tones to create a mood that is both appropriate and interesting. Evaluate students on the presentation of mood and on how well it suits the character analysis.

Extension Suggest a different color scheme to each of several small groups. Then have each group create a plot for a play that could be expressed by that color scheme. Encourage groups to consider how color schemes can communicate the mood and atmosphere of the play.

Application Activity, page 431

Performing this activity will require a considerable amount of space. Move desks and chairs to one side of the room, and have students stand to view the activity, or if possible, hold class in the auditorium. Supply heavy, corrugated cardboard from the packing boxes of appliances or other large objects. The larger the cardboard pieces that students work with, the closer this activity demonstrates the experience of actually moving flats. When groups demonstrate each method, ask them to explain what they are doing and, if possible, to tell why they are doing it in that particular way.

Application Activity, page 435

You will need to provide a large work space for this activity. In addition, you will need to provide some of the following materials: old flats or drop cloths, brushes, paints, sponges, rags, feather dusters, and possibly rulers, protractors, compasses, and other materials for making stencil templates. Also, students will need heavy paper, poster board, or other surfaces on which to paint. Students who will be painting should wear old clothes or smocks and old shoes.

When you evaluate this activity, observe how well students can explain the reasons they are using a particular process and how their techniques will help to achieve the final results they desire. Also ask them to suggest uses, moods, or themes for the types of texturing or stenciling they have created.

Application Activity, page 436

Some students might benefit from actually going to the school stage once the play is identified. There, they can more easily envision the action of the scene and the possible limitations on that action. Have students refer to their predesign checklists from the Application Activity on page 415 for the actual measurements. After students have assessed the stage and available equipment, encourage them to refer to page 436 both to identify possible problems and to suggest solutions.

FYI

One of the most celebrated set designers of the last few decades is Ming Cho Lee. In 1982 he designed the set for *K-2*, a play set on the side of a Himalayan mountain. The set represented part of the mountain's snow-covered, vertical face, and was one of the most memorable sets in the history of Broadway theater. The immensely high set was made mostly of Styrofoam™ and was so convincing that audience members reported feeling cold. Ming Cho Lee, though he won a Tony Award for the set, considered it a failure. Why? It was so dramatic and so breathtaking that he felt it drew the audience's attention away from the actual play for the first fifteen minutes of each performance.

ASSESS

Chapter Review, page 444

Summary and Key Ideas Sample Responses

1. Drama students should study stagecraft because a set provides the place in which to act, as well as the time and the setting of the play. Scenery is an integral part of contemporary play writing and production because audiences have come to expect scenery that not only presents a specific locale but also adds an essential dimension to the production in terms of detail, mood, and atmosphere.

2. The main purpose of scenery, also called sets, is to provide a place in which to act. The set also defines the time and setting of the play. In addition, a set should help inform the audience about the effects of the environment on the characters, and how, in turn, the characters' personality traits affect their surroundings. Sometimes a set might also reveal the relationships between characters, as well as characters' ranks, stations, influence, or positions. Scenery can also enhance a performance by creating mood and atmosphere.

3. Set design as we know it came into being during the Renaissance. Early Renaissance sets included painted walls showing city streets in perspective and a large central entrance that was the forerunner of the proscenium arch. Prism sets and raked stages were sometimes used. Renaissance dramatists also experimented with other backdrops, wing settings, revolving stages,

and shutters. During the Restoration, most onstage action took place on the raked apron, with little action occurring behind the proscenium in the scenery. During the nineteenth century, efforts were made to suit the scenery to the individual play. By the middle of the nineteenth century, realism began to gain influence; settings changed as the apron shrank, orchestra seats were added, painted backdrops were eliminated, and wings were closed. During the twentieth century, experimentation with scenery has been common. Naturalism peaked with the photographically accurate sets. However, designers of today often select elements that convey the idea of the locale rather than serve as an exact replica of it; this style is called selective realism. Designers typically use a proscenium set that has all of the essential entrances, such as doorways and windows, in two-sided or three-sided rooms.

4. Types of sets include the following:

   • box set, which consists of two or three walls built of flats and often covered by a ceiling

   • unit set, which consists of several scenic units that can be moved about the stage, turned, and interchanged to create several settings

   • permanent set, which can vary in design but rarely changes during a play

   • profile set, which can be constructed of screens and forms the entire perimeter of the setting

   • curtain set, which simply uses curtains as a backdrop for the play

   • skeleton set, which consists of frames and openings that can be left empty or filled by draperies, backings, and doors

5. Before designing a set, the designer must know the size and shape of the auditorium; details about the available space, including storage space and the dimensions of the apron and the wings; the number and the sizes of flats, drops, and scrims; whether they are special units, such as ramps or platforms; and what kind of lighting is available. In addition, the designer must have a good knowledge of the play and the audience.

6. Four key artistic considerations in building a set include unity (all of the elements of the set form a whole that centers on the theme of the play); emphasis (focus on a particular object, area, or furnishing); proportion (all elements are scaled realistically if realism is the goal, or distorted appropriately if nonrealism is the goal); and balance (the distribution of emphasis from one side of the stage to the other). Other artistic considerations include line, mass, and shape.

7. The steps in constructing a flat are the following:

   (1) Gathering the materials, including special stage hardware

   (2) Assembling and bracing the frame, which can be done through the use of butt joints or, preferably, miter joints

   (3) Washing the frame with a flameproof solution

   (4) Covering the frame with cloth

   (5) Sizing the cloth

   (6) Attaching a lash line

   Refer to pages 423–428 in the text for complete instructions.

8. The best fabric for covering flats is canvas, but because it is expensive to purchase, the next best choice is unbleached muslin.

9. Shifting scenery requires an experienced crew. The stage manager is responsible for all backstage activity and directs the crew members. The grips move flats, *periaktoi*, and set pieces. The flycrew raises and lowers flown scenery and draperies. Set dressers set and strike a set's finishing touches.

10. Refer to page 441 in the text for a list of general stage safety rules.

Discussing Ideas

1. Students should explain that a few well-designed and well-constructed pieces are more powerful and effective in creating a mood, projecting a theme, or revealing character and setting than numerous items that have been assembled without sufficient planning or care.

2. To facilitate the discussion, urge students to analyze every choice made by the designer. When analyzing color choice, students should reflect some of the ideas that are presented on page 422. In their discussion of number and types of sets, students should consider how elaborate or simple the scenery was and which factors in the play and theater influenced the designer's decisions.

3. Discussion should include the idea that a realistic set will include the features of an actual balcony, such as the appropriate height, size, and shape. The realistic balcony might look as if it were actually found in Verona, Italy, in the late Middle Ages, which is the established setting of the play.

Review Workshop, page 445

Independent Activities

A Play Without Scenery Before students begin this activity, lead a class discussion to brainstorm ideas of plays that will be appropriate. If you make this a group activity, make sure each group has a different play or at least different scenes of the same play. Before students begin sketching, encourage groups to discuss the best ways of using limited resources. Suggest, also, that students use the stages of the writing process—prewrite, write, and revise—as they write their explanations. These steps will help students logically evaluate and revise their stage plans. Note how well students use a limited setting to emphasize the mood and the atmosphere of the scenes. Commend creativity.

Visual Metaphor Introduce this activity by reviewing the term *metaphor* and generating some examples with the class. Allow students to select a symbol or metaphor. You might also review the term *perspective drawing*, referring students to page 407 in the text for an example. Encourage students to title their drawings with the name of the play and to label key parts of the set. In addition, suggest that students also write a caption explaining the purpose and content of the drawing. Assess student work on the appropriateness of the metaphor or the symbol they chose and on the representation of it in their sets.

Cooperative Learning Activity

Troubleshooting Students should begin by reading the play and then discussing the demands of physical space it makes. Encourage students to present only realistic suggestions for what might or might not be built or added. Once each group has made recommendations, the class as a whole might discuss the total amount of labor needed and the financial cost required to bring about such changes.

Across the Curriculum Activities

Woodworking Talk with students about optimal sizes for models. While larger models might be easier to create and be less demanding in terms of woodworking skills, smaller models may look more attractive and be easier to display. Inform students that they can construct models from heavy cardboard or poster board, using craft sticks, toothpicks, and glue to create smaller objects on the set. Sets should be practical for the play chosen.

Art To streamline this activity, divide the class into small groups and have each group demonstrate just one method of texturing, such as spattering, rag rolling, stippling, featherdusting, or dry brushing. In addition, have one group demonstrate gridding and one demonstrate using papier-mâché. Evaluate students on their knowledge of the technique and the final outcome of their projects.

CLOSE

Final Activity

As a final activity, have students return to the sketches they created for the Motivating Activity at the beginning of the chapter. Ask students to refine their sets by applying what they have learned in this chapter. Refinements might be made by changing or adding scenic elements, such as furnishings, props, colors, and textures. Also, the placement of such things might be changed.

Then have students look analytically at the sets they created, and have them write about how they should be altered and improved. In the written analysis, students should include the types of sets they would use, for example, box sets or unit sets. Also, have students address the style used to create the sets, such as symbolism, selective realism, or naturalism. Would they place their living room on an open stage or a proscenium arch? Have they designed their set for another type of stage?

Discuss the differences in design for the different styles and sets chosen. Also, discuss the importance of knowing the type of stage on which the set will be placed.

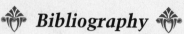

Bibliography

Books

Aronson, Arnold. *American Set Design.* New York, NY: Theatre Communications Group, Inc., 1985. The achievements of eleven American set designers, including Ming Cho Lee, Santo Loquasto, and Marjorie Bradley Kellogg, are catalogued here. In accessible style, Aronson combines research, commentary, and interviews. There are over one hundred photographs.

Bay, Howard. *Stage Design.* New York, NY: Drama Book Specialists, 1974. Bay has designed over one hundred Broadway productions and won prestigious awards. He gives an international overview of the development of design, staging, and lighting from the 1920s to the 1970s. Aided by many illustrations, he combines the basic aspects with aesthetic theory.

Bellman, Willard F. *Scene Design, Stage Lighting, Sound, Costume & Makeup: A Scenographic Approach.* New York, NY: Harper & Row, 1983. This is a comprehensive guide divided into ten parts: A Working Aesthetic, Physical Theater, Organization and Safety, Scenery, Properties, Use of Color, Costume and Makeup, Lighting, Sound, and Scenic Projection.

Buerki, F.A. *Stagecraft for Nonprofessionals.* Madison, WI: University of Wisconsin Press, 1983. This standard backstage text provides straightforward solutions to the basic production problems encountered by amateurs working in a variety of settings.

Friedman, Martin. *Hockney Paints the Stage.* New York, NY: Abbeville Press, 1983. This illustrated book that celebrates Hockney's inventive exploration into the 3-D world of the stage reveals Hockney's unique theatrical vision. The text is based on extensive interviews. The poet Stephen Spender contributes an essay based on his long association with Hockney. Also included are Hockney's

own imaginative plot summaries of the plays on which he worked.

Gillette, J. Michael. *Theatrical Design and Production: An Introduction to Scene Design and Construction, Lighting, Sound, Costume, and Makeup.* Mountain View, CA: Mayfield Publishing Company, 1992. A comprehensive study guide to these technical fields is given by Gillette. The book is suitable as an introduction for college students.

Parker, W. Oren, and R. Craig Wolf. *Scene Design and Stage Lighting.* Fort Worth, TX: Holt, Rinehart, Winston, 1990. With examples from English, Canadian, and American stages, this is a comprehensive reference book.

Reid, Francis. *Designing for the Theatre: Costumes, Properties, Settings and Lighting.* New York, NY: Theatre Arts Books, 1989. This is an authoritative and helpful introduction to the possibilities and processes of design for the theater. Reid treats all these aspects of theater as interconnected functions. The play and the performance space are also considered an integral part of the whole thought process.

Smith, Ronn. *American Set Design 2.* New York, NY: Theatre Communications Group, 1991. This book contains twelve illustrated profiles of contemporary scenic designers who reveal their early influences, individuality, thoughts on the future, and more during extensive interviews conducted by Smith. There is a foreword by Ming Cho Lee.

Sporre, Dennis J., and Robert C. Burroughs. *Scene Design in the Theatre.* Englewood Cliffs, NJ: Prentice Hall, 1990. Two veterans describe both the excitement and challenges in the world of scene design. The history of design, the practices, and the principles are also covered.

Sweet, Harvey. *Handbook of Scenery, Properties, and Lighting, Vol. I, Scenery and Props*. Boston, MA: Allyn Bacon, 1995. A manual containing illustrations, examples, and practical, step-by-step techniques and instructions for creating scenery and properties quickly, easily, and economically is provided by Sweet.

_____. *Handbook of Scenery, Properties, and Lighting, Vol. II*. Boston, MA: Allyn Bacon, 1995. A continuation of Volume I, this book includes practical solutions for lighting staged events—with special emphasis on design and implementation.

Thomas, Terry. *Create Your Own Sets*. Englewood Cliffs, NJ: Prentice Hall, 1985. Aimed at schools and amateur theater groups, this authoritative and comprehensive book goes from basic designing and construction to effective control of scenery in a performance.

Welker, David. *Stagecraft: A Handbook for Organization, Construction and Management*. Boston, MA: Allyn & Bacon, 1987. Welker thoroughly details every phase of set construction from early drawings to painting and shop management, and then to set-up and strike. There are dozens of examples, and the text is suitable for students with no previous experience.

Videotapes and Films

Blithe Spirit. 1945. This film version of Noël Coward's comedy-fantasy stars Rex Harrison and Constance Cummings and is directed by David Lean. The movie won an Oscar in the Special Effects category. It is listed in Critic's Choice Video 1-800-367-7765. Video, colorized; 96 minutes.

Camelot. 1967. Richard Harris and Vanessa Redgrave star in this version which has a score by Lerner and Loewe. It won Oscars for Costumes, Scoring, and Art Direction/Set Decoration. It is listed in Critic's Choice Video 1-800-367-7765. 2 videocassettes, color; 178 minutes.

Signature: Marsha Norman. The viewer follows Norman backstage as she works with actors, designers, composers, and producers. This video is available through Annenberg/CPB Multimedia Collection 1-800-LEARNER. Video, color; 60 minutes.

Theatre Fundamentals. Bloomington, IN: Indiana University Audio-Visual Center, 1979. This series of four films on techni-

cal theater includes the following titles: *Backstage: Is it Safe?*; *Breath of Performance*; *Stage and Lighting*; and *Costumes on Stage*. 16mm films, color; averaging 20 minutes.

Journals

TCI. New York, NY: Theatre Crafts International. This is a professional journal that provides international, in-depth coverage of design and technology for theater, opera, and dance.

Technical Brief. New Haven, CT: Yale University. This professional journal contains articles by and for technical theater practitioners and also includes mechanical drawings that represent solutions to technical theater problems.

Internet

The New York Studio of Karen TenEyck. This is an Internet site created by the class of '91 graduates of the Yale Drama School who studied Set Design with Ming Cho Lee. Viewers will see set designs for the theater, past and present, and also meeting rooms where collaboration on future shows is in progress. The Internet address is http://www.inch.com/~kteneyck

The International Theatre Design Archive. This site offers examples of innovative scene, lighting, and costume designs from professional designers. The Internet address is http://www.siue.edu/PROJECT2000/

Rose Brand Online. Rose Brand offers a full line of theatrical fabrics, stage draperies, and scenic and production supplies for sale online. The Internet address is http://www.rosebrand.com/

CD-ROM

Sound Library Pro. Mac/Win (Hybrid). Published by Wayzata Technologies, there are over 1200 different sounds on this CD-ROM. It is available from EDUCORP Multimedia 1-800-843-9497.

Sound Library 2000. Macintosh. Published by Wayzata Technologies. There are over 2000 sounds and more than 140 MB of auditory files on this CD-ROM. It is available from EDUCORP Multimedia 1-800-843-9497.

CHAPTER

11 Lighting and Sound

Framework

Lighting and sound are key elements in establishing the mood, atmosphere, and setting of a play. Effective lighting aids in conveying a particular interpretation of a script. While the lighting technician might be the only one who needs to know the technical aspects of the equipment, everyone involved in the play should understand how lighting affects other elements of a production—notably costumes, makeup, and setting. Without a sound system, most audiences would not be able to hear the actors. Setting this system up can be a challenge, from choosing the proper microphones to setting the proper levels to arranging the speakers so there will be a balanced sound for the audience. Sound effects, too, play an important role. The sound of slamming a door in anger, of traffic in the background, of a bell tolling—these help the audience enter the world of the play.

Teaching Note

Activities found in the **Review Workshop** at the end of the chapter often require some planning or preliminary work by students. Be sure to check these activities, and make sure students have adequate time in which to complete them.

In this chapter students will explore both the technical and the interpretive aspects of stage lighting and sound. The text illustrates and describes some common lighting equipment before discussing the dramatic effects that can be created with light. The chapter also addresses practical planning considerations and proposes solutions to some common theatrical lighting problems. After covering basics in microphone selection, the text details other pieces of equipment necessary to sound production and recording.

Students who might not be interested in performing are often intrigued by the wide array of possibilities offered by the technical aspects of stage production, two of which are lighting and sound. Encourage students with skills or interests in engineering or electronics to learn more about the responsibilities of stage lighting and sound technicians.

Instructional Objectives

- To know the basic lighting equipment used in theatrical productions and to understand the capabilities each has for enhancing a performance
- To understand the principles of light and color and to apply them to specific dramatic situations
- To prepare and interpret a lighting plan, a lighting plot, and a cue sheet
- To understand the types of equipment used in sound recording and amplification
- To learn the factors involved in setting up sound equipment and setting levels
- To prepare and interpret a sound plot and a sound cue sheet

Vocabulary

spotlight a metal-encased lighting instrument that can be focused, having a lens and a mirror that give out a concentrated light and can be directed specifically; used to light acting areas

dimmer an electrical device that controls the amount of current flowing into a lighting instrument, thus increasing or decreasing the intensity of the light

light panel a console from which the brightness of light is controlled

cable heavily insulated wire for joining instruments to electrical outlets or to a switchboard

connector a device for joining cables to each other or to instruments

ellipsoidal reflector spotlight a highly efficient lighting instrument with a reflector shaped like an ellipsoid

follow spot a long-range, high-wattage lighting instrument capable of picking up or following a person moving on the stage, with a beam strong enough to stand out against normal stage lighting; may be xenon, carbon arc, quartz, or incandescent types

floodlight or flood a high wattage lighting instrument with a metal shell open at one end, the inner surface of which is painted white, is polished metal, or has a mirror to reflect the nonfocused light

Fresnel a spotlight featuring a Fresnel or stepped lens, which projects a clear, strong light with a soft edge

portable striplight a light used for sidelighting, backing, entrance lighting, or cyclorama lighting requiring three circuits

roundel a transparent color media placed on striplights to produce different colors

gelatin or gel a transparent color medium placed on lighting instruments to produce different colors

key light the strong source of light aimed at an acting area

fill light the light that fills shadows, aimed opposite a key light

sidelight light produced by instruments behind the tormentor for facial modeling and costume accent

backlight light from above and behind performers to accent them and set them apart from the background

scrim a drop made of fabric that appears almost opaque when frontlit and semitransparent when backlit

light plot diagram showing the placing of the instruments and plugging system and where the beams from all the instruments fall

lighting cue sheet a document prepared after the light plot; indicates what lighting changes are to take place and when

acoustics qualities of a theater that determine the audiability and trueness of sound

microphone a device that receives sound waves and changes them into electronic impulses

amplifier an electronic device that receives a small signal from a mike or another source, increases the strength of the signal, and outputs it to a speaker or another destination

speaker a cone-shaped device driven by electromagnets that convert electrical impulses into sound

tweeter the speaker cone that reproduces high-pitched sounds

midrange the speaker cone that reproduces sounds from the middle range

woofer the speaker cone that reproduces low-pitched sounds

feedback the loud, ear-piercing sound caused by the amplified sound being fed back into the mikes that are picking up the original sound

intercom system a system that allows communication between the stage manager and members of the stage crew

sound-effects board a board equipped with several appliances, such as a doorbell, a door chime, a buzzer, and an old-fashioned phone bell, to create sound effects

sound plot a sheet that shows the pieces of equipment and their settings for each sound in the show, including music, actors' dialogue, and sound effects

sound cue sheet a sheet that includes each sound effect, its cue number, the script page number, the name of the effect, the volume level, and the length in seconds of the effect

Ancillaries

Forms, Models, and Activities Blackline Masters, pages 51–57

Resource Lists and Bibliographies

Chapter Test, pages 19–20

Transparency 19

Motivating Activity

A variety of dramatic effects can be created by using light in different ways. This activity will help you demonstrate a few of these techniques to students. You will need a flashlight, a piece of clear glass (approximately a four-inch square), some baby powder, and a can of hair spray.

Darken the room and turn on the flashlight. Point it upward and hold it under your chin. Ask students what effect is created (a grotesque or fearful effect, such as one used in a horror movie). Then hold the flashlight above and in front of your head, pointing the light downward on your face. Ask students what effect is created (a pleasant, appealing effect, such as one used in a love story). Next hold the flashlight directly behind your head and ask what effect is created (a serious, sober effect, such as one used to conceal a person's identity in an interview).

Shine the flashlight through the piece of glass. Have students note the appearance of the light. Then shake some baby powder on the glass. Remove the excess powder and shine the flashlight through the glass again. Have students note how the light has changed. Clean the glass and repeat the demonstration using hair spray. In both instances students should observe that the light has become softer and less glaring.

Discuss how these various lighting effects might be used in a play to achieve a particular atmosphere or mood.

TEACH

FYI

The characteristics of light are still unknown. Various schools of scientific thought claim that light consists of particles, waves, electromagnetic pulses, or a combination of all three. One supporter of the wave theory was a French physicist named Augustin Jean Fresnel (1788-1827). Based on the wave theory, Fresnel developed a lens with concentric rings that produced a beam of light with a short focal length. This type of lens concentrates light and is therefore useful in illuminating objects. The Fresnel lens is commonly found in lighthouse beacons, automobile headlights, and, of course, the stage lights discussed in this chapter.

Application Activity, page 452

Copy several pages of a lighting catalog, and distribute them to students for use with this activity. It is important that the prices be current so that the budgets are realistic. It might be more practical to divide students into three groups and to assign each group a specific budget. For example, one group might have a budget of $10,000; another group, $20,000; and the last group, $30,000.

Extension One or more students might investigate the possibility of purchasing used equipment. They can begin by contacting a theater to find out how they dispose of old equipment. Also, trade publications often run advertisements for sales or auctions of used equipment.

Application Activity, page 459

For this activity, use a strong light source and darken the classroom as much as possible. Challenge students to predict the colors that the various combinations of fabrics and colored lights will produce. Discuss how a lighting director can use color and shadow to alter the audience's perception of an actor. For example, when an actor wears makeup that is the same color as the dominant light, the makeup will remain unseen until the actor is highlighted with a different color of light. This technique is effective to show a character's transition from good to evil.

▶ **Additional Application Activity**

Demonstrate the effects of backlighting by aiming an instrument slightly toward the audience and having a member of the class stand so that the light causes a glow or halo around the head and shoulders.

Application Activity, page 465

To help students with this activity, prepare an inventory of your school's lighting resources and distribute it to students. If possible, provide students with a simple sketch of the stage area, similar to the one shown in the lighting plot on page 461. Also, distribute copies of the lighting cue sheet on page 54 of **Forms, Models, and Activities Blackline Masters.** Students should include the available inventory list in their light plots. Students should also mark on their cue sheets each acting area as well as appropriate cues from the play.

Application Activity, page 473

To begin this activity, ask students to close their eyes and to listen to the sounds within your classroom. Add variety by pacing across the floor, opening and closing a door, or making other noises. After a few minutes, ask students to share what they heard and what thoughts they had. For example, did the pacing make them nervous? As you list their ideas, explain that you want to set a tense scene in this room. Which sounds would they include, and how would these sounds fit the scene?

Extension Choose a sound plot and a sound cue sheet that have enough sounds for approximately half of your students. After you have assigned the speaking roles, divide the remaining students into pairs. Provide each pair with a sound cue sheet, and explain that each pair will take a sound effect. One person will cue the sound effect, and the other will produce it. After you have rehearsed the script once, allow pairs to switch their roles.

 ASSESS

Chapter Review, page 474

Summary and Key Ideas Sample Responses

1. Responses will vary but should explain that lighting enhances a performance by affecting the mood and atmosphere. For example, the exuberant nature of a musical is magnified by the cheerfulness of a brightly illuminated stage. The chilling effect of a mystery is heightened by dark shadows and highlighted fog. Moreover, numerous special effects can be created by carefully matching lighting with costumes and makeup.

2. Answers will vary depending on the circumstances of your school. However, all answers should reflect a concern for flexibility, efficiency, and economy. A complete answer should include the following equipment: light panel, cables and connectors, ellipsoidal reflector spotlight, follow spot, floodlight, Fresnel, and striplights. Backlight units and color frames are also desirable equipment.

3. For a more complete discussion of lighting equipment, see pages 449–452.

   • **Fresnel**   a spotlight with a stepped lens, which projects a clear, strong light with a soft edge

   • **floodlight**   a high wattage lighting instrument with a metal shell open at one end, the inner surface of which is highly reflective to reflect the non-focused light

- **striplights** lamps arranged in metal troughs, usually with three or four circuits

4. The most common error in the lighting of high school plays is attempting to eliminate all shadows with a generalized bright light. The result is a huge flat glow.

5. A lighting plan and a lighting plot show the location of each lighting instrument and the area or object each illuminates. The lighting plot also indicates how the light board is to be set up for each scene. The cue sheet gives a chronological listing of the changes to be made, which controls and instruments are involved, which settings to use, and the length of time each change will take. The cue sheet also includes warning cues, execution cues, and timing cues. The sound cue sheet includes each sound effect, its cue number, the script page number, the name of the effect, the volume level, and the length in seconds of the effect.

6. For a more complete discussion of microphones, see pages 466–468.

- **general purpose microphone** used for speeches or backstage lines or announcements; it picks up sound one to two feet away

- **close-up microphone** a cordless variety is often used for singers; it picks up sounds from two to ten inches away

- **apron microphone** often used in musicals, this mike has a reception range 45 degrees left and right of center (horizontal and vertical); it picks up sounds from ten to fifteen feet away

- **rifle microphone** this mike has a long, sensitive range but a narrow pick-up pattern

- **overhead microphones** used with shows having few scene changes

- **radio microphone** powered by a battery pack and requiring its own receiver, this mike hides conveniently in costumes; it is the most commonly used mike

Discussing Ideas

1. Because there are many possible approaches to creating atmosphere, allow students some flexibility in this discussion, provided that their suggestions are consistent with the information in the chapter. Students might mention the following:

- Achieve a supernatural atmosphere by using cool colors, possibly blues and greens; create deep shadows by using low fill light.

- An eerie atmosphere can be created by placing a spotlight above or below the figure to distort the features or behind the figure to cast a shadow on the side visible to the audience. The figure might appear aggressive if highlighted in red.

- A figure can appear comic in bright, warm colors, such as red, orange, and yellow, that bounce unpredictably around the stage.

2. This discussion should focus on the fact that light affects the appearance of the color and the texture of fabric, makeup, and paint. Costume designers, makeup artists, and set designers need to work with lighting crews to create desired effects. Poor communication might result in colors that clash, that are absorbed and become ineffective, or that create an effect different from the one that is desired.

3. Natural light sources might create a pasteboard-figure effect if they are not paired with a second light from the opposite direction. Usually the lighting instrument creating the natural light uses warm colors while a lighting instrument coming from the opposite direction uses cool colors. A light plot would need to include both the source of the natural light and an instrument paired with it.

4. Speakers must be placed so that the audience has the illusion that the sound is coming from the prop or the actor. Although placement is typically to the right and left of the audience, the crew must work with the configuration of the size and shape of the auditorium to create the proper balance. If speakers are facing each other or are placed too close to microphones, feedback can result.

Review Workshop, page 467

Independent Activity

Supporting Pantomime A good response to this activity will exemplify one or more of the fundamental principles of lighting covered in this chapter. For example, students should not suggest using a bright white light because it will wash out both the pantomime's white costume and white makeup. Be certain that students explain their lighting choices and submit a complete and detailed light plot. Students may resist the idea of including sound with the pantomime. If this is the case, explain that they are creating a new theater style that includes sound. Students should be able to explain how their sound effects and musical choice contributed to the mime's routine. Students may explain that they are accentuating one of the mime's emotions.

Music and Sound Effects Encourage students to use creativity in adapting everyday items for sound effects. For example, inverting two plastic cups and rapping them against the floor sounds like a horse's hooves; rubbing together two blocks mounted with sandpaper sounds like a train; and rattling peas in a box sounds like rain. The local library may have sound effects on record or CD, and some computers have sound files. The key to this activity is for students to identify sounds that will add to the mood of the poem.

Cooperative Learning Activity

Creating Mood and Atmosphere A good response should include creativity supported by a strong rationale. Have each group appoint a member to explain the group's plan. Compare the various plans for each of the situations and discuss which group presented the most effective lighting and sound plan.

Across the Curriculum Activities

Science You might want to select certain students to share their reports with the class. Be sure that the reports include both the scientific explanation for what is happening to the light and a practical plan for creating that effect with stage lights. It might be useful to give a few stage directions to help students focus their efforts. For example, ask students to prepare a light plan for these situations:

Act I, scene 1   [The kitchen of an old home at sunrise]

Act I, scene 2   [The same kitchen that evening]

Act II, scene 1   [Another room in the house. As the action takes place, a storm gradually gathers outside.]

History Any number of creative combinations of intensity, color, and distribution are possible. Suggest that interested students research the costumes and colors common to the period. The contrast between the colorful luxury of the nobility and the drabness of the serfs offers many lighting possibilities. Accept any response that reflects thorough research and an understanding of the lighting principles and equipment covered in the chapter.

CLOSE

Final Activity

Explain to students that Shakespeare typically established the moods for his plays in Act I, Scene 1. When these plays were originally performed, most theater technology did not exist: costuming was very limited, and lighting technology had not been discovered. The mood for a play, then, had to be established primarily through the use of words, usually delivered by the chorus or a minor character. Modern performances of Shakespeare, though, have the potential of using a wide array of lighting technologies and devices to set the mood.

To explore some of the possibilities of lighting, arrange students into working groups of three or four. Have each group choose one of Shakespeare's plays. Within the groups, have students study the dialogue and stage directions in the opening scene. After the groups are familiar with this scene, have them discuss and ascertain what the mood of that scene is. Ask them to decide how lighting could be used to help set the mood of this scene.

You might want to provide each student with a copy of the lighting plan, lighting plot, and lighting cue sheet that are found on pages 52–54 in **Forms, Models, and Activities Blackline Masters.** Then, using the lighting plot found on page 461 of the textbook, have each group prepare a lighting cue sheet for the scene.

After the cue sheets are prepared, each group should work together to prepare a brief explanation of its lighting plan to present to the rest of the class. This presentation should consist of four parts:

- a description of the mood of the scene. Students should cite excerpts from the scene that support or explain their lighting suggestions.
- a description of the lighting effects as they would be perceived by the audience. This forces students to focus on the effect or result they are trying to achieve in their lighting plans.
- suggestions for the technology (procedures and equipment) that they might use to achieve the effects they desire for this scene
- step-by-step explanations of the activities and procedures listed on the lighting cue sheets they have prepared

Have the groups make their presentations to the class. Allow members of the class to ask questions, make comments, or offer advice after the presentations are made.

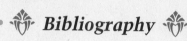

Bibliography

Books

Bracewell, John L. *Sound Design in the Theatre.* Englewood Cliffs, NJ: Prentice Hall, 1993.

Cunningham, Glen. *Stage Lighting Revealed: A Design and Execution Handbook.* Cincinnati, OH: Betterway Books, 1993. This book helps amateurs get started in setting up the lights for a performance in a relaxed and rewarding atmosphere. Information is presented in the order it is needed. Neither history nor stage lighting fixtures are discussed.

Fraser, Neil. *Lighting and Sound.* New York, NY: Schirmer Books, 1989.

Gillette, J. Michael. *Designing with Light: An Introduction to Stage Lighting.* Palo Alto, CA: Mayfield Publishing Company, 1978. Gillette emphasizes the essential design rather than the technical elements of stage lighting. The two parts of the book are Tools of the Designer and Creating the Lighting Design. The author gives many insights into a lighting designer's creative imagination.

Hood, Edmund. *Practical Handbook of Stage Lighting and Sound.* Melbourne, FL: Krieger Publishing Company, 1987.

Palmer, Richard H. *The Lighting Art: The Aesthetics of Stage Lighting Design.* Englewood Cliffs, NJ: Prentice Hall, 1994. Palmer teaches the design principles and techniques used in creating an effective and visually exciting lighting design for drama and dance. He addresses the designer rather than the technician. A practical approach for script analysis from the lighting designer's point of view is also included.

Parker, Oren W., and R. Craig Wolf. *Scene Design and Stage Lighting,* 6th ed., Fort Worth, TX: Holt, Rinehart & Winston, 1990. This highly illustrated college level textbook is updated to include the latest technology and wisdom.

Reed, Francis. *The ABC of Stage Lighting.* New York, NY: Drama Book Publishers, 1992. This is an encyclopedia of stage lighting terminology, equipment, and techniques.

Reid, Francis. *Discovering Stage Lighting.* Oxford, England: Focal Press, 1993. At the center of this book is a series of "discover" projects that ask students to use minimal resources to explore the effect of light in the theater. These projects cover all the major scenarios likely to be encountered by lighting students.

———. *Lighting the Stage: A Lighting Designer's Experiences*. Oxford, England: Focal Press, 1995. Reid is concerned with fostering good working relationships between people on a lighting team. He shows how a lighting team fits into the larger creative team putting together all the other aspects of a play production. He includes technical pieces, such as styling the light, integrating effects and mixing media, control boards, filtering light, and more.

Sellman, Hunton Dade. *Essentials of Stage Lighting*. New York, NY: Meredith Corporation, 1972. This handbook for technical directors and lighting designers is a college level introduction to lighting.

Streader, Tim. *Create Your Own Stage Lighting*. London, England: Bell & Hyman, 1985. This is a high-school level textbook with clear information and illustrations.

Walne, Graham, ed. *Effects for the Theatre*. New York, NY: Drama Book Publishers, 1995. This practical handbook divides theatrical effects into four types—scenic, sound, lighting, and special. Effects include flying people, snow, fog, ghosts, telephones ringing, and explosions. This practical text offers budget-conscious suggestions.

———. *Projection for the Performing Arts*. Boston, MA: Focal Press, 1995. This reference book deals with projected scenery and stage lighting.

Videotapes and Films

Theatre Fundamentals. Bloomington, IN: Indiana University Audio-Visual Center, 1979. This series of four films on technical theater includes the following titles: *Backstage: Is it Safe?*; *Breath of Performance*; *Stage and Lighting*; and *Costumes on Stage*. 16mm films, color; averaging 20 minutes.

Internet

Entertainment Technology Online. This Internet site was created by the publishers of TCI and Lighting Dimensions magazines. All the latest news information on production and design for theater professionals appears at this site. The Internet address is http://www.etecnyc.net/

The International Theatre Design Archive. This site offers examples of innovative scene, lighting, and costume designs from professional designers. The Internet address is http://www.siue.edu/PROJECT2000/

Sound Systems for High School Theater. This site offers troubleshooting ideas, recommended equipment, and many other suggestions to get the most out of high school theater sound systems. The Internet address is http://www.serve.com/acedkr/sschs1.html

Lighting and Electronics. This site features safety guides, authorized dealer listings, solutions to common lighting problems, and much more. The Internet address is http://www.le-us.com/

The Stage Technician's Page. This site is geared toward people with little to no experience with the technical aspects of theater. Lighting, Sound, and Special Effects are especially emphasized. The Internet address is http://www.geocities.com/Broadway/3738/

CD-ROM

Shoot Like a Pro. Mac/Win. Published by Zelos Digital Learning. This CD-ROM presents an experienced team of video consultants, directors, camera people, and lighting experts who show how to manage camcorder controls, create special effects, compose shots, make the best of available lighting, and produce motion shots using everyday objects. It is available from EDUCORP Multimedia 1-800-843-9497.

Costuming

Framework

From masks worn in Greek tragedies to the elaborate ensembles found in productions such as The Phantom of the Opera, *effective costumes enhance characterizations by giving the audience information about the characters' personalities, lifestyles, and social status. Students have probably noticed, for example, that the "bad guys" usually wear black suits, and the "good guys" wear white. Costuming is used in conjunction with the stage settings and dialogue to provide a historical and geographical context for a play. Costumes that are in harmony with the play's theme add to the visual design and the general atmosphere of a performance.*

It is important for students of drama to understand the impact that costuming has on a production. This will enable them to recognize the reasons for using a particular costume for a character, and it will foster creativity in the designing of costumes. Students will learn to consider the budget, the time, and the available skill when deciding to build costumes. This chapter also introduces different means of obtaining costumes, which will be useful if students are involved in an actual production.

This chapter will help students understand how costuming can improve or detract from the overall power of a production. They will learn to match costume with character by considering elements such as style, color, design, and setting. Also, this chapter presents options for obtaining costumes and basic considerations and instructions for building costumes.

Teaching Note

Activities found in the **Review Workshop** at the end of the chapter often require some planning or preliminary work by students. Be sure to check these activities, and make sure students have adequate time in which to complete them.

Instructional Objectives

- To learn why costuming is important to a good production
- To understand the process that costumers follow and the factors they consider
- To learn what makes a costume appropriate for a particular historical period or for a particular character
- To identify the advantages and disadvantages of renting, borrowing, and building costumes

Vocabulary

color coding matching characters by color or pattern

swatch a fabric sample

costume parade a procession during which actors wear costumes under the lights to ensure the compatibility of the colors

costume silhouette each historical period's own distinctive line and form in dress

costume plot an outline that describes the colors, fabrics, and accessories for each costume design; kept by the wardrobe manager

building the term used by costumers for making a costume

wardrobe manager the person responsible for creating the costume plot and for caring for costumes during rehearsals and performances

dressers assistants who help actors with costume changes and who help care for costumes

Ancillaries

Forms, Models, and Activities Blackline Masters, pages 58–60

Resource Lists and Bibliographies

Chapter Test, page 21

Motivating Activity

To prepare for this activity, either supply a variety of costume accessories, or ask each student to bring one accessory to class. For example, bring items such as hats, gloves, umbrellas, canes, bandannas, scarves, hard hats, or briefcases.

Taking turns, have each student choose two accessories, think about a character who might use these accessories, and then create that character. Allot each student a few minutes in front of the class to show how the character moves, gestures, speaks, and uses the accessories.

Afterward, have students discuss the type of character that used each accessory and how a single accessory can suggest a character and a setting. For example, a bandanna might be used either as a burglar's mask or as a cattle rancher's neckerchief. A cane could suggest a feeble or sick person or a debonair stroller.

Application Activity, page 486

Before students begin, suggest that they try to imagine people from their own lives, such as a friend or a relative. Students should be encouraged to provide information on the following aspects of the costumes:

- clothing style
- color
- texture or type of fabric
- condition, including fit and cleanliness

Ask students to exchange their final drawings or descriptions and to assess each other's work.

Extension Have students reconsider the same characters with one major difference—each character is a nonconformist or an eccentric. How would the costumes that the students first envisioned change?

▶ Additional Application Activity

This activity will help students think about costumes in terms of how they affect characterization. Have the students form groups. Then have each group try to imagine and describe characters that might wear specific types of dress. For example, you might suggest that students describe characters who would wear dark suits, bib overalls, or loud, colorful shirts. Students' descriptions should include each character's personality, mannerisms, and interests. Have groups compare their ideas.

Application Activity, page 491

One approach would be to ask students to bring several cloth samples to class. Pool the contributions and allow students to select their swatches from the pool. Swatches might also be obtained from a tailor, a quilter, a home economics teacher, or an interior or costume designer. Have groups present their fabric books

to the class and explain their choices. Remind groups that the colors and textures of the costumes should enhance the personality traits of the play's main characters.

Extension Have students focus only on footwear for the characters. Provide magazines, department store flyers, or illustrations of period costumes for the class to use. Students can use these resources to select footwear that might be appropriate for each character. Students might also demonstrate how characters would move in this footwear. Will the character stomp, step daintily, or stride?

▶ Additional Application Activities

- From the student edition text, have students select photographs of people in costume and explain what can be inferred about each character from his or her costume. Based on the costume, have students describe the historical period of a play in which that costume would appear and make inferences about the possible age and personality of each character. The photographs on pages 120 and 126 offer good examples for use with this exercise.

- Have students suggest costumes that would make them appear older and serious. Then have them suggest costumes that would make them appear younger and lighthearted. Have students suggest the colors and textures of the fabrics they would use for their costumes.

Application Activity, page 495

If students are unable to find an entry for "Costumes" or "Costume Houses" in local telephone directories, suggest that they look in directories for the closest large city. These directories might be available in any large business office, in a public library, or on the

Internet. If necessary, supply addresses from the list of costume suppliers in the **Teacher's Resource Binder.** Divide the class into small groups and have each student contact one costume house, requesting brochures and price lists. These will be useful for other activities and possibly for productions. Save the information students gather to use with the Application Activity on page 491.

Extension Have students determine the cost of renting costumes for a play that the school or class might produce or has produced. Students will first need to review the play to determine how many and what kind of costumes are needed. After completing the costume list, students can then determine the cost of renting costumes for all characters or for only the main characters.

Extension Have students use telephone directories or the Internet to find additional sources of clothing or accessories that might be useful in plays. These sources might include thrift stores, stores that rent tuxedos, or resale shops. Discuss the many possibilities that are available for locating costumes.

Application Activities, page 499

Activity 1 Students can begin by referring to their notes for the activity on page 486. Students can work together to select the play and then have one group research the cost of rentals, one group research the cost of purchasing costumes, and another research the cost of building their own costumes.

Activity 2 This can be a class activity with students working together to brainstorm a list of items to appear on the poster. Encourage

students to discuss the reasons behind the responsibilities and the assignment of the responsibilities. Have one student write everyone's ideas on a poster.

▶ *Additional Application Activities*

- No one's body is perfectly symmetrical. Most people have one foot larger than the other, one shoulder higher, and so forth. Have students use mirrors, tape measures, and any other means to discover their own asymmetry. Which hand is larger? Is this their dominant hand? Is the same foot larger? Afterward, have students discuss how this asymmetry or other physical differences might affect costuming.

- Have students work in pairs to take and record measurements of their partner's collar size, calf circumference, head circumference, foot outline, wrist circumference, and shoulder span. Have students refer to the chart on page 497 for instructions on how to take the measurements.

FYI

Throughout history costumes have been used to enhance characterization. In Medieval morality plays people expected to see the actor who played Vanity dressed in a costume decorated with brightly colored feathers; the actor who played Wealth was adorned with gold and silver coins. In Chinese opera, strict rules are set as to what colors are worn. Yellow is for members of the royal family, and red is specifically for emperors. White is for elderly people, and pink is for the young.

Chapter Review, page 500

Summary and Key Ideas Sample Responses

1. A costume can express the character's personality, social status, tastes and idiosyncrasies. A costume can also place a character in a historical context.

2. Color coding means matching characters by means of a particular color or pattern. This technique can help an audience understand the character's relationship to other characters in the play. For example, two lovers might always wear similar colors; two enemies might wear opposite colors.

3. A costume parade should take place after the lighting has been finalized and before the dress rehearsal takes place.

4. If the cost of making or renting historically accurate costumes exceeds the budget, the costuming could ruin the total effect of the play because some actors might be in accurate historical dress while others are not. Also, if costumes are uncomfortable, the actors might not appear natural onstage.

5. A costume silhouette is the distinctive line and form of the clothing of a certain time period. For example, women in Victorian times wore long elaborate dresses. Half a century later, clothing was lighter, shorter, and more informal. If the costume silhouette is not accurate, it will not effectively re-create the historical period.

6. For men, the important measurements include their height, waist, chest, inseam, back length and width, collar size, and arm length. For women, the important measurements include their height, bust, waist, hips, back length and width, arm length, and length from waist to shoe tops.

7. One positive aspect of renting costumes is the ability to use historical or special costumes that can enhance a production. Such costumes might include armor or formal attire. The negative aspects of renting costumes include the high cost, the possibility of ill-fitting costumes, substitutions, boot covers instead of shoes, and limited availability.

8. The major benefits of building costumes include the following: the costume wardrobe grows; the overall costume design of a play can be made more uniform; and the costumes are made to fit particular actors. In addition, the students who work on building costumes gain satisfaction and experience.

Discussing Ideas

1. A good discussion will include descriptions of clothing worn by both genders and by people of different ages and social standing. To help generate discussion, suggest different locations and events. Then ask students what type of clothing they would expect to see or wear in such places or at such events. Locations might range from different workplaces, such as factories or corporate offices, to different geographical locations. Events could also cover a broad range, from a professional sporting event to a formal wedding.

2. In discussion students should infer that the practicality of renting costumes depends on several factors: budget, time, and any special costuming requirements. If students have completed the Application Activity on page 499, they can use those figures to arrive at a decision.

3. A discussion should touch on the available resources, including budget, time, and skilled costumers. There are several ways to proceed, including sewing costumes from scratch, adapting ordinary clothing, and adjusting old clothes or costumes. Students could seek the help of various people: tailors or parents who sew, members of a local theater, actors, or members of historical organizations.

Review Workshop, page 501

Independent Activity

Show, Don't Tell   You might limit this activity by asking students to write a costume plot for only a single scene. This will enable students to produce a more detailed plot. Remind students to take into account color coding, historical context, and the characters' social status. This activity should be judged by how well the student has captured the costume silhouette of the period and the status of each character.

▶ *Additional Independent Activity*

Have each student select a historic photograph that was taken before 1950. Ask students to analyze the picture and explain what it reveals about the people in it. To what social class do they belong? What does their clothing reveal about their occupations? What else can the student determine?

Cooperative Learning Activity

Representational Costuming   This activity offers the opportunity for students to apply what they have learned about costuming. Students should demonstrate an awareness of the play's historical period and differences among characters. The styles and colors of costumes that students select will be an indication of the level of their awareness. Remind students that carefully selecting a few representative elements can be more effective than elaborate costumes.

Extension   Ask students to work together to create a unified design appropriate for the play's historical period. Have students create a simplified costume plot, as well as sketches to display their design.

Across the Curriculum Activities

Sewing/Tailoring   The basic costume should be relatively simple, but should have various eye-catching accessories. Students might suggest for men reversible jackets with one side tattered and the other impeccable. Ladies' acccessories could include ornate hats as well as parasols, gloves, and jewelry. Showing students a few scenes from the movie *My Fair Lady* might help them understand the contrast between clothing appropriate for Ascot and clothing worn by street people in London. Student designs must be practical, allow for quick changes, and personify the different characters.

History   The suggestions should show some evidence of thorough research. You might provide time for students to do research in the library. Suggest to students that they consult some of the books listed in the bibliography for this chapter. The student's work should reflect the correct costume silhouette, as well as practical suggestions for creating that look. Make sure students can explain their costuming decisions and can give suggestions for making the costumes more comfortable or reasons for the costumes' wearability.

Final Activity

This activity will allow students to understand the overall effect of costuming on a production, and to address different elements that go into costuming. After viewing the video in this activity, students will understand the impact of costuming on a production, whether positive or negative.

Show a video of a period play to the class. It might be helpful to supply students with a list of the characters so they can keep track of each character throughout the play. Ask students to take notes on costumes as they watch, observing color coding, historical accuracy, and the social status of the characters. Also, have students take into consideration the costumes' wearability. Do the actors appear natural and comfortable in the costumes, or do they seem restricted by their outfits?

After students have watched the video, have them discuss their observations, giving a critique of the costuming. Ask students if they thought the costuming was effective or ineffective, and have them give support for their opinions.

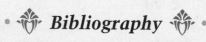

✳ *Bibliography* ✳

Books

Blumenthal, Eileen. *Julie Taymor, Playing With Fire: Theater, Opera, Film.* New York, NY: Abrams, 1996. Taymor has won many awards for her dazzling and enchanting masks. She learned much of her designing, mask making, and directing skills while in Sri Lanka, Indonesia, Bali, Japan, and Paris. This book describes several of her productions, including Shakespeare plays, and shares how she creates her visual magic.

Dryden, Deborah M. *Fabric Painting and Dyeing for the Theatre.* Portsmouth, NH: Heinemann, 1993. A book of straightforward descriptions that include the following: setting up a dye shop, painting the fabric, and aging and distressing fabric. A list of suppliers is also included.

Emery, Joy Spanabel. *Stage Costume Techniques.* Englewood Cliffs, NJ: Prentice Hall, 1981. This is a reference book for students that provides the foundation for experimentation by offering general principles. It contains numerous illustrations.

Ingham, Rosemary, and Liz Covey. *The Costumer's Handbook: How to Make All Kinds of Costumes.* New York, NY: Prentice Hall, 1983. Quick and easily executed ideas for constructing a wide variety of costumes are described in this book. It is also filled with time-saving tips such as using glue, clay, and papier mâché in the costume process.

Motley, pseud. *Designing and Making Stage Costumes.* New York, NY: Theatre Arts Books/Routledge, 1992. This book details the work of a costume designer and is full of inspiring costume sketches. The foreword is by Dame Peggy Ashcroft.

Russell, Douglas A. *Stage Costume Design: Theory, Technique and Style,* 2d ed. Englewood Cliffs, NJ: Prentice Hall, 1985. Russell provides an overview of the costume design field. Ten periods in the history of Western cultural style are explored to show a designer-in-training how to design within a specific period.

Thomas, Beverly Jane. *A Practical Approach to Costume Design and Construction, Fundamentals and Design, Vol. I.* Newton, MA: Allyn & Bacon, 1981. This practical book details eight major eras of costume design with information on the designer's role, budgeting, production schedules, and more.

Thomas, Beverly Jane. *A Practical Approach to Costume Design and Construction, Vol. II.* Newton, MA: Allyn & Bacon, 1981. Scores of ideas for adapting available garments into hard-to-find period wear, plus a multitude of scaled patterns and drawings for creating clothing and accessories are found in these pages.

Williams, John T. *Costumes and Settings for Shakespeare's Plays.* Totowa, NJ: Barnes and Noble Books, 1982. This book sets forth an application of principles to ten of Shakespeare's plays: *A Midsummer Night's Dream, The Comedy of Errors, Twelfth Night, Love's Labour's Lost, The Tempest, Romeo and Juliet, Julius Caesar, Macbeth, Hamlet,* and *Richard III.*

Videotapes and Films

Camelot. 1967. Richard Harris and Vanessa Redgrave star in this version, which has a score by Lerner and Loewe. The movie won Oscars for Costumes, Scoring, and Art Direction/Set Decoration. It is listed in Critic's Choice Video 1-800-367-7765. 2 video cassettes, color; 178 minutes.

Theatre Fundamentals. Bloomington, IN: Indiana University Audio-Visual Center, 1979. This series of four films on technical theater includes the following titles: *Backstage: Is it Safe?; Breath of Performance; Stage and Lighting;* and *Costumes on Stage.* 16mm films, color; averaging 20 minutes.

Journal

The Costumer. Indianapolis: National Costumers Association, Inc. This is a journal aimed at professional costume makers.

Internet

The Costume Page. This is an ever-expanding list of costume and costuming-related links, compiled for the benefit of those who make and/or study costumes: costumers, students, historical re-enactors, science-fiction fans, dancers, theatrical costumers, and those interested in fashion, textile art, and costume history. The Internet address is http://users.aol.com/nebula5/costume.html

Milieux: Science Fiction and Costuming. This is an on-line resource center for costumes, materials, accessories, books, and related items. Catalogued areas include Arms & Armor; Books, Video, and Patterns; Footwear & Leather; Garb; Hats & Wigs; Ornament, Metalwork & Findings; Notions, Trim, & Fabric; Costumes & Accessories; Mail-Order Sources; and more. The Internet address is http://www.milieux.com/costume/source.html

English Actors at the Turn of the Twentieth Century. This site offers a collection of pictures of more than forty turn-of-the-century British actors in costume. The Internet address is http://www.siue.edu/COSTUMES/actors/pics.html

The History of Costume. This site explores the early history of costume in cultures such as Persia, Judah, and ancient Greece and Rome. The Internet address is http://www.siue.edu/COSTUMES/history.html

The International Theatre Design Archive. This site offers examples of innovative scene, lighting, and costume designs from professional designers. The Internet address is http://www.siue.edu/PROJECT2000/

Would You Believe? This site is an on-line resource for ordering masks, makeup, costumes, and more (includes price lists). The Internet address is http://www.wyb.com/

CD-ROM

The Clothes We Wore. MPC. Published by E.M.M.E. Interactive. This is a 2 CD-ROM set that documents the history of costumes between 1750 and 1930 in images of period paintings, sketches, and photographs. It is accompanied by audio commentary and cross-referenced text. It is available from EDUCORP Multimedia 1-800-843-9497.

CHAPTER

13 *Makeup*

Framework

Makeup can greatly enhance a theatrical characterization and help to make that characterization convincing. Makeup also allows actors to portray older characters, animals (Cats), monsters (Frankenstein), or other nonhuman characters (Starlight Express).

It is important for all the members of a cast and crew to understand the fundamental aspects of stage makeup. Choices of the kind and style of makeup to use must be based on many different theatrical considerations. Lighting, stage settings, costuming, and characterizations all affect the impact that makeup has on an audience and on the audience's interpretation of a play.

Throughout the three parts of this chapter—The Basics; Straight Makeup: The Six Steps; and Special Makeup Problems—students will learn why makeup is necessary and what items comprise a makeup kit. They will also learn the six steps in applying straight stage makeup. In addition, students will receive concrete advice for dealing with special makeup problems that range from simulating aging to creating and using prosthetics.

Teaching Note

Activities found in the **Review Workshop** at the end of the chapter often require some planning or preliminary work by students. Be sure to check these activities, and make sure students have adequate time in which to complete them.

Instructional Objectives

- To understand how differences in stage settings, stage lighting, and characters affect choices in makeup
- To identify the contents of a makeup kit, and to become familiar with the six steps in applying straight stage makeup
- To understand the effects of highlights and shadows, especially in showing the process of aging
- To identify types of wigs and beards and recognize their uses and benefits

Vocabulary

chiaroscuro   the use of makeup to highlight and shadow the face

foundation   a base color in makeup

matte   the flat or dull makeup that is achieved by powdering

highlighting   the term used when applying makeup to bring out facial features

shadowing   the term used in applying makeup to bring out facial features

blocked out   a natural facial feature covered with neutral makeup to obscure it

facial mask   a plaster casting taken of the face

blender   the area where the edge of a bald wig blends with an actor's skin

prosthetics   molded latex pieces of eyelids, cheeks, noses, and other features which are attached to the skin with additional latex

Ancillaries

Forms, Models, and Activities Blackline Masters, page 61

Resource Lists and Bibliographies

Chapter Test, page 22

Transparency 20

Motivating Activity

Divide the class into pairs. Place in a box the names of several familiar characters from the stage and the screen. The characters might range from Scrooge to the wicked stepmother in "Cinderella" or any contemporary figure in the arts or politics.

Have each student choose one name from the box, but allow anyone who does not know the face of the chosen character to return it and select another. Then ask each student to look at the face of his or her partner and to make suggestions for what might be done to make the partner look like the character they have chosen. Have students include suggestions for each of the following characteristics: hair, beard or mustache (if applicable), eyes, cheeks, nose, mouth, and any other special features. Provide time for each pair of students to share their ideas with each other and with the class. Invite students to draw sketches of the character's face if they wish.

Application Activity, page 507

For this activity, provide a selection of old magazines, newspapers, and photographs. Have students select a few close-up pictures of faces to help them answer the questions presented in the activity. As students answer these questions, have them examine each facial feature one by one, including eyebrows, skin tone and texture, eyes, hair, lips, teeth, chin, and nose. As students examine each face, they might ask themselves whether any one feature dominates or whether many common features unite to create an interesting look. In short, encourage students to study each face systematically and in detail before making a generalization. Evaluate students' answers based on the detailed observations that they include in their portfolios.

Application Activity, page 515

This activity might be accomplished over a few days rather than in one session. For example, students can complete their sketches then take some time to gather the necessary makeup supplies. You might also provide time for sharing, reflecting, and rethinking between the stages of completing the worksheet and carrying out the makeup plan. Photocopy and distribute copies of the makeup worksheet found on page 59 of the **Forms, Models, and**

Activities Blackline Masters. Caution students about the dangers of sharing makeup by explaining that this practice can result in the spread of viruses, bacteria, and skin ailments. Refer students to page 507 to review the proper handling of makeup.

Extension After carefully examining their facial features and bone structure, students might suggest several characters that they are well-suited to play because their facial types are similar.

Application Activity, page 523

You will need to provide an ample amount of wool crepe in a variety of colors and shades. Straighten the crepe before it is used for the activity. Supply students with clean nylon stockings, or have them bring these items from home. One stocking can be used to create several mustaches or beards. You will also need to supply scissors and an ample amount of adhesive such as spirit gum. If you are using latex as an adhesive, caution students not to apply their beards or mustaches too close to their hair or eyebrows.

Evaluate beards or mustaches on how realistic they appear, how well they fit the wearer, and how well the colors blend to match students' natural hair colors.

Application Activity, page 526

Encourage students to enhance their sketches by using colored pencils, watercolors, or paint. When assessing this activity, be sure that students' makeup choices reflect a clear understanding of how to change, diminish, or heighten the effect of facial features and bone structure in order to accurately represent their characters.

FYI

In its first 5,000 performances alone, the popular musical *Cats* used 23,580 makeup brushes; 13,652 cosmetic/eyebrow pencils; 1,359 liquid eyeliners; and 3,409 powder puffs to dress the 193 actors who played cats. In *Phantom of the Opera,* another Broadway spectacle, 70 wigs are worn by the 36 actors—in addition to the wigs worn by the 15 life-size mannequins that appear in the show. The most famous makeup work in *Phantom of the Opera* is the mask worn by the Phantom himself. It is not, however, just one mask. The Canadian touring group that stages *Phantom of the Opera* travels with seventeen different masks, each made of molded plastic and lined with leather.

Application Activity, page 527

Remind students that their work may simply suggest an animal rather than realistically re-create it. Once students have chosen the animals they want to represent, have them brainstorm the animals' distinguishing traits and characteristics. For example, a lion is associated with pride and ferocity and is marked by its whiskers, teeth, tail, and mane. For this activity, evaluate students on how creatively they represent the animal they have chosen.

Extension Invite students to make up a face showing one side as a woman and the other side as a man. Have students use a different base for each side, creating a distinct line down the middle of the nose. Make sure students use an appropriate amount and color of makeup, especially rouge and lipstick, to represent the different genders.

ASSESS

Chapter Review, page 528

Summary and Key Ideas Sample Responses

1. Chiaroscuro is the use of makeup to highlight and shadow the face.

2. The most expressive features of the face are the eyes and the mouth.

3. Makeup can change the appearance of an actor's face to make the actor resemble the character that he or she is portraying. For example, old age makeup can help a young actor give a convincing portrayal of an older person. Also, it can help to communicate certain aspects of a character's personality.

4. Before any makeup can be applied, the face must be cleansed, and for men, shaved. Use cold water to cool the surface of the face. Apply astringent to oily skin or apply a nongreasy moisturizer under full foundation to aid with later removal.

5. The steps in applying makeup follow:

   • The first step in applying makeup is the application of the correct foundation base color.

   • Next is the application of shadows and highlights.

   • The third step is the application of rouge and lipstick.

   • Step four is the application of makeup to the eyes and eyebrows.

   • The fifth step is powdering.

   • The last step is the application of finishing touches, such as mascara and false eyelashes, and making any necessary corrections.

See pages 508–515 for a more detailed description of the six steps in applying makeup.

6. Highlighting and shadowing emphasize features, correct features, and change features to indicate age, character, or physical oddities.

7. The most difficult makeup problem for the high school stage is creating the look of aging. It is often difficult to create the semblance of old age on young faces. Another problem encountered by high school productions is heavy makeup inexpertly applied that looks "tacked on."

8. The types of beards and wigs that work best for actors are professionally made, expensive, and individually fitted. If professionally made beards and wigs are not accessible to a school, the next best choice is to construct them from wool crepe.

Discussing Ideas

1. The discussion should include the fact that dramatic lighting requires more makeup. Students should mention that stage lights can wash color out of an actor's face, creating a pasteboard effect. Additionally, if too much light comes from above it creates deep shadows that distort the actor's face, causing the eyes to appear lost in deep shadows and the nose to take on strange shapes. Also, students should mention that to plan effective makeup, the color of the light and the direction from which it comes must be taken into account.

2. Students should mention the use of light foundation colors to suggest paleness, the use of lines to create wrinkles, and the use of highlights and shadows to create

the appearance of folds in the skin. To make a young actor look convincing, students should suggest heightening or deepening any wrinkles that the actor already has and using makeup to make lips appear thinner and paler. Finally, students should suggest stippling the skin, roughing its texture, and heightening features of the hands and legs to suggest age.

Review Workshop, page 529

Independent Activity

Mime Encourage students to brainstorm a list of personal qualities they might draw on to perform a mime. Students should explore the types of actions they would perform and the types of facial expressions that would complement these actions. Once students know what they want to achieve as mimes, it will be easier for them to develop their makeup to project the desired image.

In the interest of time, this assignment can be completed on paper instead of on a face; however, this alternative does not enable students to see how their makeup will complement changing facial expressions.

Cooperative Learning Activities

Creating Special Effects Guide students in planning and discussing ideas before they begin. With features such as an open wound or a missing tooth, students might discuss the effect of placement. With features such as freckles, students should talk about both the placement and the intensity of the effect. Similarly, the degree of balding or the size and appearance of an open wound should be discussed. Both the student applying the makeup and the student being made up should share in planning the desired effect. To formalize the assignment, have students record their goals for creating the effect. Assess the results according to how well each pair achieved its goals.

Bizarre Makeup This activity provides enormous latitude in choice of materials and end results. Have students brainstorm other choices for which they can create bizarre makeup, such as an alien or a monster.

You will need to gather a large variety of unusual materials in advance, perhaps asking students to bring items from home. Display the range of materials on a large table so that students can view them as they decide what character to create. As with all makeup activities, be sure to have a large supply of paper towels and cleanup items on hand. Also, remind students to use caution when applying makeup and other materials to the face.

Extension Ask each group to plan costuming that will complement the effect they achieved with makeup. Have them sketch different views of the costume and add details with colored pencils or watercolors.

Across the Curriculum Activities

History In order to create an effective presentation, have students photocopy photographs that show a progression in aging. Be sure they have at least one photograph that was taken during the person's youth. Students can also arrange the photographs on a time line that represents the person's life span. The time line should show not only the dates of each photograph but also significant events in history that were occurring at the time.

Evaluate the makeup demonstrations based on the appropriateness of the selected techniques and the materials used. You might also make your evaluation on the basis of the range of techniques. For example, some students might confine themselves to facial wrinkling, while others might include changes in skin tone, and, possibly, changes to the lips, arms, legs, and hands.

Art Assure students that they are not being asked to re-create the person pictured but rather the person's basic characteristics, such as hair and skin tone, as well as the feeling or mood created by the artist.

Extension Some students might experiment with costuming to more completely re-create the mood of the portrait they have selected.

● ## Final Activity

Students can demonstrate what they have learned in this chapter by portraying with makeup the main character from a play, a story, a biography, or a current event. Begin by helping students to narrow their choice range. For example, students who are especially interested in bizarre effects might select a children's story, myth, or fairy tale. Students who are interested in re-creating the process of aging might choose a biography, a television drama, or a novel that tells a life story. Students who wish to create realistic characters might select a current event or film.

Evaluate the activity according to how well the makeup suits the character. Also evaluate the activity on the basis of the process each student used to achieve the desired effect. For example, be certain that students use the makeup worksheet, the six steps in applying makeup, and the proper makeup tools.

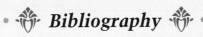

Bibliography

Books

Arnink, Donna J. *Creative Theatrical Makeup.* Englewood Cliffs, NJ: Prentice Hall, 1984. Written with beginners in mind, this book explains how to achieve striking and original makeup effects with a simple palette of three colors, a sponge, and a brush. There are plenty of hands-on exercises and hundreds of illustrations.

Buchman, Herman. *Stage Makeup.* New York, NY: A Back Stage Book, 1989. Buchman brings years of experience as a makeup artist and teacher to this very practical book. Both thorough and inspiring, it provides methods for students to build their skills.

Corson, Richard. *Stage Makeup,* 8th ed. Englewood Cliffs, NJ: Prentice Hall, 1989. Corson has written an encyclopedic collection of "how-to" ideas. The foreword was written by Hal Holbrook, and the introduction was written by Uta Hagen.

Egan, Jenny. *Imaging the Role: Makeup As a Stage in Characterization.* Carbondale, IL: Southern Illinois University Press, 1992. This book addresses both students and professionals. Attention is given to exploiting the bond between an actor and his makeup, between psyche and physical appearance. Clear illustrations show makeup use, paint, putty and prostheses. Attention is also given to ethnic characters.

James, Thurston. *The Prop Builder's Mask-Making Handbook.* White Hall, VA: Betterway Publications, Inc., 1990. James writes for both professional and amateur mask-makers. This book covers everything you need to know to make a mask and includes commedia dell'arte, character masks, and leather masks.

Swinfield, Rosemarie. *Stage Makeup: Step-by-Step.* Cincinnati, OH: Betterway Books, 1994. This book constitutes a complete guide to basic makeup, planning and designing makeup, adding and reducing age, ethnic makeup, and special effects. There are photographs on every page.

Videotapes and Films

Driving Miss Daisy. 1989. Jessica Tandy and Morgan Freeman star in this film adaptation of Alfred Uhry's stage play about aging and friendship. This movie won four Oscars: Best Screenplay, Best Makeup, Best Actress, and Best Picture. Video, color; 99 minutes.

Makeup: Aging and Hair. Pasadena, CA: Barr Films, 1973. This film presents basic makeup techniques along with the variety of available materials and also demonstrates how to effect aging, apply beards and mustaches, build up noses, and blacken eyes. 16mm film, color; 17 minutes.

Puppets

Traditional Bunraku Theater. NHK Films, 1976. Monjuro Kiritake demonstrates this classic puppet drama by showing how puppets and manipulators coordinate action and explaining the use of *shamisen* music. 16mm film, color; 29 minutes.

Internet

Minifie's Makeup—Theatre and Party Makeup. This is an Internet site created by a pharmacist in New Zealand who manufactures, sells, imports, and exports theatrical makeup. Hundreds of products are listed, with photos showing the effects of the products. There is also an area for asking questions. The Internet address is http:/www.minifie.co.nz/

The Monster Makers. This site specializes in providing ideas and materials for monster masks and special effects (includes on-line catalog). The Internet address is http://www.monstermakers.com

Would You Believe? This site is an on-line resource for ordering masks, makeup, costumes, and more (includes price lists). The Internet address is http://www.wyb.com/

Mail-order Sources for Video

Critic's Choice Video. PO Box 749, Itasca, IL 60143-0749. (1-800-367-7765). The catalog lists over 2,000 VHS/laser/8mm titles. School and library purchase orders are accepted. Free catalogs are available.

Facets Video. 1517 W. Fullerton Ave., Chicago, IL 60614. (1-800-331-6197). This is a nonprofit arts organization established in 1975. It is a source for videos of stage plays filmed as stage plays.

Filmic Archives. The Cinema Center, Botsford, CT 06404-0386. (1-800-366-1920). Thousands of feature films and educational shorts that are for sale to schools and libraries only are listed. Catalogs are free to librarians and teachers of English and history.

TLA Video. Theater of the Living Arts, 1520 Locust Street, Philadelphia, PA 19102. (1-800-333-8521). A large selection of arts videos is offered in this catalog.

The Video Catalog. PO Box 64267, St. Paul, MN 55164-0428. (1-800-733-2232). This catalog lists low- to medium-priced arts videos, documentaries, classics, international titles, British comedy, and drama. School purchase orders are accepted, and catalogs are free.

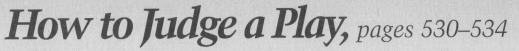

How to Judge a Play, pages 530–534

SUMMARY AND KEY IDEAS

With Sample Responses

1. What two major areas should be evaluated when judging a play? Name at least three considerations in each area.

   In judging a play one should evaluate the play itself and the production. When evaluating the play itself, consideration should be given to theme, plot, dialogue, and characterization. An evaluation of the production should include a consideration of set design, the direction, acting, and audience reaction.

2. Is it fair to judge the ultimate success of a performance by the audience's response?

   The reaction of the audience may or may not be a fair criterion of the ultimate success of a play. Although local tastes mean that all plays are not suitable for all audiences, if the audience is restless and the applause is more polite than enthusiastic something must be amiss. The average audience is usually eager to be pleased.

3. What are the three goals a scenic designer must strive toward in order to achieve a successful production?

   A scenic designer strives to create atmosphere, to establish a center of interest, and to help carry out the fundamental purpose of the play.

DISCUSSING IDEAS

1. Review the lists of questions following each section in the text. Which questions do you feel are the most important considerations in judging a play? Can many or all the questions be combined into a single, underlying question? Be prepared to defend your choice.

   Responses will vary. A good response will cite certain underlying principles of evaluation. One such principle is the need for consistency among the author's purpose, the characters, situations, and dialogue. In addition, a good response will take into account the need for a harmonious relationship among the elements of production, the direction, the acting, and the author's intentions.

2. Why is the director the most important factor in the success of a play?

   Discussion should touch on the following points: The director is responsible for seeing that all parts of a production are in harmony with one another and that the production develops a clearly focused interpretation of a theme. The director is responsible for making the parts of the production consistent. Stated briefly, the director is ultimately responsible for all facets of the performance.

ACTIVITIES

- Read several reviews by one critic. They can be reviews of a play or a movie. Can you find patterns or preferences in the critic's evaluations? Do you think the reviewer makes fair assessments, or does he or she display too much bias? Write a brief review of the critic.

- Read and compare several reviews of the same performance. What does one critic praise that another condemns? What might account for the differences in the reviewers' assessments?

- View a recently released movie. Without consulting your classmates, write a brief review. Conclude your review by giving the movie from one to four stars using the following scale:

  *   Don't bother. It's a waste of time.
  **   Occasionally interesting, but generally rather boring.
  ***   Good, but not great.
  ****   Outstanding! Don't miss it.

Part Five

Adapting and Interpreting Drama

CHAPTER 14
Theater and Other Media   133

CHAPTER 15
Theater and Other Art Forms   143

Media and Culture   153

14 Theater and Other Media

Framework

Technological advances in the late nineteenth and twentieth centuries have led to the invention of two new forms of media, film and television. Both of these media provide their own distinct style of entertainment. Until the invention of movies, the stage provided the sole arena for viewing dramatic productions. The conventions of theater had to be adapted to suit film and later television.

This chapter explores the history of film and television. By studying the differences among theater, film, and television productions, students will be able to determine the elements unique to each of these media. They will understand that actors in each media must have different talents, and that a fine stage actor will not necessarily be an equally successful film or television actor. Students will also learn how the dramatic structure of a play differs from that of a movie or television show.

After reading this chapter, students should understand the influences of theater on modern film and television productions. They should also see that critics and audiences play an important role in determining the success of current stage, film, and television productions.

Instructional Objectives

- To learn about the history and development of film and to determine the unique elements and processes of film productions
- To learn about the history and development of television and to determine the unique elements and processes of television productions
- To understand the differences among acting for theater, film, and television productions
- To study the assessment of theater, film, and television productions, particularly the role critics and audience members play in determining the success or failure of a production

Vocabulary

animation the concept of making drawn or inanimate objects appear to live and move

live-action film a motion picture in which the action is provided by living creatures

close-up a shot taken at a very close distance

zoom a camera technique in which a zoom lens is used to change the nearness of the shot without moving the camera. To "zoom in" is to use the zoom lens to make the scene appear to move closer to the audience; to "zoom out" is to use the zoom lens to make the scene appear to move farther away from the audience

dissolve a camera technique in which one shot is superimposed onto another as the first fades away; often used to show the passage of time

crosscut shot a camera technique in which the camera switches abruptly from one scene to another to show events occurring simultaneously in different locations

story idea a few sentences that express the plot of a film; the first stage of the film and the television writing process

the treatment a narrative version of the story without dialogue; the second stage of the film and the television writing process

storyboard a comic-book version of a story that helps filmmakers visualize the screenplay

film editing choosing and sequencing various, randomly shot pieces of film to tell a coherent story; performed by the editor and the director

three-camera system the use of multiple cameras to allow the director to shoot from various camera angles and distances; may refer to the use of more than three cameras

criticism review and analysis of a dramatic, artistic, or literary work

review an evaluation that's primary function is to encourage viewers to watch or not watch a film or a television production

analysis an evaluation that considers, describes, and evaluates such elements as theme, plot, dialogue, and characterization of a film or television production

receipts the money earned from the ticket sales of a movie or a stage play; a means of measuring the success of a production

ratings the measurement of success of television productions determined by monitoring a small, theoretically representative selection of the population

Ancillaries

Forms, Models, and Activities Blackline
  Masters, pages 62–63

Resources Lists and Bibliographies

Chapter Tests, page 23

*Scenes and Monologues: From Euripides to
  August Wilson*

Motivating Activity

The following activity provides a fun way for
students to consider the difference between
stage acting and film or television acting. It
may be easier to perform in a large space, such
as an auditorium or an outside area.

Have students find a partner and think of an
emotion, such as happiness or sadness, to act
out for their partners in the most natural way
possible. Tell them they must not state directly what their emotions are: they must use
facial expressions, gestures, and dialogue to
express their emotions to their partners. Then
have one student from each pair walk approximately thirty feet away from his or her partner. Have each partner express his or her emotion to the other. Then have the students stand
within a few feet of each other and express the
emotions again, keeping in mind they should
be as natural as possible. Ask students to consider which details they saw from close up that
they couldn't see from far away. How did students compensate for their partners' not being
able to see their facial expressions?

Students should see that stage performances, in which the audience is at a distance
from the actor, require more exaggerated
movements than movie and television performances, in which the audience can see the
actor close up.

TEACH

Application Activities, page 542

Divide students into small groups and have
them draw sketches of each setting. Students
should include directions for camera angles in
the movie settings. They should keep in mind
that the audience of a stage production will
only be able to see the scene from one angle,
and will not have the benefit of close-up or
side views of the setting.

▶ Additional Application Activity

Rent *Battleship Potemkin* or another silent
classic movie from your local library or video
store. Before watching the movie, ask students to pay particular attention to the camera
angle, the dialogue, and the actor's expressions. After students watch the movie, ask
them to discuss the position of the camera and
the way dialogue is expressed.

Application Activities, page 545

Activity 1 Help students organize their
responses by suggesting they look for the following information. Students who choose to
do research on a program should find out when
the program began, who its stars are, and for
how long it ran (or has run). Students who
choose to do research on a star should find out
in which programs the star has performed,
when and for how long, and if possible, what
training the star received. Suggest students
find an interesting quote about the program or
star to include in their presentations.

Extension After students have done research
on the program or star, ask them to consider
what they think the program or star has contributed to television history.

Activity 2 Divide students into small groups
for this activity. Ask them to consider the following elements as they discuss the differences and similarities between productions
made for film and those made for television:

- **Setting:** Do the differences between on-
  site filming for movies and on-set filming
  for television productions affect the quality
  of the production?

- **Actors:** Do movies and television attract a
  different caliber of actors?

- **Overall quality of the production:** How are
  time constraints different in film and television? Do time constraints and budgets play a
  large role in the quality of the production?

▶ Additional Application Activity

In recent years, many major motion picture stars have acted in television sitcoms, dramas, and made for TV movies. Ask students to use the information provided on pages 543–545 to speculate about why this may be so. Students should note that the quality of television has improved so much that the medium now attracts stars who have successful movie careers. Have students think of examples of movie stars who have also appeared on television.

Application Activity, page 549

Before beginning this activity, have students watch a few minutes from a movie, and model analyzing this scene for students. Examine the stunts, special effects, and camera techniques. Students should include this type of information when they create their own storyboards. If possible, provide watercolors, pastels, colored pencils, and other media for students.

Application Activities, page 550

Activity 1 For this activity, students should recall the basic plot of each of their favorite movies and then write a summary of each plot in two or three sentences. Remind students that story ideas are presented to film executives, so they should be interesting as well as brief. After students have written their story ideas, ask them to read one or two to the class. Then have the class guess which movie each story idea describes.

Extension Have students write their own story ideas. Evaluate students' story ideas based on originality and appeal.

Activity 2 Ask students to watch a show that evening. Suggest they pay particular attention to what occurs in the show just prior to commercial breaks. When discussing the shows with the students, ask them to evaluate the scriptwriter based on whether or not the commercial breaks occurred at interesting places. Ask students if they wanted to keep watching the show after a commercial break.

▶ Additional Application Activity

Divide students into groups and ask each group to make a list of requirements they think film executives should look for in the story ideas and treatments they receive. For motivation, have students consider the elements that make their favorite movies so enjoyable, as well as those that make other movies less enjoyable. Have students share their lists with the class. Then ask each group to add one plot device or element they think film executives should avoid.

Application Activities, page 554

Activity 1 Have students respond to this activity as a class. Organize their responses on the board by filling in a two-column chart, with one column labeled "Attributes of Stage Acting" and the other labeled "Attributes of Film Acting." (See the answers to question 1 in Discussing Ideas.) Students' examples of actions that can be performed on the screen but not onstage should reflect an understanding of the limitations of the stage, including that the stage is not very big, that subtle actions aren't visible to the audience, that props are not always real, and that elaborate special effects aren't possible.

Extension Ask students, "Based on what you've read, which type of acting would you prefer?" Have them provide one or two reasons for their acting preferences.

Activity 2 Ask students to work in pairs to find out whether the actor they chose was trained on the stage or in film, and whether the actor has been involved in both stage and movie productions. Have them present their findings to the class, with one student discussing the actor's training and experience, and the other student discussing the actor's "big break." Evaluate students' work based on how informative and organized their presentations are.

Application Activities, page 559

Activity 1 Students should learn from this activity that reviewers do not always share the same opinion of a film, and that reviewers are not always "right." Suggest students underline the key points each reviewer makes. Tell students to look for evidence to support or refute these points as they watch the movie.

Extension Lead students in a discussion of their own experiences with movie reviews. Ask them how often they agree with reviewers, and whether they have favorite reviewers with whom they generally agree.

Activity 2   Before students begin this activity, remind them that an analysis should be more detailed than a review. Suggest analyzing a video, which will allow them to watch scenes more than once if necessary. If students have not yet studied "How to Judge a Play" (pages 530–534), read through these pages with them. Tell students that although they do not need to answer every question in their analysis, they should cover each element (except audience reaction if they choose to review a video or a television program). Students may find it helpful to organize their analyses using the elements on these pages as headings.

▶ *Additional Application Activity*

Ask students to discuss or debate the following question: Should filmmakers change their movies based on test-audience reactions? Ask students to consider that different audiences may have different reactions to a movie. To which audience should the filmmakers listen? This discussion or debate should lead students to a more general debate about the importance of profit vs. the story.

ASSESS

Chapter Review, page 560

Summary and Key Ideas Sample Responses

1. Mark Peter Roget proposed that an image that the eye perceives will remain in sight for a fraction of a second after the image is no longer present. This "persistence of vision" allows the eye to blend a series of sequential images that, if changed slightly, create the illusion of movement.

2. At first, the camera assumed the position of a member of the audience: It rarely moved and was located thirty feet from the actors. D.W. Griffith changed the film process by using a variety of shots (including the close-up and the zoom), light and shade compositions, and film editing.

3. Early television was black and white and had an extremely small screen.

4. A storyboard is a script depicted in comic-book form. It helps filmmakers visualize the screenplay and stage stunts, develop special effects, and combine different techniques on film.

5. Commercials pose special problems for TV writers because commercial breaks interrupt a show and often take up as much as eight minutes of a half-hour broadcast. Writers must make shows so compelling that viewers will want to sit through eight minutes of commercials. They must also organize the script so that a high point of interest occurs just prior to each commercial.

6. The success of theater and film productions is assessed by counting receipts, or the money earned by ticket sales. The success of television shows is assessed through ratings, determined by surveying a small number of homes that theoretically represent national viewership.

Discussing Ideas

1. In the course of the discussion, students should mention the following skills:

   For stage actors:
   - a powerful voice
   - an energetic, driven stance with exaggerated gestures
   - an especially good memory (there can be no second takes in a live performance!)

   For film actors:
   - an attention to subtlety and detail (because the camera records every muscle twitch, hesitation, breath, and gesture)
   - an ability to portray characters in a natural manner
   - a familiarity with the entire role and an ability to keep the story's order and the character's development in mind, because movies are filmed out of sequence

2. Students should realize that the stage actor has a far more intimate relationship with his or her audience than the film actor. Once filming is complete, a movie actor's job is over. A stage performance, on the other hand, is not complete until closing night. A stage actor can take note of the audience's reaction during the performance and alter his or her performance to suit this reaction.

3. In the case of film actors, natural, subtle performances are necessary. With theater actors, exaggerated gestures and loud voices are necessary to reach the audience, which is far away from the actor. Close-up camera shots mean that film audiences can see every nuance of a film actor's expression: exaggerated gestures and "over-acting," conventions of past stage performances, are not only unnecessary but undesirable.

4. Write the factors students mention on the board. Then survey class members to see which factors play a leading role in determining movies the class sees. Add any of the following that students don't mention in their discussion to the list: the leading actors, the director, reviews, the suggestions of friends and family, advertisements, newspaper or magazine articles about the movie. Ask students to think about which movies they've enjoyed the most. Can they remember which factors affected their decision to see those movies?

Review Workshop, page 561

Independent Activity

Situation Comedy Suggest that students watch the reruns of sitcoms that appear nightly on some local channels. Have them keep track of each sitcom's "situation" and characters in a journal. Students should not focus too much on one particular plot from a sitcom, but rather consider which situation and characters seem to have the most potential for interesting and amusing plots. Encourage students to be creative when writing their plans for a new sitcom. Evaluate their plans based on creativity and originality.

Film Adaptation This activity allows students to see firsthand how theater productions are adapted for film. Photocopy each page of the scene on extra large paper so that large margins surround the text. Provide students with a photocopy of the scene they've chosen to adapt. Suggest they write the camera crew's directions and music suggestions directly on the photocopy. Students' adaptations should have directions for each part of the scene.

Cooperative Learning Activity

Demonstration This activity provides an opportunity for students to see the persistence of motion theory in action. Give students an index card and have them draw one image on each side of the card. After the demonstration, explain to students that without persistence of motion, people would notice every time they blink, which occurs hundreds of times a day. Tell them that the mind doesn't notice the lids covering the eyeball for a fraction of a second because the image before the blink is retained.

Across the Curriculum Activity

Language Arts This activity allows students to understand the review process and also to see an example of the practical application of writing skills. Suggest that students make a chart or grid using the following headings: Plot, Main Characters, Actors, Costumes, Setting, and Comedic/Dramatic Elements. They can then use the chart to organize their notes during or after the performance. When grading students' reviews, keep in mind that good reviewers will provide evidence to support their evaluation.

CLOSE

Final Activity

Have students perform some of the film adaptations they prepared in the Independent Activity. For this activity, the adaptations will need to be altered slightly so they only require one camera.

Divide the class into groups and give each group a photocopy of one of the film adaptations. Each group will have actors, a cameraperson with a video camera, and a director who will also be in charge of the music.

After a rehearsal led by the director, have the cameraperson film the actors' performance. Actors will need to pay attention to the position of the camera. The cameraperson should be familiar with the directions provided on the script. The director should add music at appropriate places. Have students watch and evaluate their performances.

This activity may be adapted for schools without access to video cameras. Have the cameraperson use flashlights or large theater spotlights on wheels as cameras. Tell students that the camera is on when the light is on. The cameraperson can follow the directions on the script, for example, moving near the actor to represent a close-up. This adaptation will also allow more than one cameraperson per scene.

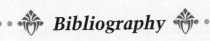

Bibliography

Books

Arijon, Daniel. *Grammar of the Film Language.* Hollywood, CA: Silman-James Press, 1976. This is a timeless source of knowledge for producers, animators, writers, students, and filmmakers. Arijon provides the reader with clear language and more than 1,500 illustrations.

Beaver, Frank Eugene. *Dictionary of Film Terms; the Aesthetic Companion to Film Analysis.* New York, NY: Twayne Publishers, 1994. This text defines the terminology of film analysis, film appreciation, techniques, genres, theoretical concepts, and styles. Contains over 100 stills from classics and contemporary films. Compact and concise, this dictionary is essential for students, teachers, and theatergoers.

Behlmer, Rudy. *Inside Warner Brothers.* New York, NY: Viking Penguin, Inc., 1985. This inside look at one of Hollywood's most successful entities contains memos, letters, and production reports about some of the finest films ever made. A great behind the scenes look at the actors and directors of Warner Brothers and Hollywood!

Bender, David L. and Bruno Leone, eds. *The Mass Media: Opposing Viewpoints.* St. Paul, MN: Greenhaven Press, 1988.

Bessy, Maurice. *Charlie Chaplin.* New York, NY: Harper & Row Inc., 1985. A study of Charlie Chaplin: screenwriter, director, actor, composer, and producer.

Bognàr, Desi K. *International Dictionary of Broadcasting and Film.* Newton, MA: Focal Press, 1995. This is a valuable guide to terminology of international radio, film, and television production. Provides informative lists of professional organizations and guilds, awards, festivals, international and national standards, and television and film systems.

Boyum, Joy Gould. *Double Exposure.* New York, NY: New American Library, 1985. Boyum argues that filmmakers can successfully translate fiction to film. The author carefully examines contemporary films to defend her belief that good novels can make good films. Boyum's analysis includes such movies as *The Great Gatsby, Slaughterhouse Five, The Innocents,* and more. Eight pages of movie stills are included.

Bushby, Alex. *A–Z of Film, Television and Video Terms*. London: Blueprint, 1994. This pocket size guide is essential to those interested in the film, television, or video industries. The portable book explains the current terminology, abbreviations, phrases, acronyms, and the equipment of all three industries.

Culhane, Shamus. *Animation from Script to Screen*. New York, NY: St. Martin's Press, 1988. Written for students of animation, this book explains the process from "script to screen" with clear, vivid language. Culhane exposes the tricks of the trade without alienating the reader with technical terms and jargon.

Davies, Anthony. *Filming Shakespeare's Plays: The Adaptations of Laurence Olivier, Orson Welles, Peter Brook and Akira Kurosawa*. New York, NY: Cambridge University Press, 1988. Considering the popularity of Shakespeare's plays in the classroom, this is an excellent book for the drama or film teacher. Davies focuses on Orson Welles's *Macbeth, Othello,* and *Chimes at Midnight;* Olivier's *Henry V, Richard III,* and *Hamlet;* Peter Brook's *King Lear;* and Akira Kurosawa's *Throne of Blood.* The advantages and disadvantages of adapting drama to film are discussed, as is the influence these specific adaptations had on later films. The book includes stills from the four directors' films and a selected filmography.

DeGaetano, Gloria and Kathleen Bander. *Screen Smarts: A Family Guide to Media Literacy*. New York, NY: Houghton Mifflin Company. 1996.

Diawara, Manthia, ed. *Black American Cinema: Aesthetics and Spectatorship*. New York, NY: Routledge, 1993. This book explores the African American cinema from two different standpoints. The first perspective focuses on the African American artist, community, institutions, and literature. The second perspective focuses on film spectatorship. The book includes insight from filmmakers such as Spike Lee, Oscar Micheaux, and many others.

Dick, Bernard F. *Anatomy of Film*, 2d ed. New York, NY: St. Martin's Press, 1990. Published as a supplemental text for the introductory film course, this book covers all of the basics. The topics covered include film genres, film subtext, the director, film and literature, total film, and film criticism. Examples of a student film analysis and the "basic film library" are included in the text. Specific films are cataloged in the index. This is an ideal book for students of film.

Drain, Richard, ed. *Twentieth-Century Theater: A Sourcebook*. New York, NY: Routledge, 1995. This text was designed with the performance arts student in mind. The text provides an introduction to each section that pulls the topics together and puts them into context. The book is organized around political, modernist, popular, and inner and global dimensions. Lucid and helpful notes accompany original writings from a diverse group of playwrights, directors, performers, and designers.

Falsetto, Mario, ed. *Perspectives on Stanley Kubrick*. New York, NY: Twayne Publishers, 1996. This book provides a series of contrasting critical assessments on Stanley Kubrick's films. The text contains both critical and historical aspects. With the combination of previously published reviews, written and pictorial documents, interviews, and essays to new writings, the reader receives a broad range of criticism dedicated to Stanley Kubrick's work.

Gay, Martin K. *The New Information Revolution: A Reference Handbook*. Santa Barbara, CA: ABC-CLIO, 1996.

Goldstein, Norm. *The History of Television*. New York, NY: Portland House, 1991. The exciting birth of television and its history are recorded in this book. *The History of Television* includes over 300 illustrations and text from the Associated Press.

Greenspon, Jaq. *VGM's Career Portraits: Acting*. Lincolnwood, IL: VGM Career Horizons, 1996. This is a wonderful resource for those considering a career in acting.

Hecht, Hermann, and Ann Hecht. *Pre-Cinema History: An Encyclopaedia and Annotated Bibliography of the Moving Image Before 1896.* London: Bowker-Saur, 1993. This encyclopedia and bibliography encompasses pre-cinema history from 1321. This reference tool includes quotations from contemporary literature and critical analyses.

Hollyn, Norman. T*he Film Editing Room Handbook,* 2d ed. Los Angeles, CA: Lone Eagle Publishing Company, 1990. This is an essential text for assistant editors, independent filmmakers, and students. Hollyn walks the reader through the editing process, from pre-production to post-production, and provides many illustrations. Also included is an important section on how to break into the business.

Karney, Robyn, ed. *Chronicle of the Cinema.* New York, NY: Dorling Kindersley Publishing, Inc., 1995. This book gives a year-by-year account of the first century of the cinema. Oscar winners and highlights for each year are provided. Includes over 3,000 portraits, film stills, and posters.

Katz, Ephraim, et al. *The Film Encyclopedia: The Most Comprehensive Encyclopedia of World Cinema in a Single Volume,* 3d ed. New York, NY: Harper Collins, 1998.

Kuritz, Paul. *The Making of Theater History.* Englewood Cliffs, NJ: Prentice Hall, 1988.

Lapsley, Robert, and Michael Westlake. *Film Theory: An Introduction.* Manchester: Manchester University Press, 1988. This book focuses on film theory from the late 1960s to the present. The text covers the background of film theory and emphasizes topics like narrative, realism, the avant-garde, and postmodernism.

Lichter, Robert S. and Linda S. Lichter and Stanley Rothman. *Prime Time: How TV Portrays American Culture.* Washington, D.C.: Regnery Publishing, Inc., 1994.

Malkiewicz, Kris, and Robert E. Rogers. *Cinematography: A Guide for Filmmakers and Film Teachers.* New York, NY: Van Nostrand Reinhold Company, 1992. This text concentrates on camera structure and operations; theory and practice of film and filters; use of lenses, lighting, and other related equipment; and techniques. There is a chapter on developing a film course, which could be very useful to the beginning film teacher.

Rafferty, Kevin, and Bruce Gordon. *Walt Disney Imagineering: A Behind the Dreams Look at Making the Magic Real.* New York, NY: Welcome Enterprises, Inc., 1996. This fully illustrated book gives the inside scoop on what's being served up at Disneyland! The book contains rough drafts, original artwork, trivia, and more.

Roes, Nicholas A. *Helping Children Watch TV.* Barryville, NY: NAR Publications, 1992.

Rona, Jeffrey. *Synchronization from Reel to Reel.* Milwaukee, WI: Hal Leonard Publishing Corporation, 1990. This is a "how-to" book for the musician, composer, engineer, songwriter, or anyone working in a recording studio. Jeffrey Rona, president of the MIDI Manufacturers Association, gives a step-by-step explanation of the synchronization process and the equipment involved. The book contains charts, diagrams, and photographs.

Sklar, Robert. *Film: An International History of the Medium.* New York, NY: Harry N. Abrams, Inc., 1993. Robert Sklar covers pre-cinema to the present and does so with a historical perspective, coupled with aesthetics, social impact, craft, and technology. The book analyzes directors, cinemas, producers, and more. Sklar devotes separate chapters to particular studies; for example, Soviet Silent Cinema, Italian Neo-realism, and the French New Wave. The book also includes over 750 film stills and 120 color images. A bibliography, a filmography, and a complete glossary support the text.

Smith, Wendy. *Real Life Drama: The Group Theater and America, 1931–1940.* New York, NY: Alfred A. Knopf, Inc., 1990.

Smoodin, Eric Loren. *Animating Culture: Hollywood Cartoons from the Sound Era.* New Brunswick, NJ: Rutgers University Press, 1993. Smoodin critiques cartoons and challenges the common belief that cartoons are for children; instead, he argues that these harmless animated series deal with such political and social issues as class, censorship, imperialism, gender roles, race, and labor issues.

Stone, Judy. *Eye on the World: Conversations with International Filmmakers.* Beverly Hills, CA: Silman-James Press, 1997. Interviews with more than 200 filmmakers from 40 countries are included in this work. Some of the filmmakers interviewed are Chen Kaige, Francis Ford Coppola, George Lucas, Spike Lee, and Nikita Mikhalkov.

Thomson, David. *A Biographical Dictionary of Film,* 3d ed. New York, NY: Alfred A. Knopf, 1994. David Thomson supplies his reader with over 1,000 entries on the principal actors, producers, and directors in the business.

Vardac, Nicholas. *Stage to Screen; A Theatrical Method from Garrick to Griffith.* New York, NY: Benjamin Blom, Inc., 1968.

Vena, Gary. *How to Read and Write about Drama,* 2d ed. New York, NY: Prentice Hall Trade, 1988. This is an invaluable study aid for teachers and students of drama or literature. This book covers all of the essentials needed for successful writing! Vena includes a glossary and suggested reading list in this text.

Yancey, Diane. *Life in the Elizabethan Theater.* San Diego, CA: Lucent Books, 1997.

Multimedia

Total Television. Win. CD-ROM. Published by Simon and Schuster. This CD-ROM covers the history of television from 1948 to the present. It provides an interactive journey through television and also includes a yearly guide to the Emmy awards. It is available to order on-line at http://www.cdromshop.com

Charlie Chaplin Film. Mac/Win. CD-ROM. Published by CD Titles. One of the pioneers of silent film, Chaplin was known for his writing and directing as well as his acting. These various aspects of Chaplin's life are covered in this CD-ROM that provides full-motion video of some of his films. Available to order on-line at http://www.cdromshop.com

Internet

Film.com. This comprehensive site offers information on and reviews of movies from all genres, countries, and decades. The Internet address is http://www.film.com

Film Links for *Silver Screen Texas.* This web page features links to a variety of sites with film-related topics, such as film history, films on television, and film reviews. The Internet address is http://www.history.swt.edu/Full-Time-Faculty/delateja/movie_links.htm

Kino On-Line. This site contains an on-line catalogue that offers foreign, literary, and silent films for purchase. The Internet address is http://www.kino.com/

The All-Movie Guide. This site is a searchable database of movies by title, actors' or directors' name, plotline, mood, genre, time period, and country. Includes plot synopses, casts, and lists of related movies from the beginning of filmmaking. The Internet address is http://www.allmovie.com/index.html

15 Theater and Other Art Forms

Framework

The theater is not for actors only: it is a place where musicians, artists, and dancers work together with actors to tell a story to an audience. Art forms such as music, fine art, and dance are used in theater to communicate the many elements of a story, including theme, mood, plot, characterization, and setting.

This chapter gives students a brief history of fine art, music, and dance as well as an explanation of how to interpret and enjoy these art forms. Students should understand that each of these elements has its own history, and that each may be enjoyed independently of the others.

This chapter then provides information about how these art forms have been combined in the past to achieve different artistic purposes. The influence of society and artistic philosophies on the arts is reviewed, showing how artists are connected by shared social influences. Finally, students are introduced to a study of the synthesis of all the art forms in such productions as musicals, theater, film, and dance performances.

After reading this chapter, students should appreciate that a theater production offers its audience members more than just a story. It offers them the chance to experience a multitude of art forms, which combine to create a moving and memorable experience.

Teaching Note

- Activities found in the **Review Workshop** at the end of the chapter often require some planning or preliminary work by students. Be sure to check these activities, and make sure students have adequate time in which to complete them.

- Having students perform Activity 2 on page 574 provides them with the information needed to begin the history time line in the Review Workshop.

Instructional Objectives

- To learn about the history, elements, and communication methods of fine art, music, and dance

- To determine the elements that fine art, music, and dance share

- To learn how each art form communicates theme, mood, action, character, and setting

- To determine the role society, including the prevalent social philosophies, plays in the creation of art

- To understand the role music, art, and dance play in drama

Vocabulary

composer   the author of musical compositions

melody   the main musical phrase in a composition

lyrics   words to a song

troubadours   Gothic era strolling musicians who wrote music to accompany popular poetry of the time

choreographer   the composer of dance performances who combines a series of steps to produce a work

ballet   a form of dance, which originated in France, with structured steps and poses and light, flowing movements, often communicating storyline or mood to the audience; the first dance form to be performed for an audience

modern dance   a form of dance with roots in ballet that permits less-structured movements; considered to have been founded by Isadora Duncan

tap dance   a form of dance in which dancers make rhythm and music by wearing shoes with hard soles or ones to which taps have been added; popularized by Fred Astaire

synthesis   the combination of elements to form a whole

performance art   acts that combine a wide variety of art forms, which may include music, dance, fine art, poetry, improvisation, comedy, and acting

Broadway musical   performances first shown in the playhouses of New York City's Broadway; they include dialogue and popular music and were popularized in the twentieth century

art director   the person who works with the director and the makeup, costume, and lighting designers to determine the overall look of the play

opera-buffa   a performance with dialogue and light music, offering a series of comical, satirical sketches

Ancillaries

Forms, Models, and Activities Blackline Masters, pages 64–65

Resource Lists and Bibliographies

Chapter Tests, page 24

Scenes and Monologues: From Euripides to August Wilson

Teaching Note

Explore with your students the integration of the arts, including music, dance, and theater, in *Artsource®: Performing Arts Packages* 1, 2, and 3, developed by the Music Center of Los Angeles County. Available through Glencoe, these packages combine audiotapes, videotapes, and printed material to bring to students in your classroom the richness and depth of the performing arts. See page 152 for more information.

Motivating Activity

Many dramatic productions combine theater, fine art, music, and dance. The following activity will show students how these art forms work together to communicate plot, setting, and theme to the audience.

Show students a scene from a videotaped stage performance of an opera in German, Italian, or French. (Suggestion: The first scene from Verdi's *La Traviata*, which normally includes dancing.) Before students watch the scene, explain to them that many Americans who speak only English attend performances of French, Italian, and German operas. Although subtitles may be provided, audience members will miss much of the performance if they have to read the subtitles throughout to determine the plot.

Ask students to watch the scene, looking for ways besides reading subtitles to ascertain the plot, theme, mood, action, and setting of the performance. Write "Dance," "Fine Art," and "Music" on the board. Then write students' answers under the appropriate heading. For example, if a student says mood is portrayed through the set design or the costumes, write this response under "Fine Art."

❇ TEACH ❇

Application Activity, page 566

Tell students they may choose any type of music they wish. Stress the fact that the lyrics are not the only element of music that communicates theme. Evaluate students' presentations based on their discussion of tempo, rhythm, volume, key, and harmony as well as the lyrics. Encourage class members to add their own interpretations after each presentation.

(Possible reasons a writer might compose a work include: to entertain, to communicate a social problem or emotion, or to add background music to a movie.)

Application Activities, page 569

Activity 1 Tell students that they will not be evaluated based on their dancing abilities. The important thing is to communicate a scene using body movements and gestures. Encourage students to have fun with this activity. Students should keep in mind that the music they choose to accompany their performance should fit the mood of the scene.

Extension Ask class members watching the performance to interpret the dancers' movements. Lead them in a discussion about the way certain movements and gestures express emotions. Ask them to consider what they think is challenging about determining meaning through body language.

Activity 2 Have students tell you which country or culture they've chosen to avoid repetition. Ask students to consider how they will report their findings to the class. They may like to present their information in the form of an oral presentation, with pictures of costumes and dancers as visual aids. Instead they may prefer to present their findings in the form of an illustrated booklet, which can be posted on the class bulletin board or passed around for everyone to see.

Application Activity, page 572

This activity gives students practice analyzing fine art. It may be helpful to analyze a piece of fine art as a class for practice. During the class discussion, write the headings "Mood," "Character," "Setting," and "Theme" on the board. Write any ideas students mention under the appropriate heading. Suggest that students organize their ideas by writing a similar outline in their journals. For a shorter activity, have students turn in their outlines instead of writing a complete analysis.

▶ Additional Application Activity

Art museums often display works from the same time period and artistic movement together. Have students visit a local art museum and find an exhibit of works by several artists from the same time period. Ask students to discuss how the works are similar and how they are different. If the museum has provided information about the time period or the works, ask students to read the information and write a brief summary to share with the class.

Application Activities, page 574

Activity 1 Have students choose to compare and contrast two of the following art forms: music, fine art, or dance. Ask them to consider whether the forms are visual, auditory, or both. Students might organize their papers by writing one paragraph on each art form and then comparing and contrasting them.

Extension Hold a group discussion in which you ask students to consider which art form they most enjoy and why. Then ask them which art form they think best communicates theme, mood, setting, and character, and why they think so. Students should discuss whether the art form that they think is most expressive is the same art form they most enjoy.

Activity 2 This activity allows students to see how artistic movements and social and political occurrences affect fine art, music, dance, literature, and drama. Give students a list of artistic movements, including classicism, realism, naturalism, expressionism, and modernism. (Romanticism is covered in some detail in the chapter, so it should not be an option for this assignment.) Have students find out when their chosen art movement occurred and then investigate the period. Students should discuss only those social and political occurrences they think were the most important.

For a shorter assignment, ask students to discuss how the artistic movement affected two of the following art forms: fine art, dance, music, literature, and drama.

FYI

Andrew Lloyd Webber's musical *Cats* is one of the most profitable and longest running musicals in history. *Cats* began with no real story line. In 1972, Webber found a copy of the poet T. S. Eliot's book of verses called *Old Possum's Book of Practical Cats*, which he remembered his mother reading to him when he was a young boy. Ten years later, he and director Trevor Nunn set about turning Eliot's book into a musical. As they began rehearsal, they had only a series of songs based on the book. They were at a loss about how to join their songs into a cohesive and interesting show. Late in the rehearsal, they received help from Valerie Eliot, T. S. Eliot's widow. She gave them a somewhat tattered sheet of one of her husband's unpublished poems about a cat named Grizabella. Grizabella the Glamour Cat is one of the most haunting and memorable characters in the performance.

Application Activity, page 579

After students read the scene, ask them to determine its mood and theme. Suggest that they write a list of adjectives they would use to describe the mood and theme. A list for mood, for example, might include such adjectives as "light, cheery, and funny." Encourage students to refer to this list as they look for a piece of art or an artistic style they think conveys the mood and theme of the scene. Students might want to read their lists during their reports or demonstrations.

Evaluate students' reports or demonstrations based on their reasons for choosing the work of art or artistic style.

▶ Additional Application Activity

Divide students into groups and have them create a musical performance in which all of their instruments are everyday items like those used by Stomp. Encourage students to use creativity when deciding on an "instrument." Suggest they choreograph their movements so that their performance is a visual product as well as an auditory one. Have each group perform for the class.

Application Activity, page 581

Ask students to take notes during and directly after the movie or play. Then tell them to organize their notes for a presentation. One way to do this is to write their notes about the music, set design, and choreography on index cards, which they can use as a reference during their speeches.

(Note that choreography may include the actors' gestures and body language if there is no dancing in the movie or play.)

This activity may be performed as a class instead. Show students a movie or videotape of a play of your choosing. Then have a class discussion about the music, set design, and choreography.

● Chapter 15 Review, page 582

Summary and Key Ideas Sample Responses

1. Melodies express the general or overall feeling of a composition, while lyrics express thoughts, themes, moods, and settings.

2. Ballet was the first form of professional dance—the first to be watched by an audience. Up until the formation of ballet, dance was intended for participation, not observation. Ballet was also the foundation for other forms of dance, like modern dance, jazz, and tap.

3. The main elements used in fine art to convey mood, theme, character, action, and setting are color, line, texture, shape, form, and space. It is also helpful to consider the work's historical background and any artistic movement that might have affected it.

4. The art director is responsible for the overall look of the performance. He or she achieves the desired look by working with the costume, makeup, and lighting designers and the director.

5. Artists within a certain time period often share common philosophies and apply these philosophies to the creation of their art. These philosophies are influenced by, among other things, the political events of the time.

6. Each art form communicates theme in its unique way. The synthesis of different art forms provides audience members with a multitude of visual and auditory means to determine theme.

Discussing Ideas

1. A good discussion will include details such as when and what kind of music is used. Also, ask students to discuss movies or television shows that they think make ineffective use of music. Have them consider why they think it is ineffective. Such productions may, for example, use music simply because it is popular, without considering whether or not it suits the mood of the movie.

2. Most students will probably agree with this statement. They should note that dance relies on body movement to communicate to the audience. Accept any reasonable responses from students who disagree with this statement. (Some may feel, for example, that knowledge of technique is more important that random movement.)

3. It may be helpful to have students first state their interpretation of the theme and mood of the work. Then lead them through the elements listed (line, color, etc.) and have them discuss these elements in relation to the theme and mood on which they've decided. Students may form different opinions as the discussion proceeds. Encourage students to share their ideas. Tell them there are no right or wrong answers.

4. Some students may feel that artists are a product of the time in which they live, and hence their artwork must also be a product of that time. Others may feel that society and history do not always affect an artist's works and that universal emotions like love, hatred, and jealousy can be depicted in such a way that artists can construct "timeless" art.

based on how effectively the set design, lighting, costume, and makeup work together to convey the mood and theme. Encourage students to pay particular attention to color as they plan their stage designs.

Review Workshop, page 583

Independent Activity

Children's Musical This activity may be divided into three steps.

First, have students write a brief summary or "treatment" (see Chapter 14) of the story they've chosen. As they write their summaries, they should note where they feel a song would be appropriate.

Second, have students write the names of the songs they've chosen in a bright color in the margins of their summaries.

Third, ask students to write a "Cast of Characters." Have them make a chart with two columns. In the left-hand column, have them list the main characters; in the right-hand column, have them write the actors they've chosen to play these main characters.

Extension Ask students to make posters advertising their musicals. They may use original art, a photocopy of a piece of fine art, or a photograph of one of the actors.

You Are the Art Director Remind students that the art director works in collaboration with the lighting, costume, and makeup designers. Stage designs should be judged

Cooperative Learning Activity

Music Video Remind students that rock songs and ballads often tell a story. Students may decide to tell this story visually in their video by using actors to convey the emotions of the scene. If students decide to use actors in their videos, their group should consist of a director, an art director, a camcraperson, and actors. Have each group begin by listening to the chosen song, and describing the song's story.

Across the Curriculum Activity

History To complete this time line, students may use the information they collected in the Application Activity on page 574. Suggest that students use encyclopedias, literature anthologies, and the Internet to determine the most influential artists of the time.

CLOSE

Final Activity

This activity will allow students to compare the different means of expressing story elements (in this case, mood). Divide the class into groups, and assign each group an art form. Then tell the class that their goal is to express misery (or elation, or whatever you choose) using their assigned art form. Each group will present its interpretation of the mood to the class.

Encourage students to work together to produce a piece of art, a musical composition,

or a dance performance that communicates the assigned mood. If the students who have been assigned music have not had formal musical education, they may decide to use an existing piece of music, but they should be ready to discuss how the tempo, rhythm, volume, key, and harmony of the chosen piece communicate the mood.

Have students evaluate the performances, discussing which groups did the best job of communicating the mood and why.

Books

Alpert, Hollis. *Broadway! 125 Years of Musical Theatre.* New York, NY: Arcade Publishing, Inc., 1991. This is a wonderfully written historical survey of Broadway. Alpert provides a detailed history beginning with the first hit in 1866 to *Miss Saigon* of 1991. Illustrations include scenes from the best shows, set designs, and other theater memorabilia.

Anawalt, Sasha. *The Joffrey Ballet: Robert Joffrey and the Making of an American Dance Company.* Chicago, IL: University of Chicago Press, 1997. This book was published in unison with the company's fortieth anniversary. Anawalt provides a detailed account of Robert Joffrey's life and the dance troupe he created.

Anderson, Jack. *Ballet and Modern Dance: A Concise History,* 2d ed. Pennington, NJ: Princeton Book Company, 1992. This book is a great reference for students! Anderson maps the development of Western theatrical dance from the Renaissance to the early 1990s. Photos and biographical profiles are included.

Atkins, Robert. *Artspeak: A Guide to Contemporary Ideas, Movements and Buzzwords.* New York, NY: Abbeville Press, 1990. Afraid to stop in for coffee because you can't speak the language? With Atkin's guide, you will never be left in the dark again. This book addresses and defines every word, from *Neo-Dada* to *Zeitgeist,* and gives an insightful look into the world of art.

Balanchine, George, and Francis Mason. *Balanchine's Complete Stories of the Great Ballets.* New York, NY: Doubleday & Company, Inc., 1977.

Cohen, Selma Jeanne. *Dance as a Theatre Art: Source Readings in Dance History from 1581 to the Present,* 2d ed. Pennington, NJ: Princeton Book Company, 1992. Cohen, the author of *The International Encyclopedia of Dance,* has produced a history of Western dance. The book is divided into sections, with a historical and critical essay by the author, and traces the history and development of dance from sixteenth-century Europe to the present. The book contains original writings from the most prominent choreographers, dancers and theorists of Western dance. Included in the book are personal statements from Isadora Duncan, Ruth St. Denis, Doris Humphrey, and Martha Graham. This second edition boasts a new section, "Breaking Boundaries," with articles from Steve Paxton, Twyla Tharp, Mikhail Baryshnikov, and many others.

Conway Greene Company. *Art & Design Scholarships: A Complete Guide.* Cleveland, OH: Conway Greene Publishing Company, 1995. This reference book is an impressive collaboration of over 2,300 art and design scholarships. Students interested in fields such as photography, toy design, or even art therapy can discover sources for financial aid to over 900 colleges.

Emery, Lynne Fauley. *Black Dance From 1619 to Today,* 2d ed. Princeton, NJ: Princeton Book Company, 1988.

Everett, Carole J. *The Performing Arts Major's College Guide,* 2d ed. New York, NY: Macmillan, 1994. The former Director of Admissions at the Juilliard School developed this college guide. The reference book includes information about entry requirements and program choices. Students interested in pursuing a career in any of the dramatic arts should find this book very helpful.

Foster, Susan Leigh. *Reading Dancing.* Los Angeles, CA: University of California Press, Ltd., 1986.

Friedman, Martin. *Hockney Paints the Stage.* New York, NY: Abbeville Press, 1980.

Gänzl, Kurt. *The Blackwell Guide to the Musical Theatre on Record*. Cambridge: Basil Blackwell, Inc., 1990. The book is divided into ten chapters that examine the early forms of comic opera in Britain and France, Viennese operetta, developments in Britain and Europe after WWI, the birth of the modern American musical, and the trends of the 1980s. Each chapter is accompanied with a guide to the author's recommended recordings.

Green, Stanley. *Encyclopædia of the Musical Theatre*. New York, NY: Dodd, Mead & Company, 1976. Green chronicles the musical theater of New York and London from the late 19th century to 1975. This reference book contains information about backgrounds, plots, descriptions of over 1,000 songs, credits of musicals, and casts. Green also provides biographies of over 600 composers, librettists, lyricists, performers, directors, producers and many more prominent characters in the business.

Gruber, Paul, ed. *The Metropolitan Opera Guide to Recorded Opera*. New York, NY: W.W. Norton and Company, 1993. This guide evaluates 150 different operas. Paul Gruber, from the Metropolitan Opera Guild, furnishes important information about the casts, dates, and the best recordings and their availability. There is an index by artist included in this guide.

Kendall, Elizabeth. *Where She Danced*. Berkeley, CA: University of California Press, 1984. Kendall's study revolves around the life of Ruth St. Denis. Kendall records the history and development of interpretive dance.

Kerner, Mary. *Barefoot to Balanchine: How to Watch Dance*. New York, NY: Doubleday, 1990.

Lahti, N.E. *Plain Talk about Art: The Language of Art from A to Z*, 4th ed. Crooked River Ranch, OR: York Books, 1994. This is a helpful resource for students or art enthusiasts. Lahti explains art terms and movements. The book includes an alphabetized list of people, places, trends, concepts and more!

Lerner, Alan Jay. *The Musical Theater*. New York, NY: Da Capo Press, Inc., 1986.

Malone, Jacqui. *Steppin' on the Blues: The Visible Rhythms of African American Dance*. Chicago, IL: University of Illinois, 1996. This is a detailed history of black dance. The book, written by a former dancer, discusses the importance of African American influence on the art forms of American culture as a whole. Malone expresses the significance dance played in the survival of the African American culture, and the importance vocal groups, marching bands, and stepping teams had on the development of the art form.

Mazo, Joseph H. *Prime Movers*. Princeton, NJ: Princeton Book Company, 1977. Joseph H. Mazo tells the story of the birth of a new dance form. The history of American modern dance begins with Loie Fuller. Sections in the text are devoted to Isadora Duncan, Ruth St. Denis, Ted Shawn, Doris Humphrey, Martha Graham, Merce Cunningham, Twyla Tharp, and the other "primary movers" of modern dance.

New York Public Library. *The New York Public Library Performing Arts Desk Reference*. New York, NY: Macmillan, 1994. This is an exquisite reference source for the performing arts. The book is divided into three sections, featuring theater, music, and dance. Each section includes essays, definitions, awards, and more.

Percival, John. *Modern Ballet*. New York, NY: Harmony Books, 1980.

Russell, Mark, ed. *Out of Character: Rants, Raves, and Monologues from Today's Top Performance Artists*. New York, NY: Bantam Books, 1997.

Steinberg, Michael. *The Symphony: A Listener's Guide*. New York, NY: Oxford University Press, 1995. This guide to the symphony provides analysis of over 118 works by 36 composers. Steinberg provides a detailed biographical reference to the composers, and this insight allows the reader to experience the music of these remarkable composers from a more personal level.

Suskin, Steven. *Show Tunes, 1905–1991: The Songs, Shows and Careers of Broadway's Major Composers*, 2d ed. New York, NY: Limelight Editions, 1992. This reference book provides a complete look at Broadway's major composers. The book provides information about more than 750 songs and over 6,000 careers on Broadway. Composers included in this text are Bob Merrill, George Gershwin, Andrew Lloyd Webber, and more.

Swain, Joseph Peter. *The Broadway Musical: A Critical and Musical Survey.* New York, NY: Oxford University Press, Inc., 1990.

Theatre Communications Group, Inc. *Theatre Directory 1997–98.* Vol. 25. New York, NY: Theatre Communications Group, Inc., 1997. This pocket guide to theater provides useful information for theatergoers and actors. Theater addresses, phone numbers, and seasons and schedules are included in this concise guide. There is a regional index of theaters by state included.

Waugh, Alexander. *Opera: A New Way of Listening.* London: De Agostini Editions, 1996. This introduction to opera is accompanied by a compact disk. Waugh focuses on eight of the most famous operas, including Bizet's *Carmen.* The compact disk walks the listener through the opera step-by-step, and discusses the crucial aspects of the work. This is a well-designed introduction into the world of opera.

Wold, Milo, et al. *An Introduction to Music and Art in the Western World*, 10th ed. Chicago, IL: Brown & Benchmark Publishers, 1996.

Woll, Allen. *Black Musical Theatre.* Baton Rouge, LA: Louisiana State University Press, 1989. Allen Woll traces the history of black musical theater from the turn of the century to the late eighties. The key players in the development of this art form are included: performers, lyricists, choreographers, composers, and directors.

Multimedia

Great Composers for Children. CD-ROM. Mac/Win. Published by Zane Publishing/ZCI. This three CD-ROM set includes over 1,130 images, 140 minutes of musical excerpts, and 275 interactive questions and answers. It covers the lives and music of several of the world's best-known composers. Available to order on-line at http://www.cdromshop.com

History of Music. CD-ROM. Win. Published by Voyetra Technologies. This CD-ROM contains information on the lives and works of well-known composers and includes information about their different cultures and the social and political occurrences of the time. This CD-ROM is available to order on-line at http://www.cdromshop.com

History Through Art Volumes 1 and 2. Mac/Win. CD-ROM. Published by Zane Publishing/ZCI. This two-volume, eight-disk set includes art history from ancient Greece through the Pre-Modern era. View thousands of famous art works along with history of the time. Available to order on-line at http://www.cdromshop.com

Age of Evolution Art and Music. Mac/Win. CD-ROM. Published by Zane Publishing/ZCI. This CD-ROM explores the connections between the movements in art and music, from the Middle Ages to the Renaissance. Available to order on-line at http://www.cdromshop.com

Art and Music. Win. CD-ROM. Published by Zane Publishing/ZCI. This four-disc collection features over 160 minutes of multimedia presentations, 2000 photos, and 85 musical excerpts that cover the Medieval era, the Renaissance, the Baroque era, and the eighteenth century. It is available to order on-line at http://www.cdromshop.com

Picture Atlas of the World. Mac/Win. CD-ROM. Published by National Geographic Society. This CD-ROM contains fascination audio and video clips that demonstrate languages, music, and cultural traditions of nations around the globe. Available from Glencoe/McGraw-Hill 1-800-334-7344.

Internet

Art History. Yahoo's search engine links you to some of the most interesting art history sites on the Internet. Topics include Artists, Collections, Criticism and Theory, Periods and Movements, and Themes. The Internet address is http://www.yahoo.com/Arts/Art_History

Don's Dance Links. This site provides an extensive list of dance sites. Topics include dance companies; dancers; choreographers; dance supplies; dance discussions, publications, and reference sources; and miscellaneous. The Internet address is http://www.rpi.edu/~ruberd/dancelnk.html

MusicLink. This site offers links to music sites of various topics including classical music, music education and therapy, and popular genres. The Internet address is http://toltec.lib.utk.edu/~music/www.html

STOMP. This official web site of STOMP offers cast information, performance schedules, and much more. The Internet address is http://usinteractive.com/stomp/

Glencoe Products

Introducing Art; Exploring Art; Understanding Art © 1999. Each of these three books presents the fine arts in a meaningful, engaging manner. The instruction helps students develop their own artistic natures and explore a number of arts-related careers. Each book includes a Performing Arts Handbook, based on the *Performing Arts Packages,* helping students further appreciate how the arts are integrated in performance. Each book is available from Glencoe/McGraw-Hill 1-800-334-7344.

Artsource®: The Music Center Study of Los Angeles County Guide to the Performing Arts: Performing Arts Packages 1, 2, and 3 © 1999. Further explore the integration of art forms in Glencoe's *Performing Arts Packages.* Developed by the Music Center Education Division of Los Angeles county as part of *Artsource®: The Music Center Study Guide to the Performing Arts,* these packages introduce your students to accomplished artists from diverse cultures. Audiotapes and videotapes illustrate samples of these artists' works. Discussion questions lead students to a deeper appreciation and understanding of the artists and their work. Each package highlights a variety of different artists that include dancers, musicians, and puppeteers, in addition to many other types of performers. Available from Glencoe/McGraw-Hill 1-800-334-7344.

Media and Culture, pages 584–587

SUMMARY AND KEY IDEAS

With Sample Responses

1. Name two plays that address social issues. What issues do they address?

   Answers might include two of the following: dramatizations of Uncle Tom's Cabin *by Harriet Beecher Stowe dealt with the horrors of slavery.* Showboat *caused people to think about family and how we treat one another.* Rent *deals with AIDS. Students might list other plays with which they are familiar.*

2. Why do plays now have less influence on society than movies and television have?

   Answers should include the idea that because television is transmitted to millions of TV receivers and movies are shown in thousands of theaters at once, fewer people see plays. Also, television and movies depict events more realistically than stage plays do.

3. How does television help educate? Give an example.

   Answers might include that television teaches through educational programming or documentaries. It also educates through all programming by modeling behavior or providing information. Television also familiarizes an entire nation with social changes and new information, thereby unifying the culture. Examples will vary, but students might cite programs such as newscasts and news magazines, National Geographic documentaries, children's programming such as Sesame Street, or any sitcom or drama that deals with contemporary life and issues.

4. What can you do if you are displeased with television programming?

   To voice an opinion on programming, you can write, phone, or e-mail local television stations, networks, or producers of the show in question. You can also address your complaints to groups such as the Federal Trade Commission or sponsors of the programming.

DISCUSSING IDEAS

1. How does the media shape our perception of reality?

   Answers might include that because the depiction of life on the media is often realistic, viewers assume that it is real and try to model themselves after what they see (for example, teenage girls trying to look like actresses or models). It is difficult to actually see into the lives of other people, but the media bombards us with images of the lives of others, so these become models.

2. What controls, if any, should there be on access to electronic information, such as the Internet? Explain your arguments.

   Students might disagree on this issue. Some might feel that it's a constitutional issue. They might feel any kind of censorship is wrong and we should have access to any information we want. Others might take the position that people, especially children, should be protected from questionable programming.

3. Discuss some ways that electronic media might influence your future or the future of the next generation.

   Students might discuss the use of electronic media to educate in our schools and at home, as well as to communicate between home and school. They can discuss the impact of electronic media on their private lives as well. Encourage them to use their imaginations.

ACTIVITY

- Have students interview an older person (or perhaps more than one person) with the purpose of determining what communication technology was like in the forties, fifties, sixties, etc. Have students share their findings with the class. Then as a class make some generalizations about progress in communications over the last fifty years. Based on the generalizations, make some predictions of possible changes in the next fifty years.

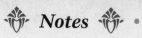

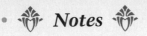

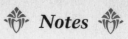

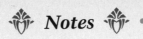

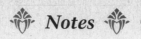